ISBN 0-8373-3159-5

C-3159 CAREER EXAMINATION SERIES

This is your PASSBOOK® for...

Fish & Wildlife Technician

Test Preparation Study Guide

Questions & Answers

National Learning Corporation

212 Michael Drive, Syosset, New York 11791

(516) 921-8888
(800) 632-8888
(800) 645-6337
FAX: (516) 921-8743
www.passbooks.com
info @ passbooks.com

PRINTED IN THE UNITED STATES OF AMERICA

PASSBOOK®

NOTICE

This book is SOLELY intended for, is sold ONLY to, and its use is RESTRICTED to *individual*, bona fide applicants or candidates who qualify by virtue of having seriously filed applications for appropriate license, certificate, professional and/or promotional advancement, higher school matriculation, scholarship, or other legitimate requirements of educational and/or governmental authorities.

This book is NOT intended for use, class instruction, tutoring, training, duplication, copying, reprinting, excerption, or adaptation, etc., by:

(1) Other publishers

(2) Proprietors and/or Instructors of "Coaching" and/or Preparatory Courses

(3) Personnel and/or Training Divisions of commercial, industrial, and governmental organizations

(4) Schools, colleges, or universities and/or their departments and staffs, including teachers and other personnel

(5) Testing Agencies or Bureaus

(6) Study groups which seek by the purchase of a single volume to copy and/or duplicate and/or adapt this material for use by the group as a whole without having purchased individual volumes for each of the members of the group

(7) Et al.

Such persons would be in violation of appropriate Federal and State statutes.

PROVISION OF LICENSING AGREEMENTS. — Recognized educational commercial, industrial, and governmental institutions and organizations, and others legitimately engaged in educational pursuits, including training, testing, and measurement activities, may address a request for a licensing agreement to the copyright owners, who will determine whether, and under what conditions, including fees and charges, the materials in this book may be used by them. In other words, a licensing facility exists for the legitimate use of the material in this book on other than an individual basis. However, it is asseverated and affirmed here that the material in this book *CANNOT* be used without the receipt of the express permission of such a licensing agreement from the Publishers.

NATIONAL LEARNING CORPORATION
212 Michael Drive
Syosset, New York 11791

Inquiries re licensing agreements should be addressed to:

The President
National Learning Corporation
212 Michael Drive
Syosset, New York 11791

PASSBOOK® SERIES

THE *PASSBOOK® SERIES* has been created to prepare applicants and candidates for the ultimate academic battlefield – the examination room.

At some time in our lives, each and every one of us may be required to take an examination – for validation, matriculation, admission, qualification, registration, certification, or licensure.

Based on the assumption that every applicant or candidate has met the basic formal educational standards, has taken the required number of courses, and read the necessary texts, the *PASSBOOK® SERIES* furnishes the one special preparation which may assure passing with confidence, instead of failing with insecurity. Examination questions – together with answers – are furnished as the basic vehicle for study so that the mysteries of the examination and its compounding difficulties may be eliminated or diminished by a sure method.

This book is meant to help you pass your examination provided that you qualify and are serious in your objective.

The entire field is reviewed through the huge store of content information which is succinctly presented through a provocative and challenging approach – the question-and-answer method.

A climate of success is established by furnishing the correct answers at the end of each test.

You soon learn to recognize types of questions, forms of questions, and patterns of questioning. You may even begin to anticipate expected outcomes.

You perceive that many questions are repeated or adapted so that you can gain acute insights, which may enable you to score many sure points.

You learn how to confront new questions, or types of questions, and to attack them confidently and work out the correct answers.

You note objectives and emphases, and recognize pitfalls and dangers, so that you may make positive educational adjustments.

Moreover, you are kept fully informed in relation to new concepts, methods, practices, and directions in the field.

You discover that you are actually taking the examination all the time: you are preparing for the examination by "taking" an examination, not by reading extraneous and/or supererogatory textbooks.

In short, this PASSBOOK®, used directedly, should be an important factor in helping you to pass your test.

FISH AND WILDLIFE TECHNICIAN

DUTIES

As a **Fish and Wildlife Technician 1**, you would, under supervision, perform technical work in fish and wildlife management, research and propagation and in environmental protection. At times, this work might involve the supervision of laborers and seasonal technicians. You would assist in the development and maintenance of habitat management programs; the measure of biological/physical/ chemical habitat attributes; the capture and transportation of fish and wildlife; the operation or use of nets, electrical shocking and other sampling devices; the operation and maintenance of equipment; the collection, tabulation and preliminary analysis of biological and statistical data; and the occasional preparation of reports and presentations.

You might conduct fish propagation activities, including securing eggs and milt, and fertilizing, incubating, rearing and distributing fish stock; conduct biological surveys using various types of equipment to obtain samples of biota, water, soil, sediment, etc.; record basic data from field samples, including identification of biota and measurements taken on samples; conduct user surveys and compile, summarize, prepare, and proof resulting data; construct and repair habitat improvement structures and equipment utilized; and conduct checks for compliance with conditions of minor agency permits.

As a **Fish and Wildlife Technician 2**, you might supervise, coordinate and assist with the collection of biological, water, and soil specimens for identification, abundance, size and quality; compile and summarize data collected from such sample collections/surveys; supervise the construction and repair of habitat structures; respond to nuisance wildlife complaints; coordinate and supervise deer and waterfowl check stations; assist in the preparation of media brochures; schedule, develop, and display public presentations; conduct field investigations to determine compliance with conditions of environmental permits; coordinate deed and tax map reviews related to wetlands; and determine wetland boundaries based on field examination for routine cases.

SUBJECT OF EXAMINATION

The written test will be designed to test for knowledge, skills, and/or abilities in such areas as:

1. Fisheries and wildlife biology;
2. Operation of mechanical devices;
3. Understanding and interpreting written material related to freshwater fish, wildlife, and marine species;
4. Office record keeping;
5. Communicating and interacting with the public; and
6. Supervision.

U.S. Fish and Wildlife Service

The United States Fish and Wildlife Service is the principal agency through which the Federal Government carries out its responsibilities for managing the Nation's wild birds, mammals, and fish for the enjoyment of all people.

The Service's national responsibilities for fish and wildlife go back over 100 years to the establishment in 1871 of a predecessor agency, the Bureau of Fisheries. First created as an independent agency, the Bureau of Fisheries was later placed in the Department of Commerce. A second predecessor agency, the Bureau of Biological Survey, was established in 1885 in the Department of Agriculture.

The two Bureaus and their functions were transferred in 1939 to the Department of the Interior. They were consolidated into one agency and redesignated the Fish and Wildlife Service in 1940. Further reorganization came in 1956 when the Fish and Wildlife Act created the United States Fish and Wildlife Service and provided for it to replace and succeed the former Fish and Wildlife Service. The Act established two Bureaus within the new Service: the Bureau of Commercial Fisheries and the Bureau of Sport Fisheries and Wildlife.

In 1970, the Bureau of Commercial Fisheries was transferred to the Department of Commerce. The Bureau of Sport Fisheries and Wildlife remained in Interior and was designated by Act of Congress in April 1974 as the United States Fish and Wildlife Service.

Today the Service consists of a headquarters office in Washington, D.C.,

six regional offices, an Alaska area office, and over 700 field units and installations. These include more than 375 national wildlife refuges comprising more than 33 million acres; 35 fish and wildlife research stations and laboratories; 45 cooperative research units at universities across the country; nearly 100 national fish hatcheries; and a nationwide network of wildlife law enforcement agents and wildlife biologists.

Program activities include:

—Biological monitoring through scientific research; surveillance of pesticides, heavy metals and thermal pollution; studies of fish and wildlife populations; ecological studies.

—Environmental impact assessment through river basin studies, including hydroelectric dams, nuclear powersites, stream channelization, and dredge and fill permits; associated research; environmental impact statement review.

—Area planning and preservation involving river basin and wilderness areas; special studies such as oil shale and geothermal energy.

—Migratory birds; wildlife refuge management for production, migration, and wintering; game law enforcement; bird banding, harvest and survival rate studies; breeding, migrating, and wintering surveys; disease studies.

—Mammals and nonmigratory birds; wildlife refuge management of resident species (primarily big game); law enforcement; research on disease and population distribution, including marine mammals and species transplants; technical assistance.

—Animal damage control; operational measures through cooperative programs

to control predator, rodent, and bird depredations on crops and livestock; research on nonlethal control methods and predator-prey relationships.

—Cooperative fish and wildlife research units located at universities to conduct research and supervise graduate student research, complementing the Service's wildlife and fishery research programs.

—Coastal anadromous fish; hatchery production; research on nutrition, disease, and habitat requirements in 16 of the 24 coastal States.

—Great Lakes fisheries; hatchery production of lake trout; fishery management in cooperation with

Canada and the States; research; sea lamprey control.

—Inland and reservoir fisheries; hatchery production; management of Federal, military and Indian waters; control of fish diseases and undesirable fish; technical assistance; training; research on fish diseases; genetics, nutrition, taxonomy and cultural methods.

—Providing national and international leadership in the area of endangered fish, wildlife, and plants from the standpoint of both restorations as well as preventive measures involving threatened species. This program includes development of species lists; research on propagation methods; distribution, genetics, and behavior; operation of wildlife refuges; law enforcement; foreign importation and exportation enforcement; consultant services to foreign countries; consultan[t] services to other Federal agencies and cooperative management with the States.

—Youth programs to further the development of the natural resources o[f] the United States and to provide meaningful employment for young men and women. This program is operated i[n] joint participation with the U.S. Department of Labor.

CAREERS
in the U.S. Fish and Wildlife Service

The interrelationships of fish and wildlife with water, land, industry, and people are very complex. Occupations in the Service require specialized education and/or experience. While an interest in conservation is desirable, academic training in fish and wildlife biology is essential for most positions.

Service managers make every effort to place employees in positions for which they are best qualified and in which they will have a chance to develop to their full potential. Most competitive appointments in the Service are to such positions as wildlife biologist, fishery biologist, refuge manager, special agent, technical aid, as well as administrative, clerical, secretarial, and other support positions.

Because of the wide variety of diversified fish and wildlife programs administered by the Service in all States and the trust territories, career and executive development concepts highlight job mobility. Accordingly, professional employees appointed in the Service must be mobile and available for transfer to various locations throughout their career.

Wildlife Biologist

Wildlife biologists study the distribution, abundance, habits, life histories, ecology, mortality factors, and economic values of birds, mammals, and other wildlife. They plan or carry out wildlife management programs, determine conditions and problems affecting wildlife, apply research findings to the management of wildlife, restore or develop wildlife habitats, regulate wildlife populations, and control wildlife diseases.

Fishery Biologist

Fishery biologists study the life history, habits, classification, and economic relations of aquatic organisms. They manage fish hatcheries and fishery resources and gather data on interrelations between species of fish and the effects of natural and human changes in the environment on the survival and growth of fish. Fishery biologists determine rearing and stocking methods best adapted for maximum success in fish hatchery operations and devise methods to regulate fishing to secure an optimum sustained yield.

Research Positions

Wildlife biologists, fishery biologist, ecologists, and other related specialists at research facilities conduct detailed research in environmental contaminate evaluation, migratory bird and marine mammal studies, population ecology and habitat evaluation and assessment, fish husbandry including nutrition and genetics, and related studies concerning fish and wildlife populations.

Refuge Manager

Refuge managers manage national wildlife refuges to protect and preserve migratory and native species of birds, mammals, endangered species, and other forms of wildlife. They are responsible for providing a balanced wildlife management program at the refuge as well as public use programs.

Special Agent (Wildlife) and Special Agent (Wildlife)(Pilot)

Special agents investigate violations of Federal laws within the enforcement jurisdiction of the Department of the Interior for the protection and conservation of wildlife, including birds, mammals, fishes, reptiles, mollusks, and crustacea. Investigations involve surveillance, participation in raids, interviewing witnesses, interrogating suspects, searching for physical evidence and clues, seizing contraband, making arrests, and other enforcement activities. Special Agent (Wildlife)(Pilot), in addition to the above duties, pilot aircraft in connection with law enforcement activities. See page 10 for additional information.

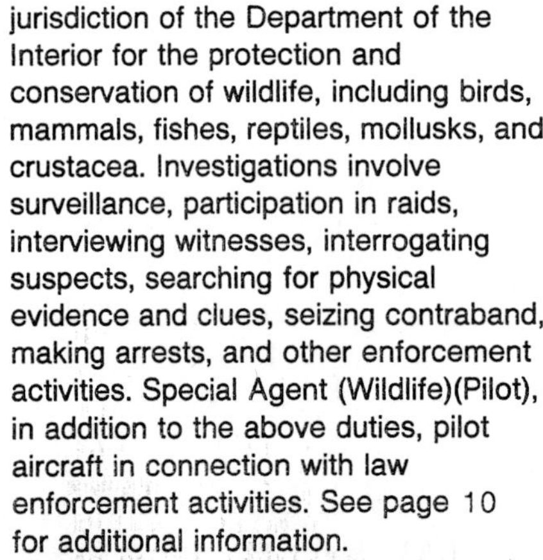

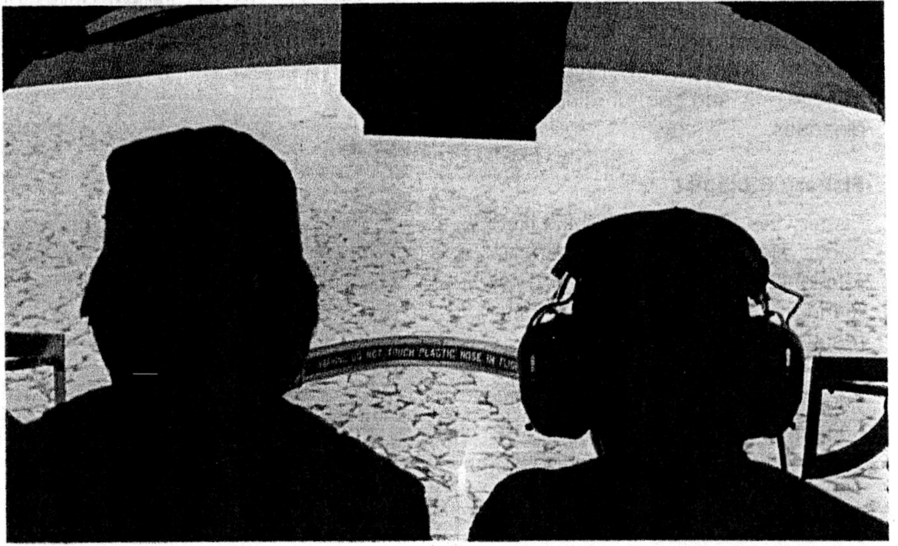

Aid-Type Positions

Fish and wildlife aids and technicians provide support to professional biologists in a wide range of laboratory and field station operations such as laboratory analysis and testing, field surveys, and numerous paraprofessional activities.

District Field Assistant

District field assistants are employed in the Western States and are engaged in various duties associated with controlling damage by predatory animals and rodents.

Because this work is conducted in cooperation with States, counties, livestock associations, and others, district field assistant positions are not under the competitive Civil Service system. Inquiries concerning employment opportunities may be addressed to the Service offices listed on page 15.

Opportunities in Trades and Crafts

Maintenance workers, light and heavy equipment operators, laborers, and some skilled trade workers are employed at wildlife refuges, fish hatcheries, and research laboratories. Hiring is conducted through local offices of the Civil Service Commission from eligible candidates on appropriate Civil Service registers. Salaries are based on prevailing wages in the local hiring area.

Summer Employment

Most summer positions are at field station locations. Positions at grades GS–1 through GS–4 are filled by eligibles from the Civil Service Commission Summer Employment Examination. The examination announcement may be obtained from local offices of the Civil Service Commission in the fall of each year.

Appointments in the Fish and Wildlife Service

Most positions in the Service are under the competitive Civil Service system; that is, positions are filled by candidates who are on U.S. Civil Service registers as a result of establishing eligibility through a competitive Civil Service examination. Initial appointment in a permanent position is followed by a probationary or trial period of one year. Appointments are made to positions in the U.S. Fish and Wildlife Service without regard to race, color, age, religion, politics, national origin, sex, or any other nonmerit factor.

General Qualification Requirements

The table below shows examples of basic qualifications for most professional positions:

GRADE	MINIMUM REQUIREMENTS
GS–5	Bachelor's degree in an appropriate field.
GS–7	Bachelor's degree with B or better average, or Bachelor's degree plus 1 year of appropriate experience or 1 full year of graduate study.
GS–9	Bachelor's degree plus: 2 years appropriate experience, or 2 full years of graduate study, or 1 year of appropriate experience, and 1 full year of graduate study.
GS–11	Bachelor's degree plus: 3 years appropriate experience, or 2 years appropriate experience, and 1 full year of graduate study, or 1 year of appropriate experience, and 2 full years of graduate study, or Ph.D.

Specific College Course Requirements

Wildlife Biologist:

30 semester hours, or equivalent, in biological sciences, including
9 semester hours in wildlife subjects
12 semester hours in zoology
9 semester hours in botany or related plant sciences

Fishery Biologist:

30 semester hours, or equivalent, in biological sciences, including
6 semester hours in aquatic subjects
12 semester hours in animal sciences

Refuge Manager:

9 semester hours, or equivalent, in zoology
6 semester hours in wildlife courses
9 semester hours in botany

Additional course work is required for wildlife and fishery research positions. Refer to the current Civil Service Commission examination announcement for these additional requirements.

Qualifications Requirements for Special Agents

Except for the substitutions provided below, candidates must have had experience of the length shown in the table and of the nature described in the paragraphs following:

Grade	General experience (years)	Specialized experience (years)	Total experience (years)
GS–5	3	0	3
GS–7	3	1	4
GS–9	3	2	5
GS–11 and above	3	3	6

General Experience

Progressively responsible experience which has demonstrated ability to work and deal effectively with individuals or groups of persons; skill in collecting and assembling pertinent facts; ability to prepare clear and concise reports; and, ability and willingness to accept responsibility. Professional level work in one of the biological sciences meets the general experience requirement.

Specialized Experience

Progressively responsible experience in criminal or comparable investigative activity which demonstrated initiative, ingenuity, resourcefulness, and judgment in collecting, assembling, and developing facts; ability to logically and objectively analyze and evaluate facts, evidence, and related information; skill in preparing written and oral reports and presenting investigative findings in a clear and concise manner; and, tact, discretion, and capability in obtaining cooperation and confidence of others. One year of professional experience in one of the biological sciences equivalent to at least grade GS–5 will meet the specialized experience requirement for grade GS–7.

NOTE: Experience as a U.S. Deputy Game Warden is not acceptable as qualifying for either general or specialized experience.

To qualify for a Special Agent (Wildlife position at GS–11 and above, candidates must have previous experience in the investigation and enforcement of fish and wildlife laws.

Substitution of Education for Experience

General Experience

Study successfully completed in an accredited college or university may be substituted at the rate of 1 year of stud (30 semester hours or equivalent) for 9 months of experience up to 4 years of study for 3 years of general experience Therefore, a 4-year college degree, in any major, is fully qualifying at the GS- level.

Specialized Experience

One full year of graduate study in an accredited college or university in law enforcement, police administration, criminology, biological science, or in a criminal justice discipline may be substituted for the one year specialized experience requirement at the GS–7 level. Two full years of graduate work or the completion of the requirements for a master's degree in one of the above-mentioned majors may be substituted for the two-year specialized experience requirement at the GS–9 level. Completion of a total of at least 6 years of legal and prelegal education which meets all the requirements for an LL.B or J.D. degree will also provide eligibility, in full, at the GS–9 level.

Physical Requirements

Candidates for Special Agent (Wildlife) positions must meet the physical standards prescribed for this occupation and once employed, are included in a comprehensive physical examination program throughout their career. The medical standards for these positions are not waived for any candidate. Preemployment physical examination is at the candidate's expense. Copies of the medical standards are available upon request.

Investigation of Suitability

During the one-year probationary period, new employees undergo a full field background suitability investigation. A satisfactory full field investigation must be completed for all nonprobationary candidates prior to appointment.

Rating Procedures

Candidates at the GS–5 and GS–7 levels from outside the Federal service must pass a written test in addition to meeting the experience requirements. Procedures for applying to take the test are explained in CSC Announcement 432. The announcement is available at local CSC Federal Job Information Centers. Candidates at the GS–9 and above levels from outside the Federal service apply under the appropriate Mid- and Senior-Level Civil Service Examination in Washington, D.C. No written test is required.

All applicants must possess a valid automobile license at the time of appointment and retain such license throughout his/her tenure as a Special Agent (Wildlife).

Fish and Wildlife Management Training

Colleges and universities in many States offer courses in fish and wildlife management or closely related fields. The schools of your choice can furnish information on courses and degrees offered.

Other Positions

Appointment to most positions, other than professional positions in the biological sciences, requires a written test as prescribed by the appropriate examination announcement.

We suggest that you contact the nearest Civil Service Commission office to obtain a copy of the examination announcement in which you are interested. Ask for the announcement by job or examination title.

The announcement will tell you what the jobs pay, where they are located, what the work is like, and what experience and training are required.

Workweek

The basic workweek consists of five eight-hour days, usually Monday through Friday. At some field stations it is necessary to adjust the working days to provide coverage seven days a week. This is essential to handle visitor use at a facility or to provide for the care and security of fish or confined wildlife, or a combination of both.

The Service has field operations of some type in every State. Listed on page 15 of this booklet are the addresses of the regional offices of the Service.

HOW TO TAKE A TEST

I. YOU MUST PASS AN EXAMINATION

A. WHAT EVERY CANDIDATE SHOULD KNOW

Examination applicants often ask us for help in preparing for the written test. What can I study in advance? What kinds of questions will be asked? How will the test be given? How will the papers be graded?

As an applicant for a civil service examination, you may be wondering about some of these things. Our purpose here is to suggest effective methods of advance study and to describe civil service examinations.

Your chances for success on this examination can be increased if you know how to prepare. Those "pre-examination jitters" can be reduced if you know what to expect. You can even experience an adventure in good citizenship if you know why civil service exams are given.

B. WHY ARE CIVIL SERVICE EXAMINATIONS GIVEN?

Civil service examinations are important to you in two ways. As a citizen, you want public jobs filled by employees who know how to do their work. As a job seeker, you want a fair chance to compete for that job on an equal footing with other candidates. The best-known means of accomplishing this two-fold goal is the competitive examination.

Exams are widely publicized throughout the nation. They may be administered for jobs in federal, state, city, municipal, town or village governments or agencies.

Any citizen may apply, with some limitations, such as the age or residence of applicants. Your experience and education may be reviewed to see whether you meet the requirements for the particular examination. When these requirements exist, they are reasonable and applied consistently to all applicants. Thus, a competitive examination may cause you some uneasiness now, but it is your privilege and safeguard.

C. HOW ARE CIVIL SERVICE EXAMS DEVELOPED?

Examinations are carefully written by trained technicians who are specialists in the field known as "psychological measurement," in consultation with recognized authorities in the field of work that the test will cover. These experts recommend the subject matter areas or skills to be tested; only those knowledges or skills important to your success on the job are included. The most reliable books and source materials available are used as references. Together, the experts and technicians judge the difficulty level of the questions.

Test technicians know how to phrase questions so that the problem is clearly stated. Their ethics do not permit "trick" or "catch" questions. Questions may have been tried out on sample groups, or subjected to statistical analysis, to determine their usefulness.

Written tests are often used in combination with performance tests, ratings of training and experience, and oral interviews. All of these measures combine to form the best-known means of finding the right person for the right job.

II. HOW TO PASS THE WRITTEN TEST

A. NATURE OF THE EXAMINATION

To prepare intelligently for civil service examinations, you should know how they differ from school examinations you have taken. In school you were assigned certain definite pages to read or subjects to cover. The examination questions were quite detailed and usually emphasized memory. Civil service exams, on the other hand, try to discover your present ability to perform the duties of a position, plus your potentiality to learn these duties. In other words, a civil service exam attempts to predict how successful you will be. Questions cover such a broad area that they cannot be as minute and detailed as school exam questions.

In the public service similar kinds of work, or positions, are grouped together in one "class." This process is known as *position-classification*. All the positions in a class are paid according to the salary range for that class. One class title covers all of these positions, and they are all tested by the same examination.

B. FOUR BASIC STEPS

1) Study the announcement

How, then, can you know what subjects to study? Our best answer is: "Learn as much as possible about the class of positions for which you've applied." The exam will test the knowledge, skills and abilities needed to do the work.

Your most valuable source of information about the position you want is the official exam announcement. This announcement lists the training and experience qualifications. Check these standards and apply only if you come reasonably close to meeting them.

The brief description of the position in the examination announcement offers some clues to the subjects which will be tested. Think about the job itself. Review the duties in your mind. Can you perform them, or are there some in which you are rusty? Fill in the blank spots in your preparation.

Many jurisdictions preview the written test in the exam announcement by including a section called "Knowledge and Abilities Required," "Scope of the Examination," or some similar heading. Here you will find out specifically what fields will be tested.

2) Review your own background

Once you learn in general what the position is all about, and what you need to know to do the work, ask yourself which subjects you already know fairly well and which need improvement. You may wonder whether to concentrate on improving your strong areas or on building some background in your fields of weakness. When the announcement has specified "some knowledge" or "considerable knowledge," or has used adjectives like "beginning principles of..." or "advanced ... methods," you can get a clue as to the number and difficulty of questions to be asked in any given field. More questions, and hence broader coverage, would be included for those subjects which are more important in the work. Now weigh your strengths and weaknesses against the job requirements and prepare accordingly.

3) Determine the level of the position

Another way to tell how intensively you should prepare is to understand the level of the job for which you are applying. Is it the entering level? In other words, is this the position in which beginners in a field of work are hired? Or is it an intermediate or advanced level? Sometimes this is indicated by such words as "Junior" or "Senior" in the class title. Other jurisdictions use Roman numerals to designate the level – Clerk I, Clerk II, for example. The word "Supervisor" sometimes appears in the title. If the level is not indicated by the title, check the description of duties. Will you be working under very close supervision, or will you have responsibility for independent decisions in this work?

4) Choose appropriate study materials

Now that you know the subjects to be examined and the relative amount of each subject to be covered, you can choose suitable study materials. For beginning level jobs, or even advanced ones, if you have a pronounced weakness in some aspect of your training, read a modern, standard textbook in that field. Be sure it is up to date and has general coverage. Such books are normally available at your library, and the librarian will be glad to help you locate one. For entry-level positions, questions of appropriate difficulty are chosen – neither highly advanced questions, nor those too simple. Such questions require careful thought but not advanced training.

If the position for which you are applying is technical or advanced, you will read more advanced, specialized material. If you are already familiar with the basic principles of your field, elementary textbooks would waste your time. Concentrate on advanced textbooks and technical periodicals. Think through the concepts and review difficult problems in your field.

These are all general sources. You can get more ideas on your own initiative, following these leads. For example, training manuals and publications of the government agency which employs workers in your field can be useful, particularly for technical and professional positions. A letter or visit to the government department involved may result in more specific study suggestions, and certainly will provide you with a more definite idea of the exact nature of the position you are seeking.

III. KINDS OF TESTS

Tests are used for purposes other than measuring knowledge and ability to perform specified duties. For some positions, it is equally important to test ability to make adjustments to new situations or to profit from training. In others, basic mental abilities not dependent on information are essential. Questions which test these things may not appear as pertinent to the duties of the position as those which test for knowledge and information. Yet they are often highly important parts of a fair examination. For very general questions, it is almost impossible to help you direct your study efforts. What we can do is to point out some of the more common of these general abilities needed in public service positions and describe some typical questions.

1) General information

Broad, general information has been found useful for predicting job success in some kinds of work. This is tested in a variety of ways, from vocabulary lists to questions about current events. Basic background in some field of work, such as sociology or economics, may be sampled in a group of questions. Often these are principles which have become familiar to most persons through exposure rather than through formal training. It is difficult to advise you how to study for these questions; being alert to the world around you is our best suggestion.

2) Verbal ability

An example of an ability needed in many positions is verbal or language ability. Verbal ability is, in brief, the ability to use and understand words. Vocabulary and grammar tests are typical measures of this ability. Reading comprehension or paragraph interpretation questions are common in many kinds of civil service tests. You are given a paragraph of written material and asked to find its central meaning.

3) Numerical ability

Number skills can be tested by the familiar arithmetic problem, by checking paired lists of numbers to see which are alike and which are different, or by interpreting charts and graphs. In the latter test, a graph may be printed in the test booklet which you are asked to use as the basis for answering questions.

4) Observation

A popular test for law-enforcement positions is the observation test. A picture is shown to you for several minutes, then taken away. Questions about the picture test your ability to observe both details and larger elements.

5) Following directions

In many positions in the public service, the employee must be able to carry out written instructions dependably and accurately. You may be given a chart with several columns, each column listing a variety of information. The questions require you to carry out directions involving the information given in the chart.

6) Skills and aptitudes

Performance tests effectively measure some manual skills and aptitudes. When the skill is one in which you are trained, such as typing or shorthand, you can practice. These tests are often very much like those given in business school or high school courses. For many of the other skills and aptitudes, however, no short-time preparation can be made. Skills and abilities natural to you or that you have developed throughout your lifetime are being tested.

Many of the general questions just described provide all the data needed to answer the questions and ask you to use your reasoning ability to find the answers. Your best preparation for these tests, as well as for tests of facts and ideas, is to be at your physical and mental best. You, no doubt, have your own methods of getting into an exam-taking mood and keeping "in shape." The next section lists some ideas on this subject.

IV. KINDS OF QUESTIONS

Only rarely is the "essay" question, which you answer in narrative form, used in civil service tests. Civil service tests are usually of the short-answer type. Full instructions for answering these questions will be given to you at the examination. But in case this is your first experience with short-answer questions and separate answer sheets, here is what you need to know:

1) Multiple-choice Questions

Most popular of the short-answer questions is the "multiple choice" or "best answer" question. It can be used, for example, to test for factual knowledge, ability to solve problems or judgment in meeting situations found at work.

A multiple-choice question is normally one of three types—

- It can begin with an incomplete statement followed by several possible endings. You are to find the one ending which *best* completes the statement, although some of the others may not be entirely wrong.
- It can also be a complete statement in the form of a question which is answered by choosing one of the statements listed.

- It can be in the form of a problem – again you select the best answer.

Here is an example of a multiple-choice question with a discussion which should give you some clues as to the method for choosing the right answer:

When an employee has a complaint about his assignment, the action which will *best* help him overcome his difficulty is to

A. discuss his difficulty with his coworkers
B. take the problem to the head of the organization
C. take the problem to the person who gave him the assignment
D. say nothing to anyone about his complaint

In answering this question, you should study each of the choices to find which is best. Consider choice "A" – Certainly an employee may discuss his complaint with fellow employees, but no change or improvement can result, and the complaint remains unresolved. Choice "B" is a poor choice since the head of the organization probably does not know what assignment you have been given, and taking your problem to him is known as "going over the head" of the supervisor. The supervisor, or person who made the assignment, is the person who can clarify it or correct any injustice. Choice "C" is, therefore, correct. To say nothing, as in choice "D," is unwise. Supervisors have and interest in knowing the problems employees are facing, and the employee is seeking a solution to his problem.

2) True/False Questions

The "true/false" or "right/wrong" form of question is sometimes used. Here a complete statement is given. Your job is to decide whether the statement is right or wrong.

SAMPLE: A roaming cell-phone call to a nearby city costs less than a non-roaming call to a distant city.

This statement is wrong, or false, since roaming calls are more expensive.

This is not a complete list of all possible question forms, although most of the others are variations of these common types. You will always get complete directions for answering questions. Be sure you understand *how* to mark your answers – ask questions until you do.

V. RECORDING YOUR ANSWERS

Computer terminals are used more and more today for many different kinds of exams.

For an examination with very few applicants, you may be told to record your answers in the test booklet itself. Separate answer sheets are much more common. If this separate answer sheet is to be scored by machine – and this is often the case – it is highly important that you mark your answers correctly in order to get credit.

An electronic scoring machine is often used in civil service offices because of the speed with which papers can be scored. Machine-scored answer sheets must be marked with a pencil, which will be given to you. This pencil has a high graphite content which responds to the electronic scoring machine. As a matter of fact, stray dots may register as answers, so do not let your pencil rest on the answer sheet while you are pondering the correct answer. Also, if your pencil lead breaks or is otherwise defective, ask for another.

Since the answer sheet will be dropped in a slot in the scoring machine, be careful not to bend the corners or get the paper crumpled.

The answer sheet normally has five vertical columns of numbers, with 30 numbers to a column. These numbers correspond to the question numbers in your test booklet. After each number, going across the page are four or five pairs of dotted lines. These short dotted lines have small letters or numbers above them. The first two pairs may also have a "T" or "F" above the letters. This indicates that the first two pairs only are to be used if the questions are of the true-false type. If the questions are multiple choice, disregard the "T" and "F" and pay attention only to the small letters or numbers.

Answer your questions in the manner of the sample that follows:

32. The largest city in the United States is
    - A. Washington, D.C.
    - B. New York City
    - C. Chicago
    - D. Detroit
    - E. San Francisco

1) Choose the answer you think is best. (New York City is the largest, so "B" is correct.)
2) Find the row of dotted lines numbered the same as the question you are answering. (Find row number 32)
3) Find the pair of dotted lines corresponding to the answer. (Find the pair of lines under the mark "B.")
4) Make a solid black mark between the dotted lines.

VI. BEFORE THE TEST

Common sense will help you find procedures to follow to get ready for an examination. Too many of us, however, overlook these sensible measures. Indeed, nervousness and fatigue have been found to be the most serious reasons why applicants fail to do their best on civil service tests. Here is a list of reminders:

- Begin your preparation early – Don't wait until the last minute to go scurrying around for books and materials or to find out what the position is all about.
- Prepare continuously – An hour a night for a week is better than an all-night cram session. This has been definitely established. What is more, a night a week for a month will return better dividends than crowding your study into a shorter period of time.
- Locate the place of the exam – You have been sent a notice telling you when and where to report for the examination. If the location is in a different town or otherwise unfamiliar to you, it would be well to inquire the best route and learn something about the building.
- Relax the night before the test – Allow your mind to rest. Do not study at all that night. Plan some mild recreation or diversion; then go to bed early and get a good night's sleep.
- Get up early enough to make a leisurely trip to the place for the test – This way unforeseen events, traffic snarls, unfamiliar buildings, etc. will not upset you.
- Dress comfortably – A written test is not a fashion show. You will be known by number and not by name, so wear something comfortable.

- Leave excess paraphernalia at home – Shopping bags and odd bundles will get in your way. You need bring only the items mentioned in the official notice you received; usually everything you need is provided. Do not bring reference books to the exam. They will only confuse those last minutes and be taken away from you when in the test room.
- Arrive somewhat ahead of time – If because of transportation schedules you must get there very early, bring a newspaper or magazine to take your mind off yourself while waiting.
- Locate the examination room – When you have found the proper room, you will be directed to the seat or part of the room where you will sit. Sometimes you are given a sheet of instructions to read while you are waiting. Do not fill out any forms until you are told to do so; just read them and be prepared.
- Relax and prepare to listen to the instructions
- If you have any physical problem that may keep you from doing your best, be sure to tell the test administrator. If you are sick or in poor health, you really cannot do your best on the exam. You can come back and take the test some other time.

VII. AT THE TEST

The day of the test is here and you have the test booklet in your hand. The temptation to get going is very strong. Caution! There is more to success than knowing the right answers. You must know how to identify your papers and understand variations in the type of short-answer question used in this particular examination. Follow these suggestions for maximum results from your efforts:

1) Cooperate with the monitor

The test administrator has a duty to create a situation in which you can be as much at ease as possible. He will give instructions, tell you when to begin, check to see that you are marking your answer sheet correctly, and so on. He is not there to guard you, although he will see that your competitors do not take unfair advantage. He wants to help you do your best.

2) Listen to all instructions

Don't jump the gun! Wait until you understand all directions. In most civil service tests you get more time than you need to answer the questions. So don't be in a hurry. Read each word of instructions until you clearly understand the meaning. Study the examples, listen to all announcements and follow directions. Ask questions if you do not understand what to do.

3) Identify your papers

Civil service exams are usually identified by number only. You will be assigned a number; you must not put your name on your test papers. Be sure to copy your number correctly. Since more than one exam may be given, copy your exact examination title.

4) Plan your time

Unless you are told that a test is a "speed" or "rate of work" test, speed itself is usually not important. Time enough to answer all the questions will be provided, but this does not mean that you have all day. An overall time limit has been set. Divide the total time (in minutes) by the number of questions to determine the approximate time you have for each question.

5) Do not linger over difficult questions

If you come across a difficult question, mark it with a paper clip (useful to have along) and come back to it when you have been through the booklet. One caution if you do this – be sure to skip a number on your answer sheet as well. Check often to be sure that you have not lost your place and that you are marking in the row numbered the same as the question you are answering.

6) Read the questions

Be sure you know what the question asks! Many capable people are unsuccessful because they failed to *read* the questions correctly.

7) Answer all questions

Unless you have been instructed that a penalty will be deducted for incorrect answers, it is better to guess than to omit a question.

8) Speed tests

It is often better NOT to guess on speed tests. It has been found that on timed tests people are tempted to spend the last few seconds before time is called in marking answers at random – without even reading them – in the hope of picking up a few extra points. To discourage this practice, the instructions may warn you that your score will be "corrected" for guessing. That is, a penalty will be applied. The incorrect answers will be deducted from the correct ones, or some other penalty formula will be used.

9) Review your answers

If you finish before time is called, go back to the questions you guessed or omitted to give them further thought. Review other answers if you have time.

10) Return your test materials

If you are ready to leave before others have finished or time is called, take ALL your materials to the monitor and leave quietly. Never take any test material with you. The monitor can discover whose papers are not complete, and taking a test booklet may be grounds for disqualification.

VIII. EXAMINATION TECHNIQUES

1) Read the general instructions carefully. These are usually printed on the first page of the exam booklet. As a rule, these instructions refer to the timing of the examination; the fact that you should not start work until the signal and must stop work at a signal, etc. If there are any *special* instructions, such as a choice of questions to be answered, make sure that you note this instruction carefully.

2) When you are ready to start work on the examination, that is as soon as the signal has been given, read the instructions to each question booklet, underline any key words or phrases, such as *least*, *best*, *outline*, *describe* and the like. In this way you will tend to answer as requested rather than discover on reviewing your paper that you *listed without describing*, that you selected the *worst* choice rather than the *best* choice, etc.

3) If the examination is of the objective or multiple-choice type – that is, each question will also give a series of possible answers: A, B, C or D, and you are called upon to select the best answer and write the letter next to that answer on your answer paper – it is advisable to start answering each question in turn. There may be anywhere from 50 to 100 such questions in the three or four hours allotted and you can see how much time would be taken if you read through all the questions before beginning to answer any. Furthermore, if you come across a question or group of questions which you know would be difficult to answer, it would undoubtedly affect your handling of all the other questions.

4) If the examination is of the essay type and contains but a few questions, it is a moot point as to whether you should read all the questions before starting to answer any one. Of course, if you are given a choice – say five out of seven and the like – then it is essential to read all the questions so you can eliminate the two that are most difficult. If, however, you are asked to answer all the questions, there may be danger in trying to answer the easiest one first because you may find that you will spend too much time on it. The best technique is to answer the first question, then proceed to the second, etc.

5) Time your answers. Before the exam begins, write down the time it started, then add the time allowed for the examination and write down the time it must be completed, then divide the time available somewhat as follows:
   - If 3-1/2 hours are allowed, that would be 210 minutes. If you have 80 objective-type questions, that would be an average of 2-1/2 minutes per question. Allow yourself no more than 2 minutes per question, or a total of 160 minutes, which will permit about 50 minutes to review.
   - If for the time allotment of 210 minutes there are 7 essay questions to answer, that would average about 30 minutes a question. Give yourself only 25 minutes per question so that you have about 35 minutes to review.

6) The most important instruction is to *read each question* and make sure you know what is wanted. The second most important instruction is to *time yourself properly* so that you answer every question. The third most important instruction is to *answer every question.* Guess if you have to but include something for each question. Remember that you will receive no credit for a blank and will probably receive some credit if you write something in answer to an essay question. If you guess a letter – say "B" for a multiple-choice question – you may have guessed right. If you leave a blank as an answer to a multiple-choice question, the examiners may respect your feelings but it will not add a point to your score. Some exams may penalize you for wrong answers, so in such cases *only*, you may not want to guess unless you have some basis for your answer.

7) Suggestions
   a. Objective-type questions
      1. Examine the question booklet for proper sequence of pages and questions
      2. Read all instructions carefully
      3. Skip any question which seems too difficult; return to it after all other questions have been answered
      4. Apportion your time properly; do not spend too much time on any single question or group of questions

5. Note and underline key words – *all, most, fewest, least, best, worst, same, opposite,* etc.
6. Pay particular attention to negatives
7. Note unusual option, e.g., unduly long, short, complex, different or similar in content to the body of the question
8. Observe the use of "hedging" words – *probably, may, most likely,* etc.
9. Make sure that your answer is put next to the same number as the question
10. Do not second-guess unless you have good reason to believe the second answer is definitely more correct
11. Cross out original answer if you decide another answer is more accurate; do not erase until you are ready to hand your paper in
12. Answer all questions; guess unless instructed otherwise
13. Leave time for review

b. Essay questions
1. Read each question carefully
2. Determine exactly what is wanted. Underline key words or phrases.
3. Decide on outline or paragraph answer
4. Include many different points and elements unless asked to develop any one or two points or elements
5. Show impartiality by giving pros and cons unless directed to select one side only
6. Make and write down any assumptions you find necessary to answer the questions
7. Watch your English, grammar, punctuation and choice of words
8. Time your answers; don't crowd material

8) Answering the essay question

Most essay questions can be answered by framing the specific response around several key words or ideas. Here are a few such key words or ideas:

M's: manpower, materials, methods, money, management
P's: purpose, program, policy, plan, procedure, practice, problems, pitfalls, personnel, public relations

a. Six basic steps in handling problems:
1. Preliminary plan and background development
2. Collect information, data and facts
3. Analyze and interpret information, data and facts
4. Analyze and develop solutions as well as make recommendations
5. Prepare report and sell recommendations
6. Install recommendations and follow up effectiveness

b. Pitfalls to avoid
1. *Taking things for granted* – A statement of the situation does not necessarily imply that each of the elements is necessarily true; for example, a complaint may be invalid and biased so that all that can be taken for granted is that a complaint has been registered

2. *Considering only one side of a situation* – Wherever possible, indicate several alternatives and then point out the reasons you selected the best one
3. *Failing to indicate follow up* – Whenever your answer indicates action on your part, make certain that you will take proper follow-up action to see how successful your recommendations, procedures or actions turn out to be
4. *Taking too long in answering any single question* – Remember to time your answers properly

IX. AFTER THE TEST

Scoring procedures differ in detail among civil service jurisdictions although the general principles are the same. Whether the papers are hand-scored or graded by machine we have described, they are nearly always graded by number. That is, the person who marks the paper knows only the number – never the name – of the applicant. Not until all the papers have been graded will they be matched with names. If other tests, such as training and experience or oral interview ratings have been given, scores will be combined. Different parts of the examination usually have different weights. For example, the written test might count 60 percent of the final grade, and a rating of training and experience 40 percent. In many jurisdictions, veterans will have a certain number of points added to their grades.

After the final grade has been determined, the names are placed in grade order and an eligible list is established. There are various methods for resolving ties between those who get the same final grade – probably the most common is to place first the name of the person whose application was received first. Job offers are made from the eligible list in the order the names appear on it. You will be notified of your grade and your rank as soon as all these computations have been made. This will be done as rapidly as possible.

People who are found to meet the requirements in the announcement are called "eligibles." Their names are put on a list of eligible candidates. An eligible's chances of getting a job depend on how high he stands on this list and how fast agencies are filling jobs from the list.

When a job is to be filled from a list of eligibles, the agency asks for the names of people on the list of eligibles for that job. When the civil service commission receives this request, it sends to the agency the names of the three people highest on this list. Or, if the job to be filled has specialized requirements, the office sends the agency the names of the top three persons who meet these requirements from the general list.

The appointing officer makes a choice from among the three people whose names were sent to him. If the selected person accepts the appointment, the names of the others are put back on the list to be considered for future openings.

That is the rule in hiring from all kinds of eligible lists, whether they are for typist, carpenter, chemist, or something else. For every vacancy, the appointing officer has his choice of any one of the top three eligibles on the list. This explains why the person whose name is on top of the list sometimes does not get an appointment when some of the persons lower on the list do. If the appointing officer chooses the second or third eligible, the No. 1 eligible does not get a job at once, but stays on the list until he is appointed or the list is terminated.

X. HOW TO PASS THE INTERVIEW TEST

The examination for which you applied requires an oral interview test. You have already taken the written test and you are now being called for the interview test – the final part of the formal examination.

You may think that it is not possible to prepare for an interview test and that there are no procedures to follow during an interview. Our purpose is to point out some things you can do in advance that will help you and some good rules to follow and pitfalls to avoid while you are being interviewed.

What is an interview supposed to test?

The written examination is designed to test the technical knowledge and competence of the candidate; the oral is designed to evaluate intangible qualities, not readily measured otherwise, and to establish a list showing the relative fitness of each candidate – as measured against his competitors – for the position sought. Scoring is not on the basis of "right" and "wrong," but on a sliding scale of values ranging from "not passable" to "outstanding." As a matter of fact, it is possible to achieve a relatively low score without a single "incorrect" answer because of evident weakness in the qualities being measured.

Occasionally, an examination may consist entirely of an oral test – either an individual or a group oral. In such cases, information is sought concerning the technical knowledges and abilities of the candidate, since there has been no written examination for this purpose. More commonly, however, an oral test is used to supplement a written examination.

Who conducts interviews?

The composition of oral boards varies among different jurisdictions. In nearly all, a representative of the personnel department serves as chairman. One of the members of the board may be a representative of the department in which the candidate would work. In some cases, "outside experts" are used, and, frequently, a businessman or some other representative of the general public is asked to serve. Labor and management or other special groups may be represented. The aim is to secure the services of experts in the appropriate field.

However the board is composed, it is a good idea (and not at all improper or unethical) to ascertain in advance of the interview who the members are and what groups they represent. When you are introduced to them, you will have some idea of their backgrounds and interests, and at least you will not stutter and stammer over their names.

What should be done before the interview?

While knowledge about the board members is useful and takes some of the surprise element out of the interview, there is other preparation which is more substantive. It *is* possible to prepare for an oral interview – in several ways:

1) Keep a copy of your application and review it carefully before the interview

This may be the only document before the oral board, and the starting point of the interview. Know what education and experience you have listed there, and the sequence and dates of all of it. Sometimes the board will ask you to review the highlights of your experience for them; you should not have to hem and haw doing it.

2) Study the class specification and the examination announcement

Usually, the oral board has one or both of these to guide them. The qualities, characteristics or knowledges required by the position sought are stated in these documents. They offer valuable clues as to the nature of the oral interview. For example, if the job involves supervisory responsibilities, the announcement will usually indicate that knowledge of modern supervisory methods and the qualifications of the candidate as a supervisor will be tested. If so, you can expect such questions, frequently in the form of a hypothetical situation which you are expected to solve. NEVER go into an oral without knowledge of the duties and responsibilities of the job you seek.

3) Think through each qualification required

Try to visualize the kind of questions you would ask if you were a board member. How well could you answer them? Try especially to appraise your own knowledge and background in each area, *measured against the job sought*, and identify any areas in which you are weak. Be critical and realistic – do not flatter yourself.

4) Do some general reading in areas in which you feel you may be weak

For example, if the job involves supervision and your past experience has NOT, some general reading in supervisory methods and practices, particularly in the field of human relations, might be useful. Do NOT study agency procedures or detailed manuals. The oral board will be testing your understanding and capacity, not your memory.

5) Get a good night's sleep and watch your general health and mental attitude

You will want a clear head at the interview. Take care of a cold or any other minor ailment, and of course, no hangovers.

What should be done on the day of the interview?

Now comes the day of the interview itself. Give yourself plenty of time to get there. Plan to arrive somewhat ahead of the scheduled time, particularly if your appointment is in the fore part of the day. If a previous candidate fails to appear, the board might be ready for you a bit early. By early afternoon an oral board is almost invariably behind schedule if there are many candidates, and you may have to wait. Take along a book or magazine to read, or your application to review, but leave any extraneous material in the waiting room when you go in for your interview. In any event, relax and compose yourself.

The matter of dress is important. The board is forming impressions about you – from your experience, your manners, your attitude, and your appearance. Give your personal appearance careful attention. Dress your best, but not your flashiest. Choose conservative, appropriate clothing, and be sure it is immaculate. This is a business interview, and your appearance should indicate that you regard it as such. Besides, being well groomed and properly dressed will help boost your confidence.

Sooner or later, someone will call your name and escort you into the interview room. *This is it.* From here on you are on your own. It is too late for any more preparation. But remember, you asked for this opportunity to prove your fitness, and you are here because your request was granted.

What happens when you go in?

The usual sequence of events will be as follows: The clerk (who is often the board stenographer) will introduce you to the chairman of the oral board, who will introduce you to the other members of the board. Acknowledge the introductions before you sit down. Do not be surprised if you find a microphone facing you or a stenotypist sitting by. Oral interviews are usually recorded in the event of an appeal or other review.

Usually the chairman of the board will open the interview by reviewing the highlights of your education and work experience from your application – primarily for the benefit of the other members of the board, as well as to get the material into the record. Do not interrupt or comment unless there is an error or significant misinterpretation; if that is the case, do not hesitate. But do not quibble about insignificant matters. Also, he will usually ask you some question about your education, experience or your present job – partly to get you to start talking and to establish the interviewing "rapport." He may start the actual questioning, or turn it over to one of the other members. Frequently, each member undertakes the questioning on a particular area, one in which he is perhaps most competent, so you can expect each member to participate in the examination. Because time is limited, you may also expect some rather abrupt switches in the direction the questioning takes, so do not be upset by it. Normally, a board member will not pursue a single line of questioning unless he discovers a particular strength or weakness.

After each member has participated, the chairman will usually ask whether any member has any further questions, then will ask you if you have anything you wish to add. Unless you are expecting this question, it may floor you. Worse, it may start you off on an extended, extemporaneous speech. The board is not usually seeking more information. The question is principally to offer you a last opportunity to present further qualifications or to indicate that you have nothing to add. So, if you feel that a significant qualification or characteristic has been overlooked, it is proper to point it out in a sentence or so. Do not compliment the board on the thoroughness of their examination – they have been sketchy, and you know it. If you wish, merely say, "No thank you, I have nothing further to add." This is a point where you can "talk yourself out" of a good impression or fail to present an important bit of information. Remember, *you close the interview yourself.*

The chairman will then say, "That is all, Mr. _______, thank you." Do not be startled; the interview is over, and quicker than you think. Thank him, gather your belongings and take your leave. Save your sigh of relief for the other side of the door.

How to put your best foot forward

Throughout this entire process, you may feel that the board individually and collectively is trying to pierce your defenses, seek out your hidden weaknesses and embarrass and confuse you. Actually, this is not true. They are obliged to make an appraisal of your qualifications for the job you are seeking, and they want to see you in your best light. Remember, they must interview all candidates and a non-cooperative candidate may become a failure in spite of their best efforts to bring out his qualifications. Here are 15 suggestions that will help you:

1) Be natural – Keep your attitude confident, not cocky

If you are not confident that you can do the job, do not expect the board to be. Do not apologize for your weaknesses, try to bring out your strong points. The board is interested in a positive, not negative, presentation. Cockiness will antagonize any board member and make him wonder if you are covering up a weakness by a false show of strength.

2) Get comfortable, but don't lounge or sprawl

Sit erectly but not stiffly. A careless posture may lead the board to conclude that you are careless in other things, or at least that you are not impressed by the importance of the occasion. Either conclusion is natural, even if incorrect. Do not fuss with your clothing, a pencil or an ashtray. Your hands may occasionally be useful to emphasize a point; do not let them become a point of distraction.

3) Do not wisecrack or make small talk

This is a serious situation, and your attitude should show that you consider it as such. Further, the time of the board is limited – they do not want to waste it, and neither should you.

4) Do not exaggerate your experience or abilities

In the first place, from information in the application or other interviews and sources, the board may know more about you than you think. Secondly, you probably will not get away with it. An experienced board is rather adept at spotting such a situation, so do not take the chance.

5) If you know a board member, do not make a point of it, yet do not hide it

Certainly you are not fooling him, and probably not the other members of the board. Do not try to take advantage of your acquaintanceship – it will probably do you little good.

6) Do not dominate the interview

Let the board do that. They will give you the clues – do not assume that you have to do all the talking. Realize that the board has a number of questions to ask you, and do not try to take up all the interview time by showing off your extensive knowledge of the answer to the first one.

7) Be attentive

You only have 20 minutes or so, and you should keep your attention at its sharpest throughout. When a member is addressing a problem or question to you, give him your undivided attention. Address your reply principally to him, but do not exclude the other board members.

8) Do not interrupt

A board member may be stating a problem for you to analyze. He will ask you a question when the time comes. Let him state the problem, and wait for the question.

9) Make sure you understand the question

Do not try to answer until you are sure what the question is. If it is not clear, restate it in your own words or ask the board member to clarify it for you. However, do not haggle about minor elements.

10) Reply promptly but not hastily

A common entry on oral board rating sheets is "candidate responded readily," or "candidate hesitated in replies." Respond as promptly and quickly as you can, but do not jump to a hasty, ill-considered answer.

11) Do not be peremptory in your answers

A brief answer is proper – but do not fire your answer back. That is a losing game from your point of view. The board member can probably ask questions much faster than you can answer them.

12) Do not try to create the answer you think the board member wants

He is interested in what kind of mind you have and how it works – not in playing games. Furthermore, he can usually spot this practice and will actually grade you down on it.

13) Do not switch sides in your reply merely to agree with a board member

Frequently, a member will take a contrary position merely to draw you out and to see if you are willing and able to defend your point of view. Do not start a debate, yet do not surrender a good position. If a position is worth taking, it is worth defending.

14) Do not be afraid to admit an error in judgment if you are shown to be wrong

The board knows that you are forced to reply without any opportunity for careful consideration. Your answer may be demonstrably wrong. If so, admit it and get on with the interview.

15) Do not dwell at length on your present job

The opening question may relate to your present assignment. Answer the question but do not go into an extended discussion. You are being examined for a *new* job, not your present one. As a matter of fact, try to phrase ALL your answers in terms of the job for which you are being examined.

Basis of Rating

Probably you will forget most of these "do's" and "don'ts" when you walk into the oral interview room. Even remembering them all will not ensure you a passing grade. Perhaps you did not have the qualifications in the first place. But remembering them will help you to put your best foot forward, without treading on the toes of the board members.

Rumor and popular opinion to the contrary notwithstanding, an oral board wants you to make the best appearance possible. They know you are under pressure – but they also want to see how you respond to it as a guide to what your reaction would be under the pressures of the job you seek. They will be influenced by the degree of poise you display, the personal traits you show and the manner in which you respond.

ABOUT THIS BOOK

This book contains tests divided into Examination Sections. Go through each test, answering every question in the margin. We have also attached a sample answer sheet at the back of the book that can be removed and used. At the end of each test look at the answer key and check your answers. On the ones you got wrong, look at the right answer choice and learn. Do not fill in the answers first. Do not memorize the questions and answers, but understand the answer and principles involved. On your test, the questions will likely be different from the samples. Questions are changed and new ones added. If you understand these past questions you should have success with any changes that arise. Tests may consist of several types of questions. We have additional books on each subject should more study be advisable or necessary for you. Finally, the more you study, the better prepared you will be. This book is intended to be the last thing you study before you walk into the examination room. Prior study of relevant texts is also recommended. NLC publishes some of these in our Fundamental Series. Knowledge and good sense are important factors in passing your exam. Good luck also helps. So now study this Passbook, absorb the material contained within and take that knowledge into the examination. Then do your best to pass that exam.

EXAMINATION SECTION

EXAMINATION SECTION
TEST 1

DIRECTIONS: Each question or incomplete statement is followed by several suggested answers or completions. Select the one that BEST answers the question or completes the statement. *PRINT THE LETTER OF THE CORRECT ANSWER IN THE SPACE AT THE RIGHT.*

1. All of the following are *true* of parking nodes EXCEPT: 1.____

   A. They should be limited to straight or long sweeping curved sections of channel
   B. They should be limited to channels whose width does not exceed fifty feet
   C. Minimum distance between nodes should not be less than 400 feet
   D. Channel flow should not be directed into the opposite bank
   E. The general shape of nodes should be streamlined

2. *Which* of the following methods is MOST successful in eliminating undesirable fish in lakes? 2.____

   A. Netting B. Trapping C. Spearfishing
   D. Commercial fishing E. Liberalized harvest regulations

3. *What* is the MAIN disadvantage of sodium arsenite in the control of aquatic weeds? 3.____

   A. It is only really effective under acid conditions
   B. Results are too variable
   C. It is very corrosive
   D. It is highly toxic to fish, birds, and mammals
   E. Polyneuritis results from prolonged skin contact

4. *What* is the PRINCIPAL target species of greentree reservoirs? 4.____

   A. Turkey B. Deer C. Quail D. Raccoon E. Duck

5. *What* is the MOST practical way of reducing algae growth in guzzlers? By: 5.____

   A. *Maintaining* adequate chemical levels in the tank
   B. *Locating* them under a cover of trees
   C. *Facing* the open end of the tank in a northerly direction
   D. *Placing* the guzzler in a gully where it will collect silt
   E. *Adding* synthetic dyes to the cistern

6. All of the following are *good* herbaceous marsh plants *EXCEPT* 6.____

   A. cattails B. arrowheads C. bulrushes
   D. smartweed E. snowberry

7. *Which of* the following aquatic plants are classified as emersed plants? 7.____

   I. Cattails
   II. Pondweeds
   III. III Bulrushes
   IV. Waterweed
   V. Sedges

   The CORRECT answer is:

A. I, IV, V
B. I, III, V
C. I, IV
D. I, II, III
E. II, III, IV, V

8. *What* are the *most common* chemicals used to control emersed plants? 8.____

I. 2,4-D ester formulations
II. Silvex
III. Dalapon
IV. Copper sulfate
V. Dichlone

The CORRECT answer is:

A. I, IV
B. I, II, III
C. I, III
D. I, III, V
E. I, II, IV

9. All of the following are true of the selection of a site for a greentree reservoir EXCEPT: The 9.____

A. area should be close to a low gradient stream
B. area should be flat
C. area should contain absorbent soil
D. area should have a mast-bearing oak timber that is adapted to flooding
E. water supply must be ample and dependable

10. *Where* do guzzlers have their greatest value? In 10.____

A. areas with sufficient rainfall to supply them
B. semi-arid regions where natural water is widely spread
C. areas where the soil is heavy clay and difficult to drain
D. areas that can be managed for a variety of wildlife
E. areas that do not offer the required arrangement of nearby cover and nottoodistant foods

11. *Which* tree species is probably the *single most important* mast producer through the country? 11.____

A. Oak
B. Hickory
C. Beech
D. Gum
E. Cherry

12. *Which* of the following are floating-leafed plants? 12.____

I. Water buttercups
II. Duck weed
III. Water shield
IV. Pond weed
V. Water weed

The CORRECT answer is:

A. I, III, IV
B. I, IV, V
C. II, III, IV
D. II, III
E. II, IV, V

13. *Why* is fishing water fertilized? To 13.____

I. produce more game fish poundage
II. control or eliminate submersed aquatic weeds
III. control or eliminate algal growths
IV. decrease turbidity
V. produce greater natural reproduction of lake fish

The CORRECT answer is:

A. I, II B. I, III C. I, IV, V D. I, V E. I, II, III, V

14. *Which* of the following species of trees are considered *good* food producers for waterfowl? 14.____

I. Cherrybark oak
II. Elm
III. Hackberry
IV. Sycamore
V. Willow oak

The CORRECT answer is:

A. I, V
B. I, II, IV
C. II, III, IV
D. II, IV
E. I, III, V

15. A guzzler is similar *to* a 15.____

A. corridor
B. dugout
C. spillway
D. cistern
E. cesspool

16. *Where* should a wood duck nest be placed so that it is *least likely* to be usurped by starlings? 16.____

A. On trees
B. On stumps
C. On posts over water
D. In open parklike woods
E. In dense woods

17. *Which of* the following are true of phytoplankton in lakes and ponds? 17.____

I. They are tiny one-celled plants
II. They are attached to the bottom or lie on submerged objects
III. They can cause taste or odor problems in the water
IV. When they die or are broken loose, they entrap gas bubbles and are floated upward to accumulate on the surface
V. They produce toxins capable of killing fish, birds, and mammals

The CORRECT answer is:

A. I, II, III
B. I, III, IV
C. I, III, V
D. II, III
E. I, II, III, IV

18. *What* dangers are involved in the use of fertilizers? 18.____

I. The resulting increase in plankton production may cause serious depletion of oxygen
II. Inorganic fertilizers may cause clay particles to settle out of muddy ponds
III. Use of commercial fertilizers in nesting areas of spiny-ray fish may cause some of the embryos to die
IV. Fertilization may upset an efficient natural food chain
V. Fertilization may result in excessive production of filamentous algae

The CORRECT answer is:

A. I, II, III
B. II, III
C. I, II, IV, V
D. I, IV, V
E. II, III, IV, V

19. *Which* species of trees should be *avoided* for use in a green-tree reservoir? 19.____

I. Boxelder
II. Pine
III. Soft maple
IV. Pin oak
V. Tupelo

The CORRECT answer is:

A. II, IV
B. I, II, III
C. II, III, IV
D. II, IV, V
E. I, II, V

20. The tanks used for guzzlers are usually made of 20.____

I. concrete
II. rubber
III. asphalt
IV. plastic
V. plywood

The CORRECT answer is:

A. I, III
B. II, IV, V
C. IV, V
D. II, IV
E. I, IV

21. *What* is the MAJOR drawback of beechnut mast? 21.____

A. The nuts are bitter
B. Few species prefer them
C. The nuts do not withstand freezing
D. The nuts do not last through the critical season
E. Production is not consistent

22. *What* type of algal growth forms a floating surface mat and is referred to as "pond scum?" 22.____

A. Phytoplankton
B. Filamentous algae
C. Branched algae
D. Submersed algae
E. Macrophytes

23. *Which* of the following are *true* of direct lake fertilization with lime? 23.____

I. In areas where total water hardness is low, lime should be applied prior to general fertilization projects
II. Calcium is almost immediately available when agricultural lime is used in place of hydrated lime
III. Liming is recommended for unproductive, acid, highly-colored bog lakes
IV. Lime may eliminate fish parasites
V. Best results are obtained when lime and phosphate are added at the same time

The CORRECT answer is:

A. I, IV, V
B. III, IV, V
C. I, II, IV
D. I, III, IV, V
E. I, III, IV

24. *What* is the MOST important consideration in providing artificial nesting sites for water fowl? 24.____

A. Placement
B. Construction
C. Installation
D. Design
E. Maintenance

25. *What* determines the size of the water-collecting apron to fill a guzzler? 25._____

A. Minimum annual rainfall
B. Average annual rainfall
C. Maximum annual rainfall
D. The water shed's target species
E. The site location

26. The procedure used to release durable browse plants from the competition of less desirable species *mainly* depends upon 26._____

A. geological formation
B. the time and intensity of the application
C. plant ecology
D. the action of biological agents
E. climate conditions

27. *Which* of the following are submersed plants? 27._____

I. Pond weed
II. Waterweed
III. Pickerel weed
IV. Cattails
V. Coontails

The CORRECT answer is:

A. I, II, III
B. I, II
C. IV, V
D. II, IV
E. I, III, V

28. All of the following are the results of dry fall of drainable basins EXCEPT: 28._____

A. Release of phosphates and other fertilizers from insoluble bonds with iron and other minerals
B. Control of overpopulations of forage fish
C. Increase in decomposition
D. pH is increased
E. Release of various fertilizers from organic colloidal systems

29. *Which* of the following are true of nesting cover for waterfowl? 29._____

I. Bare shorelines should be replaced with closely-grazed pastures
II. Openings should be created when lakes or ponds are closely surrounded with dense brush cover
III. Reservoir drawdown is an effective method of manipulating cover
IV. Aquatic vegetation can be improved with deep water along the shoreline
V. The easiest way to provide brook cover is to leave trees and shrub growth uncut when the reservoir is constructed

The CORRECT answer is:

A. I, III, V
B. I, II, III
C. I, IV, V
D. II, III
E. All of the above

30. Reservoirs intended for use by water fowl should 30._____

I. have gently sloping shorelines
II. have shllow areas with mud flats
III. have desirable emergent vegetation
IV. have tree cover
V. not offer a desirqble habitat for small game

The CORRECT answer is:

A. I, II, V
B. I, II, III, V
C. I, III, III, IV
D. I, II, IV
E. All of the above

31. The field width of a chaining operation intended to release browse is determined by all of the following EXCEPT 31.____

A. density of the vegetation
B. type of vegetation
C. weight and length of the anchor chain
D. size of the tractors used
E. topography

32. Physical control of aquatic weeds involves: 32.____

I. Adding synthetic dyes to lakes
II. Using a hand sickle or scythe
III. Adding nutrients to the water
IV. Spreading opaque black polyethylene sheeting over thesurface or bottom of the pond or lake
V. Stocking water with herbivores of aquatic vegetation

The CORRECT answer is:

A. I, II
B. II, V
C. II, IV
D. I, II, IV
E. I, III, IV

33. An ideal wetland for water fowl has _______ open water, _______ marsh. 33.____

A. 1/2, 1/2
B. 1/4, 3/4
C. 1/3, 2/3
D. 2/3, 1/3
E. 3/4, 1/4

34. *Which* of the following are the *essential* elements of the wildlife habitat? 34.____

I. Food
II. Topography
III. Water
IV. Soil
V. Cover

The CORRECT answer is:

A. II, III, IV
B. I, III, V
C. I, II, III
D. I, II
E. II, IV, V

35. *Which* of the following are true for selecting reservoir sites? 35.____

I. Reservoirs for wildlife should be no longer than are needed to serve the forage area
II. The most suitable soil is straight, clay soils
III. The watershed above the dam should not be large enough for flood damage to occur
IV. The channel grade immediately above the dam should have a fairly steep slope
V. Access to the water should be limited to the target species

The CORRECT answer is:

A. I, II, III
B. I, II, III, V
C. I, III
D. I, III, IV
E. III, IV, V

36. *What* determines the size of the chain used to thin browse? The 36.____

A. width of the field
B. topography
C. degree of kill desired
D. density of the target species
E. size of the tractors used

37. *What* are the disadvantages of creating organic turbidity as a means of aquatic weed control? It 37.____

I. results in reduced use of the lake by swimmers and fishermen
II. is not practical on waters larger than small ponds or pot holes
III. can cause winterkill of fish
IV. is only practical for control of emersed plants
V. can cause development of filamentous algae

The CORRECT answer is:

A. I, II, III B. I, II, IV C. I, V D. III, V E. I, II, V

38. *What* are the MOST important items to consider in a pond or pothole program? 38.____

I. Soil type
II. Slope of the pond margins
III. Water quality and quantity
IV. Nesting sites
V. Plant species

The CORRECT answer is:

A. I, II
B. III, IV
C. I, II, III
D. I, II, IV
E. All of the above

39. *Which* of the following are important to the design of spring developments? 39.____

I. At least one escape route to and from the water should be provided
II. Protective fences should be negotiable by wildlife
III. Fenceposts should be pointed to discourage perching by avian predators
IV. Natural cover should be cleared from the watering area surroundings
V. Protective fences should be negotiable by domestic livestock

The CORRECT answer is:

A. I, III, V
B. I, IV
C. I, II, III
D. I, III, IV
E. All of the above

40. *What* is the *minimum* width of the top of all dams constructed for reservoir sites? _______ feet. 40.____

A. 5 B. 10 C. 20 D. 30 E. 40

41. Browse is most *effectively* thinned by chaining when 41.____

A. moisture has thoroughly saturated the soil
B. the ground is not frozen
C. there is no danger of frost
D. the first several inches of soil are devoid of moisture
E. soil moisture is minimal

42. *Which* of the following methods are most *effective* in controlling duckweeds? Use of 42.____
    I. wild ducks
    II. domestic muscovy ducks
    III. 2,4-D ester mormulations in an oil carrier
    IV. kerosene
    V. minnow seine

The CORRECT answer is:

A. I, III, V
B. II, III
C. I, II, III
D. III, IV, V
E. I, III

43. *What* are the benefits of ditching marshes? It 43.____
    I. *increases* the variety of habitat for furbearers and waterfowl
    II. *helps* animals find food and cover during dry periods
    III. *facilitates* access for hunters
    IV. *provides* necessary openings
    V. protects prey fish from predators

The CORRECT answer is:

A. I, III, IV
B. I, III, IV, V
C. III, IV, V
D. I, II, III
E. All of the above

44. *What* is the purpose of installing ramps in the drinking troughs of spring developments? To 44.____

A. make them accessible to the target species
B. control access to them by wildlife
C. allow access to the public
D. provide access for maintenance purposes
E. provide safety from wildlife drownings

45. *Which* of the following are *essential* to constructing spillways of reservoirs? 45.____
    I. The spillway should have a capacity equaling that required to handle the largest known volume of runoff
    II. It should be designed to allow the water level to rise just to the top of the dam
    III. It should be wide and flat-bottomed
    IV. It should be protected from washing by riprapping
    V. The entrance should be narrow, and the grade of the spillway channel steep so that the water will pass through rapidly

The CORRECT answer is:

A. I, II, IV
B. I, IV
C. I, II, V
D. III, IV
E. II, III, IV

46. *Which* of the following methods can effectively be used to remove competition from rocky browse sites? 46.____

A. A hula dozer
B. Mechanical scalping
C. A wheatland plow
D. Hand scalping
E. Cabling

47. *What* is the most *common* algacide? 47.____

A. Copper sulfate
B. Sodium arsenite compounds

C. Sodium and potassium salts of endothal
D. Silvex
E. Diquat

48. *What* are the *advantages* of dredging as a method of ditch construction? 48.____
I. Dredged ditches are shallower than blasted ditches
II. There are lesser quantities of muck loosened along the edge of the ditch
III. High spoil banks are not created
IV. It is more expeditious and economical than blasting
V. Ditches are less susceptible to wave and wind erosion

The CORRECT answer is:

A. I, III
B. II, V
C. I, II, IV, V
D. I, II, III
E. None of the above

49. *Which* of the following principles should guide the installation of a guzzler? 49.____
I. It should not be placed in a gully
II. The tank should be placed with its open end toward the prevailing wind
III. It is more effective if an escape cover of trees is immediately adjacent
IV. When possible, the open end of the tank should face away from a northerly direction
V. The size of the water-collecting apron should be proportioned so that the tank will maintain an adequate water supply

The CORRECT answer is:

A. I, V
B. II, III, IV
C. III.V
D. II, IV
E. All of the above

50. When reservoirs are built in drainages where the chances are high that the tank will be filled with sand, 50.____

A. the bottom should be salted to encourage "puddling" the soil by livestock trampling
B. bentonite should be spread over the bottom and sides of the pit and face of the dam
C. a pipeline should be installed through the dam during construction
D. the reservoir should be built for the greatest possible ratio of depth to area
E. utilize fencing specifications which will prevent the tank from becoming clogged.

KEY (CORRECT ANSWERS)

1.	B	11.	A	21.	E	31.	B	41.	E
2.	D	12.	D	22.	B	32.	E	42.	B
3.	D	13.	A	23.	E	33.	C	43.	D
4.	E	14.	E	24.	A	34.	B	44.	E
5.	C	15.	D	25.	A	35.	C	45.	D
6.	E	16.	E	26.	B	36.	C	46.	D
7.	B	17.	C	27.	B	37.	D	47.	A
8.	B	18.	D	28.	A	38.	E	48.	B
9.	C	19.	B	29.	D	39.	C	49.	A
10.	B	20.	E	30.	C	40.	B	50.	C

EXAMINATION SECTION
TEST 1

DIRECTIONS: Each question or incomplete statement is followed by several suggested answers or completions. Select the one that BEST answers the question or completes the statement. *PRINT THE LETTER OF THE CORRECT ANSWER IN THE SPACE AT THE RIGHT.*

1. Which of the following statements are TRUE of stream improvement? 1.____
   I. The term denotes procedures for correcting an environmental deficiency or man-made problem
   II. Its prime purpose is increased fishfood production.
   III. It includes any treatment of the watershed that results in a favorable influence upon fish habitat.
   IV. It corrects conditions that continue to be aggravated by damaging floods.
   V. It may, under favorable conditions, improve shelter and spawning conditions.

   The CORRECT answer is:

   A. I, II, III B. I, III C. I, III, IV D. I, II, III, V
   E. All of the above

2. Why are deflectors preferable to dams? They 2.____
   I. are less subject to destruction
   II. are less disturbing to the stream bottom
   III. allow vegetation to be established on deposits formed to one side of the stream
   IV. help to protect eroding banks
   V. cut off side channels or direct the flow to a more suitable channel

   The CORRECT answer is:

   A. II, IV, V B. III, IV, V C. I, II D. II, IV
   E. All of the above

3. Fishways may not be justified where: 3.____
   I. There is not enough satisfactory upstream area to justify the cost
   II. Streams are populated with anadromous species
   III. There are insurmountable problems in getting a satisfactory return of downstream migrants to the ocean
   IV. The flow fluctuates considerably
   V. It is more economical to provide hatching channels below a dam

   The CORRECT answer is:

   A. I, II, IV B. II, III, V C. III, IV D. I, III, V E. II, IV

4. The most expensive structure used *to* prevent bank erosion next to roads is: 4.____

   A. Parking nodes
   B. Log revetments
   C. Gabion revetments
   D. Gabion matting
   E. Riprap

5. All of the following are harmful effects of turbidity EXCEPT: 5.____

   A. Sight-feeders are disadvantaged
   B. There is a decrease in dissolved nitrogen levels
   C. There is a reduction in bottom organisms
   D. There is destruction of sedimentation in spawning areas
   E. Removal of algae and plants occurs

6. When erosion products reach streams, they 6.___
   I. fill ponds
   II. cause the removal of algae, plants, and bottom food organisms
   III. block fish passage
   IV. destroy cover
   V. increase turbidity

   The CORRECT answer is:

   A. I, V B. II, III, V C. III, V D. I, IV, V E. II, IV, V

7. Which of the following prescriptions should guide random boulder placement? 7.___
   I. Boulder placement is most effective in narrow, shallow, and moderate-to-low velocity stream channels
   II. Boulder placement should be avoided in narrow channels with unstable banks
   III. Boulders should be two-thirds of a cubic yard or larger
   IV. All boulders should be placed so that they may be opera- tional in high water periods
   V. The number of boulders placed should be at least one per 300 square feet of channel

   The CORRECT answer is:

   A. I, II, IV B. II, III C. II, III, IV, V D. III, V
   E. I, II, III, V

8. A type of fish ladder that consists of a series of ascending boxes set in a chute is: 8.___

   A. Pool and weir ladders
   B. Pool and orifice ladders
   C. Denils
   D. Alaskan steeppasses
   E. Fish locks and elevators

9. What is the MAIN reason for providing fish cover in lakes? It 9.___

   A. helps lower water temperatures
   B. offers protection from bird and mammal predators
   C. attracts fish
   D. produces greater natural reproduction
   E. decreases evaporation

10. Turbidity control for stream improvement is usually accomplished by 10.___

    A. increasing water flow
    B. removal of shade
    C. use of instream devices
    D. chemical treatment
    E. improvement of riparian vegetation

11. Direct channel improvement projects have been unsuccessful for all of the following reasons EXCEPT: 11.___

    A. Methods well-adapted to a one region gave poor results elsewhere
    B. Limitations imposed by steep gradients and extreme fluctuations in flow were ignored
    C. Abused watersheds were treated before or during the stream project work
    D. Improper devices were selected
    E. Devices were improperly installed

12. One of the MOST expensive deflectors is a ______ deflector. 12.____

A. sheet piling
B. rock
C. trash piling
D. cabled tree
E. gambion

13. What type of fish ladder is used *mainly* for passing small runs of fish over high barriers? 13.____

A. Denils
B. Alaskan steeppasses
C. Pool and weir ladders
D. Pool and orifice ladders
E. Fish locks and elevators

14. How may the buildup of undesirable fish population be determined? By: 14.____

I. Installing natural or artificial barriers
II. Creel censuses
III. Netting surveys
IV. Draining small lakes and ponds
V. Trapping surveys

The CORRECT answer is:

A. I, IV
B. I, III, IV
C. I, III
D. II, III, V
E. III, V

15. All of the following may deplete oxygen supplies EXCEPT: 15.____

A. Decrease in temperature
B. Respiration of plants and animals
C. Reactions with other gases and chemicals
D. Decomposition of organic matter
E. Presence of iron

16. Which of the following guidelines should be considered in planning a direct channel improvement project? 16.____

I. The need for improvement should be obvious
II. Bank deflectors are more susceptible to flood damage than dams
III. Log and sheet piling installations are better suited to streams with steeper gradients and larger flows than gambion structures
IV. Improvements should not be concentrated in one area but should be placed where they are most needed
V. When possible, structures should be located where solid bedrock occurs a few inches below the rubble

The CORRECT answers is:

A. I, IV
B. I, III, V
C. III, V
D. II, III, V
E. None of the above

17. Cabled tree deflectors: 17.____

I. Use only long trees
II. Use only trees with a large trunk circumference
III. Cable the trees parallel to the bank
IV. Must have the butt of the tree pointing downstream
V. Increase deflection by using trees with a maximum number of limbs The CORRECT answer is:

A. I, II, III
B. III, IV
C. III, V
D. I, II, III, IV
E. All of the above

18. What is the PRINCIPAL disadvantage of pool and orifice ladders? 18.____

A. They are unable to function where the flow fluctuates considerably.
B. Too much flashboard adjustment is required.
C. They have a tendency to plug with debris at high flows and are difficult to clean.
D. Mechanical problems and heavy maintenance often cause high operating costs.
E. They are too expensive.

19. Stratified dispersal of toxicants are required in 19.____

A. heterothermous lakes
B. lakes that cannot be completely drained
C. very deep lakes
D. lakes with both desirable and undesirable species
E. lakes with heavy cover

20. Carbon dioxide is removed from water by: 20.____

I. Reaction with other chemicals
II. Inflow of subterranean water
III. Photosynthesis
IV. Agitation of water
V. Evaporation

The CORRECT answer is:

A. III, V B. II, III C. I, II, III D. I, II E. III, IV, V

21. Which of the following are the MOST practical to use in the creation or improvement of pools? 21.____

I. Mechanical excavation
II. Digging logs
III. Deflectors
IV. Blasting
V. Dams

The CORRECT answer is:

A. I, II B. III, IV C. II, V D. II, V E. I, IV

22. Which of the following statements are TRUE of improving gravel bed for trout and salmon propagation? 22.____

I. The objective is to remove materials too small for spawning use.
II. Selected sites should not be subject to sediment from upstream sources.
III. The survival rate in cleaned riffles is 40-60% greater than before treatment.
IV. Bed stability must be controlled before cleaning procedures begin.
V. Cleaning procedures are followed by maintenance of sustained minimum flows.

The CORRECT answer is:

A. I, II, III B. I, IV, V C. I, III, V D. I, II, IV
E. All of the above

23. Which of the following are true of denils? They 23._____
    I. constitute an improved version of the Alaskan steeppass
    II. are usually built over low barriers
    III. are portable
    IV. have good entrance characteristics
    V. pass debris well

The CORRECT answer is:

A. I, II, III B. II, IV, V C. I, II, IV
D. All of the above E. None of the above

24. What are the disadvantages of aquatic plants in lakes? 24._____
    I. Certain types trap the eggs of insects and fish
    II. The decomposition of dead plants consumes oxygen
    III. Decomposing plants sometimes produce toxins which kill fish
    IV. Less fish-food is available per unit area
    V. Certain types increase turbidity

The CORRECT answer is:

A. I, III, V B. II, IV, V C. II, III D. I, III
E. II, V

25. What is the BEST *single* indicator of productivity? 25._____

A. pH B. Total hardness C. Carbon dioxide
D. Oxygen E. Turbidity

26. *Most* dam failures are due to: 26._____
    I. Omitting to bracelog dams behind trees or large boulders or extending them at least six feet into the bank
    II. Construction of low dams that are more subject to destruction by floods than high ones
    III. Building dams so high that floodwaters are forced over the bank at either end
    IV. Constructing or directing the flow through wide notches, greater than one-fourth the total width of the dam
    V. Restricting log-type dams to channel widths of 20 feet or less

The CORRECT answer is:

A. I, II, III B. I, III C. I, II, IV D. I, V
E. All of the above

27. Debris jams should be removed because they: 27._____
    I. Block fish passage
    II. Are responsible for sedimentation of channels
    III. Are unsightly
    IV. Damage fish habitat
    V. Prevent further sediment deposition downstream

The CORRECT answer is:

A. I, II, V B. I, II, III C. I, IV, V D. II, III
E. II, III, IV, V

28. Fish screens are particularly valuable in situations involving 28.____

A. harmful debris
B. small streams with large volume diversions
C. artificial spawning channels
D. high water velocities
E. fishways of the denil or Alaskan steeppass type

29. What is the purpose of regulating dams? To 29.____

A. decrease the velocity of stream channels
B. provide hiding places for fish during construction projects
C. permit scouring spring flows to remove silt and gravel
D. correct situations where normal stream flows have been pre-empted by irrigation or power diversions
E. supply satisfactory streamflows during the driest months

30. Carbon dioxide is removed from water by: 30.____

I. Reaction with other chemicals
II. Inflow of subterranean water
III. Photosynthesis
IV. Agitation of water
V. Evaporation

The CORRECT answer is:

A. III, V B. II, III C. I, II, III D. I, III E. III, IV, V

31. What type of dam is well suited to large, fast-flowing streams? The 31.____

A. gambion B. simple log C. board D. K
E. trash-catcher

32. Ladders may not pass fish if: 32.____

I. The pools are too large
II. The slope is too shallow
III. Resting areas are inadequate
IV. Hydraulic conditions are unsatisfactory
V. The entrance does not attract fish

The CORRECT answer is:

A. I, III, IV B. I, II, III C. III, IV, V D. IV, V
E. All of the above

33. Riparian vegetation is important to the fish habitat in all of the following ways EXCEPT: 33.____

A. It serves as a buffer strip to block soil movements and to trap and filter out silt
B. The root mats bind the soil in place to provide soil stability
C. When roots extend into the stream, small pools result
D. When shade is provided, it helps keep the water temperature low
E. It provides a habitat for insects

34. All of the following are true of streamflow maintenance dams EXCEPT 34.____

A. Sites must have sufficient storage capacity
B. Sites must be accessible to motor transportation

C. Sites must have an adequate amount of water that can be stored at a reasonable cost
D. The stream should have physical characteristics capable of supporting fish in reasonable quantity
E. Streams without pools do not justify development

35. What is the *most commonly* used method for control of undesirable fish? 35.____

A. Chemicals
B. Netting
C. Trapping
D. Electricabaers
E. Physicalbarriers

36. All of the following emphasize low-stream gradients EXCEPT the ______ dam. 36.____

A. K
B. board
C. trash-catcher
D. simple log
E. gambion

37. All of the following are requirements of a good fishway EXCEPT: 37.____

A. It must not create velocities which exceed the swimming capacity of the fish
B. It must dampen rapid changes in flow patterns
C. It should be deep enough so that fish may remain hidden from view
D. Those in which energy is dissipated by steeppass require resting areas about every two feet of vertical rise
E. It should operate at all stages of the river without need for manual controls

38. What is the MAIN purpose of thinning sites of dense thickets of woody riparian vegetation? 38.____

A. It improves the stand
B. It reduces the area of shade
C. It makes the site more attractive to some animals
D. The site is more productive of insects
E. It allows new species to be introduced

39. The ability of any given body of water to produce plants and animals depends MAINLY upon: 39.____

I. Its size
II. Water movement
III. Waterside
IV. Water quality
V. Its shape

The CORRECT answer is:

A. I, IV, V
B. I, II, III, IV
C. II, III, IV
D. I, V
E. I, II, IV

40. Which of the following statements are TRUE of planning water impoundments? 40.___

I. The site should readily lend itself to dam and spillway construction.
II. A minimum lake depth of 30-40 feet is recommended for greater productivity.
III. Sites which involve flooding of substantial sections of good quality trout stream habitat generally have high priority.
IV. Anticipated sediment deposition in the reservoir basin should be low.
V. Sites at lower mountain elevations are preferable.

The CORRECT answer is:

A. I, IV, V
B. I, II, III
C. III, IV, V
D. I, II, V
E. III, IV

41. Which of the following dams are considered to be relatively inexpensive? 41.___

I. K
II. Board
III. Gambion
IV. Trash-catch
V. I

The CORRECT answer is:

A. I, II, IV
B. II, IV
C. IV, V
D. I, III, IV
E. II, III, V

42. What is the MOST important factor of a fishway? 42.___

A. The angle of the slope
B. The location of the rest areas
C. The hydraulic conditions
D. Adequate maintenance
E. The location of the entrance

43. Which of the following statements are TRUE of steambank plantings of willows? 43.___

I. Successful cuttings result if made while the willows are dormant.
II. When bearer and muskrat are abundant, "hardened" cuttingsm should be used.
III. Best results are obtained when cuttings are planted on mud or silt bars.
IV. The lower end of the cutting should never be exposed to permanently wet soil.
V. Rooting success may be increased by dipping the cutting stub into a commercial root-growth hormone.

The CORRECT answer is:

A. I, II, III
B. I, III, V
C. I, II, IV
D. II, III, IV, V
E. All of the above

44. Warm-water fish do *best* at summer water temperatures near 44.___

A. 60° F.
B. 70° F.
C. 75° F.
D. 80° F.
E. 90° F.

45. Which of the following techniques produce greater natural reproduction of lake fish? 45.____

I. Placing shallow spawning boxes filled with sand and gravel
II. Artificially graveled lake bottoms
III. Manipulating water levels
IV. Manipulating water temperature
V. Placing artificial "holes" on the lake bottom

The CORRECT answer is:

A. I, IV B. I, II, V C. II, III D. II, V
E. None of the above

46. Which of the following characteristics are TRUE of gambion dams? 46.____

I. Highly effective on streams where the flow is very small
II. Best suited to rocky streams where the banks can be excavated to strata sufficiently hard to support the weight of the dam
III. Particularly well adapted to remote stream sections
IV. Extremely effective in protecting stream banks below culverts which accommodate large and highvelocity discharges
V. Extremely effective when restricted to streams less than 10 or 15 feet wide

The CORRECT answer is:

A. I, II, V B. II, III C. I, V D. II, III, IV
E. III, IV

47. Which of the following factors are important in designing weir and pool fishways? 47.____

I. Small fishways should have a water depth of 6-12 inches over the top of the weir
II. Pools that are too large increase the discharge and make the pools very turbulent
III. Fish prefer shaded and dark areas while traveling through fishways
IV. Notches in the weir crests have the effect of increasing the quantity of water required for fish passage
V. Increasing the crest differential decreases the upper limit of plunging flow

The CORRECT answer is:

A. I, II, III B. I, III, IV C. II, IV, V D. I, II, IV, V
E. All of the above

48. Which of the following are benefits of stream bottom fences? They 48.____

I. collect bedload material
II. aid in the establishment of streamside vegetation
III. reduce water velocity
IV. are important to stream improvement by their protection of existing vegetation
V. serve as allotment pasture division fences and aid in the management of livestock

The CORRECT answer is:

A. I, II, III, IV B. II, IV C. I, III, IV D. II, IV, V
E. All of the above

49. Which of the following statements are TRUE of water temperature? 49.___

I. Temperatures affect the water's ability to carry dissolved oxygen.
II. Increasing the temperature in several small tributaries usually does not affect the temperature of the larger receiving stream.
III. Removal of riparian vegetation has little effect on raising water temperature.
IV. Water temperature manipulation may be achieved by regulating reservoir outflows.
V. Both water temperature and streamflow may be increased by the clearcutting of timber in a major portion of a drainage.

The CORRECT answer is:

A. I, V B. II, III, IV C. I, IV, V D. II, IV
E. IV, V

50. Which of the following are advantages of rotenone for selective kills? It 50.___

I. is relatively inexpensive
II. has excellent vertical dispersal through stratified density in lakes
III. is effective in both warm and cold waters
IV. has a low toxicity level to other environmental forms of life
V. is not overly dangerous to the applicator

The CORRECT answer is:

A. I, II, IV B. I, IV C. II, III, IV D. IV, V
E. III, IV, V

KEY (CORRECT ANSWERS)

1. B	11. C	21. C	31. A	41. D
2. E	12. C	22. A	32. C	42. E
3. D	13. E	23. B	33. C	43. B
4. E	14. D	24. C	34. B	44. D
5. B	15. A	25. B	35. A	45. B
6. D	16. A	26. B	36. E	46. E
7. B	17. C	27. D	37. D	47. A
8. A	18. C	28. B	38. D	48. D
9. C	19. A	29. E	39. A	49. C
10. E	20. E	30. E	40. A	50. D

EXAMINATION SECTION
TEST 1

DIRECTIONS: Each question or incomplete statement is followed by several suggested answers or completions. Select the one that BEST answers the question or completes the statement. *PRINT THE LETTER OF THE CORRECT ANSWER IN THE SPACE AT THE RIGHT.*

1. *Which* of the following are the *most important* hickories for mass production? 1.____
   I. Shagbark
   II. Mockernut
   III. Butternut
   IV. Sweetnut
   V. Red Nut

   The CORRECT answer is:

   A. I, IV
   B. I, II, IV
   C. I, II, III
   D. I, IV, V
   E. II, III, IV, V

2. *What* are some of the uses for prescribed burning? It is used 2.____
   I. as the first step in seedbed preparation
   II. to stimulate regeneration of sprouts and seedlings
   III. to create openings in dense stands of brush
   IV. to produce a slight soil sterilant effect
   V. when only crown control is required

   The CORRECT answer is:

   A. III, IV, V
   B. III, IV
   C. I, II, III
   D. II, V
   E. All of the above

3. *Which* of the following are *most important* in determining the method of seed storage? 3.____
   I. Seed characteristics
   II. Time of storage
   III. Length of storage
   IV. Seed quantity
   V. Climate

   The CORRECT answer is:

   A. I, II, V
   B. I, III
   C. II, III, V
   D. I, III, IV
   E. II, III, IV, V

4. Seeds with impervious coats should be soaked in concentrated 4.____

   A. hydrogen peroxide
   B. brine solution
   C. gibberelic acid
   D. sulfuric acid
   E. sodium hydroxide

5. Palatable woody vegetation is called 5.____

   A. forage B. mast C. browse D. pasturage E. brush

6. *Which* of the following is the MAIN requirement for a successful "type conversion"? 6.____

   A. Site and plant selection
   B. Removal of nondesired cover

C. Establishment (if a desired adapted species
D. Soil preparation
E. Maintenance

7. *What* is the *most important* sondieration for rejuvenation treatment projects? 7.____

A. Treat scattered small spots or strips instead of a large single area
B. Gear the amount of forage produced to the number of animals who will be using it
C. Treat areas in a way that the value will be prolonged for a long period
D. Treatments should be rotated so that no one is manipulated more often than once in 10-20 years
E. Tailor the program to fit the actual needs of the target species

8. *What* is the *most satisfactory* method of seed testing? 8.____

A. Flotation
B. Checking the growth of the excised embryos
C. Direct germination success
D. Biochemical staining of embryos
E. Measurement of enzyme activity

9. *Which* of the following are important to the cold stratification breatment for breaking internal dormancy of seeds? 9.____
   I. A suitable moisture-retaining medium
   II. Seeds should be mixed uniformly with about one-to-threetimes their volume of the medium
   III. Containers of seeds should be subjected to below-freezing temperatures for 30-90 days
   IV. Freezing should be followed by cold treatment of around 40° F. for an additional 30-45 days
   V. After treatment, seeds should be allowed to dry thoroughly before planting

The CORRECT answer is:

A. I, II B. I, II, V C. I, II, III, V
D. III, IV, V E. All of the above

10. All of the following are true of prescribed burning EXCEPT: 10.____

A. Backfires are recommended where the trees are small
B. Flankfires are used under larger trees
C. The best condition is a constant, northerly breeze of 3-10 mph.
D. Weather conditions should be constant for a 12-hour period
E. Day burning is preferred for minimum fire intensity

11. *What* constitutes sleeping or roosting cover? 11.____

A. Vegetation offering protection from driving rains and snow
B. Vegetation from which game cannot be driven by predators
C. A place offering shade in summer and wind protection in winter
D. Grassland for some; shrubs or trees for others
E. Shrubs and trees on knolls or ridges

12. *HOW* should Bitterbrush be regenerated? By 12.____
    I. railing
    II. dozing
    III. rolling
    IV. roto-cutting
    V. pruning

    The CORRECT answer is:

    A. I, III B. II, IV C. I, III, V D. III, IV, V E. IV, V

13. All of the following are characteristics of non-viable seeds EXCEPT: They are 13.____

    A. firm
    B. blind
    C. filled with resin
    D. rancid
    E. thin

14. *Which* of the following are TRUE of rodent predation of seeds? 14.____
    I. Small plots are more vulnerable to seed-loss than larger plots
    II. Endrin-Arasan is used as a rodent repellent
    III. Gum-dipped gloves should be used in handling treated seeds
    IV. Steep slopes are less vulnerable to seed loss than flat plots
    V. Aluminum powder is added to the repellent as a marker to attract rodents

    THE CORRECT ANSWER IS:

    A. I, IV
    B. II, III, V
    C. I, II, III
    D. I, II, IV
    E. II, III, IV, V

15. *What* is the MAIN reason for the absence of wildlife in dense virgin forests? 15.____

    A. There is not enough sunlight
    B. There is not enough food
    C. There is little empty space
    D. There is inadequate moisture
    E. Ground cover is inadequate

16. Cover for any species *must* 16.____

    A. provide an escape route
    B. provide adequate food for the trapped species
    C. be dense enough to prevent continued harassment from predators
    D. be able to attract and isolate the species
    E. be abundant enough to offset shortages in other locations

17. *What* are the requirements for chaparral-type brushfields that are targeted for improvement? 17.____
    I. More than 20% of the stand should be composed of desirable browse species
    II. Slope and soil must be favorable
    III. The density of the canopy must be less than 70%
    IV. The average height of the desirable species is less than 5 feet
    V. The browse is unavailable or unpalatable due to the age of the stand

    The CORRECT answer is:

    A. I, II
    B. I, II, V
    C. II, IV, V
    D. II, III, IV, V
    E. All of the above

18. *What* is the *major* difficulty with the flotation test for seed viability? 18.____

    A. It may be injurious to seeds with thin coats
    B. Most seeds are not so heavy as water
    C. It is unreliable
    D. It is time-consuming
    E. Some seeds are permeable to water

19. *What* are the *principal* benefits of wildlife openings? Clearings 19.____
    I. *furnish* forage for elk, deer, grouse, etc.
    II. help *in* the harvest of elk, deer, and grouse
    III. provide nesting sites for turkeys and grouse
    IV. *attract* insects that young birds need for food
    V. *offer* protection from predation

    The CORRECT answer is:

    A. I, III, IV
    B. I, II, IV
    C. I, III, V
    D. II, IV
    E. I, III, IV, V

20. *Which* of the following factors that influence wildlife populations are the MOST important? 20.____
    I. Availability of food
    II. Abundance and effectiveness of predatory species
    III. Competition with other species
    IV. Disease
    V. Presence of cover

    The CORRECT answer is:

    A. I, II
    B. I, IV
    C. I, V
    D. I, II, IV
    E. I, III, IV

21. *What* areas should be *excluded* from any sagebrush control projects? Areas 21.____
    I. of low, sparse sagebrush with a good understory of grass and herbs
    II. rarely used by grouse for food or nesting
    III. of low improvement potential
    IV. adjacent to aspen or willows
    V. outside one quarter mile of strutting grounds

    The CORRECT answer is:

    A. I, II, III
    B. I, III, IV
    C. III, IV, V
    D. II, IV, V
    E. All of the above

22. Browseways and openings in chaparrel-type brushfields are constructed by all of the following ways EXCEPT: 22.____

    A. With dozers
    B. With mowers
    C. With rollers
    D. With herbicides
    E. By prescribed burning

23. All of the following are true of direct germination tests EXCEPT: 23.____

    A. Enough water is poured into the container so that the medium will absorb its capacity
    B. Temperatures should be kept constant
    C. Moisture levels should be kept constant

D. Flats should never have watertight bottoms
E. Light is not necessary

24. A protective cover of vegetation provides wildlife with ______ cover. 24.____
I. winter
II. refuge
III. loafing
IV. fawning or nesting
V. sleeping or roosting
The CORRECT answer is:

A. I, II B. III, IV, V C. II, V
D. I, III, IV E. All of the above

25. When overpopulations of game exist, *what* is the FIRST step that should be taken? 25.____

A. Provide additional food supplies not native to the area
B. Encourage natural reproduction of food plants native to the area
C. Cut down the numbers of game
D. Provide additional food supplies of the type found in the area
E. The area should be made unavailable to other wildlife

26. *Which* of the following are guidelines used in juniper-pinyon clearing projects in order to avoid damage to deer and elk habitat? 26.____
I. Leave woody vegetation covering no more than 15% of the treated area
II. Leave live juniper crowns covering 5% of the treated area
III. Do not use control methods which tend to kill deer bowse plants
IV. Treat slopes steeper than 15%
V. Do not treat northerly exposures
The CORRECT answer is:

A. I, II, IV B. I, II, III C. III, V
D. II, III, V E. I, II, III, IV

27. *What* is the MOST important *first* step in establishing herbaceous plants? 27.____

A. Timing the seeding
B. Getting a good cover of seed
C. Eliminating undesirable competing vegetation
D. Planting the seeds at the proper depth
E. Species selection

28. Seeds with seedcoat dormancy that have been successfully treated appear 28.____

A. glossy B. pitted C. shriveled D. dull E. moldy

29. The term *escape cover* generally applies to ______ cover. 29.____
I. winter
II. refuge
III. loafing
IV. fawning or nesting
V. steep or roosting
The CORRECT answer is:

A. I, II B. II, IV, V C. II, V D. II, IV E. II, III, V

30. *What* is the MOST successful way of reducing herds of big game? 30.____

A. Eventual starvation from inadequate food supplies
B. Driving the animals away from concentration areas
C. Trapping surpluses and removing the animals to underpopulated areas
D. Extending the hunting privileges in heavily populated areas
E. Euthanasia

31. Cover height of herbaceous ground cover is GREATEST for: 31.____

A. Hungarian partridge
B. Sharptail grouse
C. Bobwhite quail
D. Sage grouse
E. Prairie chicken

32. *What* is the BEST way to prepare a seedbed for herbaceous plants? By 32.____

A. *burning* the site prior to planting
B. *rolling* the area with a heavy log or with rubber tires
C. *scalping* the site
D. *discing* the soil
E. *fertilizing* the soil

33. *Which* of the following are methods to overcome seedcoat dormancy? 33.____

I. Acid treatment
II. Cold stratification
III. Warm, followed by cold stratification
IV. Mechanical stratification
V. Hotwater treatment

The CORRECT answer is:

A. I, III, V
B. I, IV
C. I, IV, V
D. II, III, IV
E. II, III, V

34. Corridors are used by wildlife for 34.____

I. shade
II. shelter
III. loafing cover
IV. fawning or nesting cover
V. sleep or roosting cover

The CORRECT answer is:

A. I, II
B. II, IV, V
C. II, V
D. II, IV
E. II, III, V

35. *Which* of the following are TRUE of forest openings? 35.____

I. Cultivated openings find their value in concentrating wildlife during restrocking
II. Natural openings provide the ecological environment under which native game thrive
III. Cultivated openings must be maintained to prevent re-invasion by und sirable plants
IV. Natural openings are maintained as areas of annual food patch plantings
V. Cultivated openings should include low ground-cover type vegetation and shrubs and trees

The CORRECT answer is:

A. I, II, V
B. I, II, III
C. III, IV, V
D. II, III, IV
E. II, III, IV, V

36. Den formation is most *directly* due to 36.____

A. the activities of the animal user
B. decay
C. the efforts of birds
D. fortuitous circumstances
E. the activities of man

37. *Which* of the following should guide grain plantings for upland game? 37.____

I. Plots should be irregularly shaped
II. Plots should be located adjacent to good cover
III. Plots should be located on steep slopes planted in narrow strips
IV. Food should be available in late fall to early winter
V. Plant every year until the grain is fully established

The CORRECT answer is:

A. I, II
B. I, II, III
C. I, III
D. I, IV, V
E. I, II, IV, V

38. *Which* of the following are TRUE of internal dormancy of seeds? 38.____

I. It is the most common type of seed dormancy
II. Germination cannot begin until there are chemical changes in the stored food or embryo
III. Seeds must be tested to determine the proper corrective method
IV. Unusually small embryos must be given time to grow before germination is possible
V. Most embryos do not develop due to lack of water and oxygen

The CORRECT answer is:

A. I, III, IV
B. I, II, IV
C. I, IV, V
D. II, IV, V
E. IV, V

39. Den trees are used for 39.____

I. nesting
II. brooding, rearing
III. hibernation
IV. shelter from the elements
V. seclusion from predators

The CORRECT answer is:

A. I, II
B. II, III
C. I, II, III
D. I, II, III, V
E. All of the above

40. *What* MAINLY determines the number and size of forest openings? The 40.____
I. presence of predators
II. habits of the target wildlife species
III. size of the wildlife population
IV. stand density encountered throughout the range
V. age and size of the stand
The CORRECT answer is:

A. I, II
B. II, III
C. I, II, III
D. I, II, III, IV
E. II, IV

41. All of the following require den trees EXCEPT: 41.____

A. Gray and fox squirrels
B. Bluebird
C. Raccoon
D. Bobwhite quail
E. Owls

42. *Which* of the following grains are valuable for waterfowl, especially where the site is flooded for part of the year? 42.____
I. Rye
II. Buckwheat
III. Millet
IV. Barley
V. Sorghum
The CORRECT answer is:

A. I, III, V
B. I, II, IV
C. I, III, IV
D. II, III, IV
E. III, V

43. *What* is the MOST common method of pre-treating seeds with impervious coats? 43.____

A. Acid treatment
B. Mechanical stratification
C. Hotwater treatment
D. Cold stratification
E. Water, followed by cold stratification

44. *What* is the PRIMARY advantage of nest boxes? They 44.____

A. are economical to build and to maintain
B. quickly correct den scarcities
C. are predation-proof
D. are designed to meet the target species specifications
E. increase the population of the target species

45. *Which* of the following are considered to be *type conversions* of existing cover? 45.____
I. Creation of a permanent treeless opening in a forest
II. Large brush fields converted to tree plantations
III. Browse release over a designated area
IV. Rejuvenation treatments
V. Modification of the forest composition
The CORRECT answer is:

A. I, II, V
B. I, II, III, V
C. I, II
D. III, IV, V
E. All of the above

46. *Which* of the following volunteer vegetation around pothole has duck food value? 46.____

I. Horsetail
II. Bindweed
III. Bulrush
IV. Bluejoint grass
V. Marsh cinquefoil

The CORRECT answer is:

A. I, IV, V
B. I, IV
C. II, III
D. II, III, IV
E. II, III, IV, V

47. *What* environment is BEST for *most* seed storage? 47.____

A. Low moisture content and low temperatures
B. low moisture content and high temperatures
C. Ordinary air temperature in dry climates
D. High moisture content and cold temperatures
E. Temperatures below freezing

48. *What* is the MOST widely used method of breaking internal formancy? 48.____

A. Acid treatment
B. Mechanical stratification
C. Hotwater treatment
D. Chemical treatment
E. Cold stratification

49. *What* are the *basic* requirements of wood duck nest boxes? 49.____

I. The opening is large enough
II. Protection from predators
III. The base will hold a clutch of eggs
IV. The box is weatherproof
V. There is enough debris to form a base and cover for the first few eggs

The CORRECT answer is:

A. I, II
B. I, III, IV
C. I, II, III
D. I, III, V
E. All of the above

50. *What* are the purposes of *type conversions of* existing cover? To 50.____

I. *create* favorable interspersions of food and cover
II. attract a target species
III. *lessen* or eliminate predation
IV. *develop* edge
V. *provide* openings with herbaceous vegetation in extensive areas of dense brush or timber

The CORRECT answer is:

A. I, IV, V
B. II, III
C. I, II, III
D. I, II, V
E. I, II, III, V

KEY (CORRECT ANSWERS)

1. C	11. E	21. B	31. D	41. D
2. C	12. D	22. E	32. D	42. D
3. B	13. A	23. B	33. C	43. A
4. D	14. C	24. A	34. A	44. B
5. C	15. B	25. C	35. B	45. C
6. A	16. C	26. D	36. B	46. C
7. E	17. B	27. C	37. A	47. A
8. C	18. C	28. D	38. B	48. E
9. A	19. B	29. A	39. E	49. D
10. E	20. C	30. D	40. E	50. A

EXAMINATION SECTION
TEST 1

DIRECTIONS: Each question or incomplete statement is followed by several suggested answers or completions. Select the one that BEST answers the question or completes the statement. *PRINT THE LETTER OF THE CORRECT ANSWER IN THE SPACE AT THE RIGHT.*

1. LEAST likely to affect specie habitation is 1.____

   A. geographic area
   B. quantity of vegetation
   C. human population
   D. diversity of vegetation
   E. types of nearby housing developments

2. Raccoons are *most likely* to be found in 2.____

   A. residential neighborhoods
   B. rural agricultural areas
   C. shores of coastal cities
   D. wooded suburbs
   E. reservoirs or other water bodies

3. A development well-endowed with wildlife benefits a developer by 3.____

   A. decreasing construction costs
   B. reducing erosion
   C. increasing property values
   D. reducing waste
   E. giving personal satisfaction

4. What do surveys of suburban and urban residents indicate about home owners' attitudes toward wildlife on their premises? 4.____

   A. Most homeowners appreciate the presence of wildlife
   B. Homeowners show no strong feeling toward the issue
   C. Homeowners appreciate wildlife in the area, but not on their premises
   D. Homeowners have a negative attitude toward wildlife
   E. Few homeowners appreciate wildlife on their premises

5. Pigeons and starlings are *less* popular than other birds because their droppings 5.____

   A. deface buildings
   B. cause deterioration of the water supply
   C. are a hazard to human health
   D. damage plants
   E. attract rodents

6. Of the following groups of wildlife, which are MOST affected by the use of pesticides in suburban homes and gardens? 6.____

   A. Birds
   B. Mammals
   C. Amphibians
   D. Reptiles
   E. Fish and other aquatic animals

7. MOST likely to adapt to an almost complete loss of its salt marsh habitat is the 7.___

A. fiddler crab
B. egret
C. mallard
D. killifish
E. osprey

8. What aspect of urbanization *particularly* affects marine species like the sea turtle? 8.___

A. High noise levels
B. Bright city lights
C. Large amount of refuse
D. Presence of humans
E. Use of pesticides

9. The BEST way of avoiding conflict between urban wildlife and human residents is by 9.___

A. correct planning to eliminate future problems
B. education of residents
C. elimination of wildlife
D. development of problem solving devices
E. reduction of wildlife

10. Reflective glass should be used in 10.___

A. buildings in wooded areas
B. buildings near water
C. areas where the buildings would normally attract nuisance birds
D. all new urban buildings
E. none of the above

11. Of little concern to the urban wildlife planner is 11.___

A. winter-feeding
B. erection of artificial nesting structures
C. habitat management
D. artificial stocking
E. transplanting of wildstock

12. The conventional subdivision type of development allows 12.___

A. more latitude in architectural design
B. more planning opportunities for the community
C. easy modification of lots
D. more diverse movement corridors
E. landscaping by individual lots

13. Wildlife have a *greater* affinity to natural coniferous woodlands rather than coniferous plantations because 13.___

A. plantations allow too much light to penetrate the woodland floor
B. plantation trees are uniformly spaced
C. the soils of plantations are too enriched
D. plantations have little understory
E. plantations lack woodland borders

14. Similar woodlands located adjacent to dissimilar habitats would exhibit 14.____

    A. no differences
    B. imperceptible differences
    C. noticeable, but insignificant, differences
    D. significant differences
    E. one cannot tell from the information given

15. The wildlife planner should locate food sources near 15.____

    A. nesting grounds
    B. water
    C. cover
    D. woodland edges
    E. residential properties

16. The types and populations of wildlife existing in an area can be determined by 16.____

    A. consulting trained biologists
    B. consulting regional and national species lists
    C. listing those species whose geographic range includes the proposed site
    D. listing *only* those species identified as common to the site
    E. conducting on-site inspections

17. Compensating for reducing the size requirements of wildlife in the area can be made by 17.____

    A. increasing the amount of cover
    B. diversifying the space
    C. maintaining a wildlife corridor system
    D. providing a high quality habitat
    E. focusing attention on the requirements of the smaller species

18. Woodlands of GREATEST value to wildlife are 18.____

    A. coniferous
    B. deciduous
    C. upland
    D. semiwood floodplains
    E. wooded floodplains

19. The value of old fields is significantly INCREASED when they are adjacent to 19.____

    A. meadows
    B. wooded areas
    C. orchards
    D. farmland
    E. developed areas

20. Nature trails should be elevated over wet areas *primarily* to 20.____

    A. keep children on the trail
    B. provide safe footing
    C. enable people to derive benefit from wildlife
    D. avoid disturbance of vegetation
    E. prevent access to wildlife

21. Pigeons and starlings successfully nest in urban areas because 21.____

    A. they do not need time to acclimate themselves to new conditions
    B. buildings provide nesting areas
    C. they are attracted to the small ornamental trees and fountains found in front of buildings
    D. they are unaffected by reflective glass
    E. their need for cover is minimal

22. Regional wildlife considerations focus *mainly* on 22.___

A. artificial stocking
B. creation of refuges
C. preservation
D. transplanting wildlife
E. predator control

23. Maintenance of a wider diversity of wildlife species is possible on a *regional* basis because 23.___

A. more money is available
B. more flexibility is allowed
C. large amounts of open space is provided
D. individual residents are not involved
E. plans are centralized

24. Which of the following contribute to making better use of urban open space? 24.___

I. Closing off little used streets
II. Using parallel rather than diagonal parking
III. Turning alley junkyards into center block paths
IV. Developing less intensive use of existing parks
V. Rehabilitating empty lots

The CORRECT answer is:

A. I, II, III
B. II, III, IV
C. III, IV, V
D. III, IV *only*
E. I, III,V

25. During clean-up operations, which of the following should be removed? 25.___

A. Dead and hollow trees
B. Trees with dead limbs
C. Trees with dead tops
D. Fallen logs and sticks
E. None of the above

26. The MOST likely reason why urban soils fail to continue to to support the growth of healthy trees is 26.___

A. inadequate fertilization
B. salt content
C. pedestrian traffic
D. nutrient depletion
E. prior construction activity

27. Species typical of urban areas can survive WITHOUT 27.___

A. cover
B. understory
C. wide corridors
D. a home range
E. all of the above

28. All of the following are examples of marsh and aquatic plants EXCEPT 28.___

A. bullrush
B. smartweed
C. widgeon grass
D. doveweed
E. spike rush

29. Many trees should be planted in natural situations in rehabilitation projects *primarily* to 29.___

A. buffer human encroachment
B. reduce the need for insecticides
C. produce an aesthetically appealing landscape
D. reduce maintenance costs
E. reduce the threat of disease

30. Remedial measures are *usually* NOT effective in the case of streams 30.____

A. degraded by siltation
B. converted into enclosed storm sewers
C. that have been channeled
D. degraded by pollution
E. all of the above

31. Better suited to cold water ponds are 31.____

I. bluegills
II. lake trout
III. catfish
IV. small mouth bass
V. large mouth bass

The CORRECT answer is:

A. I, III *only* B. II, IV *only* C. I, III, V
D. I, III, IV E. I, II, III

32. Ponds classified as cold water ponds do NOT exceed temperatures of ______ degrees F. 32.____

A. 50 B. 55 C. 60 D. 65 E. 70

33. Fish in a wildlife impoundment are denied access to nesting sites by 33.____

A. lowering water levels B. raising water levels
C. installing deflectors D. installing check dams
E. encouraging the growth of aquatic vegetation

34. A pond deemed a safety hazard is developed with 34.____

A. very sttep banks
B. thin aquatic vegetation
C. a maximum center depth of 6 feet
D. a posted sign listing vital information
E. gentle sloping bottom to the maximum depth required

35. Detention and sediment ponds should be removed 35.____

A. after the final grading of the developed site
B. after construction has been completed
C. after the removal of all sediment
D. before occupation of the site
E. at no times

36. What food should be used to attract ducks and geese to wet pits or lakes? 36.____

A. Oats and apple B. Sorghum and millet
C. Corn and green wheat D. Rice
E. Alfalfa and barley

37. Eutrophication of water results in 37.____

A. *increase* in variety of plant life
B. *decrease* biomass of the lake
C. *increase* in the transparency of the water

D. *decrease* in dissolved oxygen levels
E. excessive algae and weed growth

38. All of the following will resist tree invasion for many years EXCEPT 38.____

A. sedge B. greenbriar C. witch hazel
D. huckleberry E. gray dogwood

39. The ______ of trees saved is MOST important to wildlife. 39.____

A. species B. age C. condition
D. height E. productivity

40. All of the following are wildlife consideration regarding new airport sites EXCEPT: 40.____

A. Soil type
B. Drainage conditions
C. Type of vegetation present
D. Human disturbance
E. Land uses in surrounding areas

41. The game manager should avoid the use of a single tree species from a single source because of the 41.____

A. possibility that a replacement may be difficult to find
B. lack of aesthetic value
C. danger of epidemic disease
D. development of a monoculture
E. possibility that the species may not enhance the site

42. The MOST certain way to keep land open is by 42.____

A. zoning
B. land development ordinances
C. conservation easements
D. public acquisition
E. use of a severance tax

43. The woody plant of GREATEST value in the United States, regardless of region, is the 43.____

A. alder B. mesquite C. oak
D. dogwood E. pine

44. Which of the following is *most likely* to act as oases for small birds during migration? 44.____

A. School yards
B. Suburban water-recharge basins
C. Reservoirs
D. Crevices of buildings
E. Parks

45. The ecological stability of a residential development may be MOST accurately measured by 45.____

A. evidence of wildlife
B. presence of wooded properties

C. a wide variety of wildlife species
D. presence of nests
E. ground cover and water supply

46. The MAIN reason people are opposed to having wildlife in their vicinity is the 46.____

A. nuisance of wildlife
B. unsanitary conditions caused by them
C. deterioration of the water quality
D. hazard to human health
E. damage done to plants and property

47. Wildlife and its supporting habitat give GREATEST benefit to 47.____

A. homeowners
B. hobbyists and recreational enthusiasts
C. children
D. researchers
E. educators

48. The design of storm detention ponds should MINIMIZE 48.____

I. growth of vegetation
II. damage to property
III. hazards to children
IV. harm to the multiple uses the pond can be put
V. problems of removal

The CORRECT answer is:

A. I, II, V
B. II, III, IV
C. I, II, III, V
D. I, II, III
E. I, II, III, IV, V

49. The features of a dump site that will attract the LARGEST number of gulls are 49.____

I. large, flat surfaces
II. fresh water supply
III. trees at the edge
IV. vegetation for cover
V. an open area

The CORRECT answer is:

A. I, II, III
B. II, III, IV
C. I, II, V
D. I,II, IV
E. II, III, V

50. Basically the same for MOST wildlife species are the 50.____

I. size of the home range
II. configuration of the home range
III. food requirements
IV. cover requirements
V. water requirements

The CORRECT answer is:

A. I, III, V
B. I, II, V
C. III, IV, V
D. V only
E. None of the above

KEY (CORRECT ANSWERS)

1.	C	11.	A	21.	B	31.	B	41.	C
2.	D	12.	E	22.	C	32.	E	42.	D
3.	C	13.	D	23.	C	33.	A	43.	C
4.	A	14.	D	24.	E	34.	E	44.	E
5.	A	15.	C	25.	E	35.	E	45.	C
6.	E	16.	A	26.	E	36.	C	46.	E
7.	C	17.	D	27.	C	37.	E	47.	C
8.	B	18.	E	28.	D	38.	A	48.	B
9.	A	19.	B	29.	D	39.	A	49.	C
10.	E	20.	D	30.	B	40.	D	50.	E

EXAMINATION SECTION
TEST 1

DIRECTIONS: Each question or incomplete statement is followed by several suggested answers or completions. Select the one that BEST answers the question or completes the statement. *PRINT THE LETTER OF THE CORRECT ANSWER IN THE SPACE AT THE RIGHT.*

1. The MOST common wild mammal in an urban area is the 1.____

   A. opossum
   B. norway rat
   C. house mouse
   D. squirrel
   E. rabbit

2. The CHIEF benefit of fish and wildlife in urban and suburban areas is 2.____

   A. hunting opportunities
   B. enjoyment of fishing
   C. opportunity for hiking and nature photography
   D. people's enjoyment in day-to-day living situations
   E. enjoyment of bird watching

3. The need for better planning and environmental management measures is MOST evident in 3.____

   A. increased interest in urban wildlife research
   B. the rapid increase in developed land
   C. the high level of environmental quality demanded by the public
   D. the decrease in farmland
   E. the growth of endangered species

4. The percent of the American public that accounts for the purchase of at LEAST sixty pounds of seed a year is *approximately* 4.____

   A. 2 B. 10 C. 20 D. 45 E. 60

5. Prices paid for new housing developments are *directly* related to 5.____

   A. the presence of wildlife in the area
   B. the educational benefits derived from wildlife in the area
   C. preservation of open space and natural setting
   D. positive attitude toward wildlife
   E. the variety of the wildlife present within the area

6. Which of the following bird populations are likely to *increase* after the development of a new town on the site of sparsely populated farmland area? 6.____

   I. Mockingbirds
   II. Chipping sparrows
   III. Red-winged blackbirds
   IV. Grasshopper sparrows
   V. Song sparrows

   The CORRECT answer is:

   A. I, II, V
   B. I, III, IV
   C. I, III, V
   D. II, IV, V
   E. II, V

7. When adequate vegetation is retained, ______ may continue to flourish in urban areas. 7.__

A. squirrels
B. raccoons
C. opossums
D. rabbits
E. all of the above

8. The GREATEST number of cases of rabies have occurred in 8.__

A. dogs
B. rabbits
C. squirrels
D. skunks
E. raccoons

9. A key requirement in meeting the needs of wildlife is providing a(n) ______ habitat(s). 9.__

A. number of
B. specific type of
C. large
D. diverse
E. enclosed

10. The planner should provide *preferred* food items in order to 10.__

A. control the wildlife population to certain species
B. ensure the health of the preferred species
C. prevent damage to homeowners' property
D. compensate for lack of vegetation
E. maximize the retention of desired species

11. The key to wildlife management is 11.__

A. space
B. vegetation
C. free water
D. soil
E. predator control

12. Procedures for integrating wildlife considerations into small site design are: 12.__

I. Identify habitats of threatened species
II. Identify food plants
III. Analyze adjacent land areas
IV. Develop continuous open space wildlife corridors
V. Identify limiting factors on the site

The CORRECT answer is:

A. I, II, IV
B. I, II,V
C. I, IV, V
D. II, III,V
E. II, IV, V

13. The amount of understory is *particularly* IMPORTANT for residential developments in order to 13.__

A. compensate for inadequate overstory
B. help buffer the disturbing effects of humans and their pets
C. prevent wildlife from entering roadways
D. prevent damage to resident's property
E. attract larger mammals to the area

14. Utilized as food by wildlife are 14.____

A. twigs
B. seeds
C. bark
D. roots
E. all of the above

15. An adjacent ______ would BEST enlarge the home range of a development site. 15.____

A. cemetery
B. school yard
C. parking lot
D. farm
E. vacant lot

16. What action should the planner take when a desired species, though present in the region, does NOT exist on the site in its undeveloped stage? 16.____

A. Attempt artificial stocking
B. Retain habitats for preferred species
C. Identify limiting factors and eliminate them
D. Increase the percent of undeveloped land
E. Plan for free water on the site

17. Major wildlife corridor systems should be developed 17.____

A. perpendicular to each other, meeting near the center of the site
B. perpendicular to each other, meeting near the edge of the site
C. parallel to each other at opposite ends of the site
D. parallel to each other at the center of the site
E. in circular configuration around the perimeter of the site

18. The major corridor should 18.____

A. encircle the site
B. connect with the largest undeveloped tract adjacent to the site
C. link all the secondary and tertiary corridors
D. bisect the site
E. encourage the movement of wildlife into and through residential areas

19. To MINIMIZE *adverse* impact on wildlife, 19.____

I. road segments should be aligned to buffer human disturbance
II. road systems should be planned where the open space system is wide
III. large wooded areas should be kept intact
IV. roads should be designed to parallel major corridor systems
V. fewer roads of wider width are preferable to more numerous, narrow roads

The CORRECT answer is:

A. I, II, III
B. I, III
C. I, III, V
D. I, IV
E. II, III, IV

20. Recommended as a means to discourage the activities of children in areas of particular value to wildlife is to 20.____

A. post signs
B. plant thorny vegetation
C. erect fences
D. limit road access
E. dig trenches

21. It is preferable to place parking lots between buildings of shopping malls and the open space system because 21.___

A. the hours of activity are limited
B. human activity is directed away from the open space
C. wildlife is less sensitive to vehicles
D. the fringe of parking lots are used infrequently
E. noise and activity levels are fairly constant

22. In regional planning wildlife considerations focus *mainly* on 22.___

A. artificial stocking
B. creations of refuges
C. preservation
D. transplanting wildstock
E. predator control

23. Dystrophic conditions in a lake result in all the following EXCEPT 23.___

A. high biomass
B. great variation in specie
C. lowered available oxygen
D. a decrease in photosynthetic organisms
E. an increase in anaerobic decomposition

24. The MAIN limiting factor for wildlife in urban areas is 24.___

A. dense population
B. small amount of open space
C. pollution
D. noise levels
E. traffic

25. Of the following, the one which would be MOST affected by the removal of rotting logs from the developed area is 25.___

A. grasshoppers
B. mice
C. salamanders
D. crows
E. frogs

26. The MOST serious effect of construction activities on urban soil is 26.___

A. topsoil is mixed with subsoil
B. no consideration is given to beneficial wildlife
C. construction materials make up various percentages of the soil
D. the presence of sewage sludge
E. the use of soil for drainage

27. The BEST security measure in downtown parks is 27.___

A. lighted walkways
B. elimination of understory
C. post signs diagramming the park's walkways and exits
D. to avoid placing walkways near dense shrub plantings
E. to avoid narrow, twisting walkways

28. The preferable means of enhancing and maintaining natural diversity is 28.____

A. use of imported plant species
B. use of native plant species
C. reducing understory in favor of overstory
D. removing dead or hollow trees
E. all of the above

29. The one MOST affected by controlling the water level in an impoundment is 29.____

A. waterfowl
B. reptiles and amphibians
C. fish
D. soil
E. vegetation

30. The result of a properly designed impoundment is to 30.____

A. increase habitat diversity
B. provide recreational benefits
C. provide aesthetic benefits
D. increase real estate values

31. Fishponds are designed with steep banks to 31.____

A. discourage the growth of aquatic vegetation
B. reduce erosion
C. attract a broad variety of wildlife
D. prevent seepage
E. discourage human interference

32. A channelized stream can be developed so that the hydrolic features resemble unchannelized streams by 32.____

A. increasing aquatic vegetation
B. reducing aquatic vegetation
C. installing deflectors, and check dams
D. installing storm detention basins
E. grading the site prior to channelization

33. Which of the following are criteria for designing a multipurpose pond? 33.____

I. Pond margins have a 3:1 slope to a depth of 3 feet
II. Dense vegetation around the margins
III. Gentle slope before drop off to maximum depth
IV. Flat area exposed
V. Mtaximum depth at center is 6 feet

The CORRECT answer is:

A. I, II
B. I, III
C. I, III, IV
D. I, III, V
E. all of the above

34. Dentention and sediment ponds should be retained after housing construction is completed to 34.____

A. trap natural drainage
B. provide a valuable wetland habitat
C. minimize washouts
D. lower the cost of construction
E. none of the above

35. All of the following channel improvements eliminate important aquatic habitats EXCEPT 35.____

A. deflectors and low dams
B. excessive use of culverts
C. realignment of the stream course
D. dredging
E. use of concrete channels

36. All of the following are useful in the control of erosion and sedimentation EXCEPT 36.____

A. using soils suited for development
B. allowing the natural flow of run-off
C. leaving the soil bare for the shortest time possible
D. detaining run-off on the site to trap sediment
E. releasing run-off safely to downstream areas

37. Old fields that are dominated by brown sedge or bunchgrass can be improved by 37.____

A. irrigation
B. disking
C. fertilization
D. reseeding
E. mowing

38. Streets and highways should be routed so they do not cross 38.____

A. old fields
B. wetlands
C. reservoirs
D. woodland
E. woodland edges

39. Of the following, the one which is *most likely* to discourage wildlife from airports is 39.____

A. providing buildings with overhanging roofs
B. foundation plantings
C. building structures with flat gravel roofs
D. locating the airport on sandy land with good drainage
E. increase the number of runway marker lights

40. The one of the following which is INCORRECT is that the planner 40.____

A. should not disturb the natural aspects of the land
B. should not use biological systems to assimilate and dispose of man's wastes
C. must realize that the stability of the ecosystem is related to its diversity
D. should not expect cooperation and support of the community
E. should not consider wildlife as an option

41. The MAJOR infrastructure stimulant for urban growth *is* (are) 41.____

A. railroads
B. waste water facilities
C. highways
D. farm land
E. strip mine areas

42. Of the following, the one which would be MOST affected by road construction and subsequent traffic is (are) 42.____

A. a population denied access to its hibernating or breeding areas
B. nocturnal species
C. non-migratory populations
D. aquatic organisms
E. parasitic organisms

43. MOST wildlife species in the suburban area are able to meet their water requirements through 43.____

A. precipitation
B. ingestion of food
C. sprinklers
D. city water supplies
E. free water

44. The MOST basic approach for encouraging wildlife populations is 44.____

A. creation of refuges
B. transplanting of wild stock
C. habitat management
D. protection through regulations
E. predator control

45. An eastern area with spacious lawns and extensive landscaping is *likely* to attract 45.____

A. house sparrows
B. chickadees
C. cardinals
D. yellow-throated vireos
E. wood thrushes

46. Wildlife species show the STRONGEST affinity for 46.____

A. deciduous woodlands
B. old fields
C. creeks
D. marshes
E. woodland edges

47. The MOST important thing(s) the understory provides is(are) 47.____

A. more moisture
B. limited light
C. protection
D. food and water
E. cover and food

48. The benefit that can be derived for species on the site from adjoining open space areas is 48.____

A. increased range
B. refuge area
C. diversified food supply
D. sites for artificial nesting structures
E. predator control

49. The one of the following which is MOST difficult to determine is (are) 49.____

A. the type of wildlife existing in the *area*
B. limiting factors for the preferred species
C. habitats on the site
D. the best use of adjacent open space
E. the amount of open space required

50. Which of the following are TRUE of planning corridor systems? 50.____

I. All corridors do not have to be equal in length
II. The major corridor should connect with the largest undeveloped tracts of land adjacent to the site
III. Shrubbery should take precedence over trees
IV. All corridors should be defined at the early planning stages
V. As many corridors as possible should be planned

The CORRECT answer is:

A. I, II, V
B. I, II, IV, V
C. I, III, IV
D. II, IV, V
E. all of the above

KEY (CORRECT ANSWERS)

1.	D	11.	B	21.	D	31.	A	41.	B
2.	D	12.	D	22.	C	32.	C	42.	A
3.	B	13.	B	23.	A	33.	B	43.	E
4.	C	14.	E	24.	B	34.	B	44.	C
5.	C	15.	A	25.	C	35.	A	45.	C
6.	A	16.	C	26.	C	36.	B	46.	A
7.	E	17.	A	27.	D	37.	B	47.	E
8.	D	18.	B	28.	B	38.	B	48.	B
9.	D	19.	B	29.	E	39.	D	49.	E
10.	E	20.	B	30.	E	40.	B	50.	A

EXAMINATION SECTION
TEST 1

DIRECTIONS: Each question or incomplete statement is followed by several suggested answers or completions. Select the one that BEST answers the question or completes the statement. *PRINT THE LETTER OF THE CORRECT ANSWER IN THE SPACE AT THE RIGHT.*

1. Of the following, which would account MOST for the presence of birds in urban areas? 1.____

   A. Reservoirs
   B. Dumps
   C. Tall buildings
   D. Zoos
   E. Mast trees

2. Urbanization has helped to increase populations of amphibians and reptiles by 2.____

   I. providing ground cover
   II. eliminating natural predators
   III. creating breeding sites
   IV. draining wetlands
   V. providing a diverse habitat

   The CORRECT answer is:

   A. I, II
   B. II, III
   C. II, IV, V
   D. all of the above
   E. none of the above

3. The high urban squirrel populations can be accounted for by 3.____

   A. large, uncrowded and productive mast trees
   B. conifers
   C. reservoirs
   D. refuse dumps
   E. few predators

4. Most of the money spent on the enjoyment of nongame birds was spent on 4.____

   I. birdseed
   II. birdbaths
   III. books on birds
   IV. binoculars
   V. camera equipment

   The CORRECT answer is:

   A. I, II, III
   B. I, II, III, IV
   C. I, III
   D. I, III, IV
   E. I, IV, V

5. Trees enhance the value of property by *approximately* ______ percent. 5.____

   A. 2 B. 5 C. 10 D. 20 E. 30

6. The increase in mockingbirds in new town developments can be accounted for by an increase in 6.____

   A. coniferous woodland
   B. deciduous woodland
   C. the fruit bearing shrubs
   D. watercourses
   E. decorative landscaping

7. Man's PRINCIPAL impact on wildlife has been to alter the environment through 7.____

A. hunting and fishing
B. highway construction
C. use of pesticides and fertilizers
D. urbanization
E. applied ecology

8. The GREATEST health hazard associated with gray squirrels is the 8.____

A. transmission of rabies
B. risk of infection from bites
C. transmission of leptospirosis
D. transmission of cryptococcosis
E. spread of encephalitis from fleas

9. The area necessary to satisfy all of an animal's requirements is called its 9.____

A. territory
B. space
C. home range
D. biosphere
E. ecosystem

10. Wildlife management is defined as 10.____

A. the act of producing sustained annual crops of wildlife to achieve human goals
B. the conservation of endangered species
C. the act of creating environmental enhancement
D. the preservation of wanted species and the elimination of unwanted ones
E. the act of sustaining wildlife for environmental, recreational and scientific values

11. The house sparrow would be the dominant nesting bird in an eastern metropolis with 11.____

A. little or no empty space and few grassy areas or shrubs
B. pleasant lawns of some size and a sprinkling of shrubs
C. spacious lawns and extensive landscaping
D. grassy lawns and shade trees
E. older trees, many shrubs with mulch around them

12. The FIRST step in wildlife planning of a Planned Unit Development is to 12.____

A. identify regional species that could be present with the proper habitat
B. determine the amount of open space necessary
C. identify habitats and their relative value
D. identify limiting factors for preferred species
E. identify food plants important to wildlife

13. When two deciduous habitats are similar, the one which should be chosen for site development is the one 13.____

A. whose soil has a high moisture content
B. requiring minimum maintenance
C. with the denser understory
D. with the greater overstory
E. with less ground cover

14. The potential wildlife amenities within the proposed development and in adjacent residential areas will be MOST enhanced by 14._____

A. limiting traffic to two lane roads
B. providing movement corridors
C. increasing acreage
D. thinning the overstory canopy
E. providing woodland edges

15. A linear configuration of the wooden tracts found in residential areas is suitable to songbirds because 15._____

A. food is readily available
B. it provides much edge
C. it provides a buffer from the human population
D. these birds are nonmigratory
E. good moisture content of the soil is retained

16. The integration of wildlife habitats into the open space design begins in those areas 16._____

A. best suited to desired wildlife
B. with free water
C. adjacent to open space areas
D. that would be retained irrespective of wildlife
E. preferable for use as recreational areas

17. The species which finds value in tertiary corridors consisting of rows of trees or shrubs along a road right-of-way is 17._____

A. squirrels
B. raccoons
C. garter snakes
D. rabbits
E. none of the above

18. With respect to vehicles, MOST species will run when 18._____

A. the vehicle is moving
B. the engine is running
C. the engine is shut off
D. passengers stare out the windows
E. headlights are turned off

19. A commercial development may help buffer the larger refuge components of the open space system because 19._____

A. the activity does not affect adjacent open space areas
B. the activity is continuous
C. the grounds are landscaped
D. activity is low or nonexistent in evenings and over weekends
E. none of the above

20. The ability of nuisance birds to use urban buildings for nesting is *most* attributed to the _______ of the buildings. 20._

I. design
II. location
III. exposure
IV. construction
V. height

The CORRECT answer is:

A. I, II, III
B. I, II, V
C. I, III
D. I, IV
E. none of the above

21. Regional planners can MAXIMIZE diversity of habitats by 21._

A. preserving limited and unique habitat types
B. creating refuges
C. maintaining the soil fertility and avoiding erosion
D. managing existing vegetation and added plantings
E. modifying sensitive areas

22. The corridor system of larger-scale planning should be based on 22._

A. floodplains present
B. wooded areas
C. waterways
D. meadowlands present
E. all of the above

23. Landscaping in urban areas should be directed toward selecting plant species that fit well into the urban environment and 23._

A. provide cover
B. are aesthetically pleasing
C. have food value for wildlife
D. do not require much care
E. are desirable for erosion control

24. Which of the following are ways of protecting trees in northern cities where deicing salts are used in large quantities? 24._

I. Erecting snow fences
II. Locating trees a distance from the road
III. Improving road drainage systems
IV. Treating root systems before planting
V. Mixing salt with sand

The CORRECT answer is:

A. I, II, III
B. I, III, IV
C. I, IV, V
D. II, III, IV
E. II, IV, V

25. The SIMPLEST and MOST cost efficient method of reconditioning urban soil is 25._

A. mixing topsoil with subsoil
B. adding sewage sludge
C. adding topsoil
D. aeration
E. use of fertilizers and insecticides

26. Sensitive planting and design are CRITICAL in urban redevelopment projects because 26.____

A. of the presence of dense population
B. many buildings have reflective glass
C. people are not accustomed to the needs of wildlife
D. soils are usually poor
E. undisturbed land and water is limited

27. Most urban parks LACK 27.____

A. native plant species
B. free water
C. overstory
D. understory
E. wild seeds

28. The main reason that roads should be located far from streams is 28.____

A. to discourage recreation activities
B. accelerated erosion
C. wildlife mortality
D. noise levels
E. pollution

29. Watersheds filter strips bordering tributaries should be increased ______ feet for each one percent of slope. 29.____

A. 1 B. 2 C. 4 D. 10 E. 12

30. A depth of ______ feet around the margin of a pond discourages plant growth. 30.____

A. 2 B. 3 C. 4 D. 5 E. 6

31. Which of the following is MOST desirable for both fish and wildlife management purposes of a wildlife impoundment? 31.____

A. A control structure to prevent changing temperatures
B. A control structure to permit changing water levels
C. Seasonal vegetation
D. Shallow margins
E. Steep margins

32. Storm detention ponds and catchment basins should be installed 32.____

A. prior to the initial grading of the development site
B. after grading of the development site is completed
C. during construction of the development site
D. after construction of the development site
E. at any time

33. Water control structures and emergency spillways should be designed as permanent structures of storm detention ponds to 33.____

A. minimize possible washouts
B. meet safety requirements
C. ensure sediment is trapped
D. allow for the easy removal of sediment
E. ensure the preservation of the pond

34. What effect do the organic compounds in the effluent of septic tanks have on the receiving body of water? 34.___

A. Available nitrates are decreased.
B. CO_2 levels decrease.
C. The pH of the water increase.
D. The amount of dissolved oxygen is decreased.
E. The basic oxygen demand of the water body decreases.

35. The BEST approach to managing existing open space areas is 35.___

A. frequent mowing
B. frequent fertilization
C. periodic reseeding
D. spraying with herbicides
E. less frequent mowing

36. Food plots in old fields should be planted 36.___

A. midway between travel corridors
B. at a central location
C. under overstory
D. adjacent to good cover
E. at locations that will equally distribute wildlife over the site

37. The MOST effective way of lowering highway deaths of deer is the use of 37.___

A. tunnels underneath the highway
B. deer-proof fences
C. trenches
D. natural vegetation
E. warning signs for drivers

38. Which of the following will NOT reduce the bird hazard at airport sites? 38.___

A. Retaining the squirrel population
B. Keeping infield grass areas free of weeds
C. Keeping infield grass areas at a height of 5-8"
D. Prohibiting the growing of corn and sunflowers near the site
E. Locating the dump on the same side as bodies of water

39. The Conservation Directory is of much use to the planner because it 39.___

A. contains programs related to plant and animal species
B. provides information on services rendered by federal departments
C. provides information on wildlife planning and management
D. lists organizations concerned with conservation programs
E. lists wildlife and their habitats

40. The cultivated plant that is of the GREATEST value throughout the United States is 40.____

A. corn
B. apple
C. rice
D. cultivated cherry
E. timothy

41. One effect of conventional residential developments is that 41.____

A. smaller natural drainage channels are obliterated
B. little space is left for natural vegetation
C. bright lights confuse species' biorhythms
D. erosion occurs
E. the number of enclosed storm sewers decrease

42. ______ corridor(s) can be defined at the early planning stages. 42.____

A. Primary
B. Secondary
C. Tertiary
D. Ancillary
E. none of the above

43. The people who tend to make the LEAST use of adjacent natural open space are those in 43.____

A. townhouses
B. low bedroom-count units
C. high bedroom-count units
D. garden apartments
E. high rise apartments

44. The LEAST desirable area to locate a playground is near 44.____

A. the edge of woodland areas
B. orchards
C. larger wooded areas
D. old fields
E. open areas with little vegetation

45. The MAJOR function of large-scale planning is to 45.____

A. safeguard nesting sites
B. establish wildlife inventories
C. achieve aesthetic and environmental enhancement
D. identify key wildlife areas that should be free from development
E. review the site development plans of all developers

46. The BEST way for regional planners to identify the presence of endangered plant and animal species is by 46.____

A. wildlife inventories
B. local conservation groups
C. state museum
D. field surveys
E. fish and game departments

47. The MOST common type of regulatory mechanism to preserve open space is 47.____

A. zoning
B. requiring an Environmental Impact Statement
C. state law
D. federal law
E. individual policing and increasing awareness through education

48. Accumulation of excess salt in the root zones of urban trees can be prevented by 48.____

A. digging a shallow trench around the tree
B. fencing the planting area
C. mounding the planting area
D. flushing with water
E. mulch around planting areas

49. If reflective glass is used on buildings, it should NOT reflect 49.____

A. other buildings
B. the sky
C. water
D. vegetation
E. lights

50. Which of the following represents the BEST connecting links to planned urban open space? 50.____

I. Nearby residential areas with small adjoining backyards
II. Parkway right-of-way
III. Parking lots
IV. Railroad right-of-way
V. Alley junkyards

The CORRECT answer is:

A. I, II, IV
B. I, III, V
C. II, III, IV
D. II, IV, V
E. III, V

KEY (CORRECT ANSWERS)

1.	A	11.	A	21.	A	31.	B	41.	A
2.	B	12.	C	22.	A	32.	A	42.	A
3.	A	13.	C	23.	C	33.	E	43.	E
4.	E	14.	B	24.	A	34.	D	44.	C
5.	D	15.	B	25.	B	35.	E	45.	D
6.	C	16.	D	26.	E	36.	D	46.	D
7.	D	17.	A	27.	E	37.	B	47.	A
8.	C	18.	C	28.	B	38.	E	48.	C
9.	C	19.	A	29.	C	39.	D	49.	D
10.	A	20.	D	30.	B	40.	A	50.	A

EXAMINATION SECTION
TEST 1

DIRECTIONS: Each question or incomplete statement is followed by several suggested answers or completions. Select the one that BEST answers the question or completes the Statement. *PRINT THE LETTER OF THE CORRECT ANSWER IN THE SPACE AT THE RIGHT.*

1. ______ squirrels are found in northern urban areas where conifers predominate. 1.____

   A. Tree
   B. Red
   C. Fox
   D. Gray
   E. Flying

2. People prefer to live in communities in which wildlife has been integrated because of 2.____

   A. personal satisfaction
   B. ecological benefits
   C. environmental concerns
   D. the reduction of the insect population
   E. recreational benefits

3. Surveys indicate that the type of wildlife MOST desired by residents is 3.____

   A. squirrels
   B. birds
   C. chipmunks
   D. rabbits
   E. fish

4. The GREATEST impact on wildlife has been made by 4.____

   A. shooting and trapping of wildlife species
   B. alteration of the habitat
   C. waste disposal and pollution
   D. pesticides
   E. increased human population

5. The house sparrow population INCREASES after a new development replaces farmland because of 5.____

   A. an increase in nesting and roosting sites
   B. birdseed put out by residents
   C. the presence of deciduous trees
   D. the presence of fruit bearing shrubs
   E. an increase in insect population

6. Modification of aquatic habitats by drainage, dredging, pollution and removal of vegetation has serious effects on all amphibians EXCEPT those 6.____

   A. who are adapted to salt water
   B. whose egg and larvae stages are spent on land
   C. which are carnivorous
   D. which have internal development of eggs
   E. with dry, scaly skin

7. Animal control specialists have found that residents reporting damage by wildlife want 7.____

   A. advice on how to deal with the nuisance
   B. the animal killed
   C. the animal removed
   D. preserves set up by the authority
   E. wildlife departments to exert more control over wildlife

8. The amount and diversity of wildlife in urban and suburban areas is LIMITED by 8.____

   A. poor spatial configuration
   B. lack of connective open space
   C. failure to provide a specific type of habitat
   D. lack of small, disconnected woodlots
   E. all of the above

9. Which of the following poses the BIGGEST threat to wildlife? 9.____

   A. Free roaming cats and dogs
   B. Domestic livestock
   C. Children
   D. Indiscriminate use of poisons
   E. Presence of omnivorous opossums and raccoons

10. The planned unit development INCREASES the potential for wildlife amenities within the community because 10.____

   A. of the smaller human population
   B. unique habitat types can be preserved
   C. of the involvement of municipal and county planning departments
   D. there is more open space
   E. of better watershed planning

11. Habitat types for site planning can be identified by means of 11.____

   A. aerial photographs
   B. vegetation maps
   C. water tables
   D. field guides
   E. geographic guides

12. The habitat type that is LEAST attractive to wildlife is 12.____

   A. orchards
   B. meadows
   C. old fields
   D. farmland
   E. woodland edges

13. The purpose of tying a development to adjacent open space areas is that 13.____

   A. populations of wildlife are increased
   B. habitats can be improved
   C. movement corridors are unnecessary
   D. species requiring larger home ranges can be accommodated
   E. species can be isolated from human population

14. The planner can retain species sensitive to human disturbance by 14.____

A. maintaining wooded tracts
B. providing a high quality habitat
C. providing acreage greater than that required under normal conditions
D. providing food close to human occupied areas
E. providing food far from human occupied areas

15. The MAIN purpose of developing corridor systems that meet near the center of the site is 15.____

A. wider corridors are possible
B. wildlife amenities are more concentrated
C. less light penetration
D. protection from human population
E. equitable distribution of wildlife amenities

16. Evergreen shrubs are preferable for supplemental planting because they 16.____

I. provide cover and screening all year
II. are more resistant to disease
III. are less conducive to erosion
IV. reduce noise levels
V. attract insects

The CORRECT answer is:

A. I, II, III
B. I, II, V
C. I, III
D. I, IV
E. I, V

17. ______ noise and movement have had the least effect on most species. 17.____

A. Discontinuous
B. intermittent
C. Continuous
D. Sudden
E. Furtive

18. To MINIMIZE the effects on wildlife, parking areas for small commercial facilities should be 18.____

A. at the rear of the buildings
B. in the front of the buildings
C. evenly distributed around the building
D. placed as buffers for the open space
E. restricted to roadways

19. Runoff from agricultural land will have its GREATEST genetic effect on 19.____

A. filter feeders
B. photosynthetic organisms
C. primary consumers
D. bacteria
E. predatory animals at the top of the food chain

20. MOST useful in evaluating wildlife habitats for large scale planning are 20.___

A. aerial photographs
B. vegetation maps
C. wildlife inventories
D. field surveys
E. fish and game departments

21. Efforts on the regional level should be directed toward MAXIMIZING retention of large areas interconnected by smaller corridors to 21.___

A. protect species from natural predators
B. protect species from human intervention
C. better distribute wildlife
D. ensure retention of most species in the region
E. accommodate species with large home range requirements

22. Plant selection in urban areas should attract 22.___

A. squirrels
B. songbirds
C. insects
D. house sparrows
E. all of the above

23. The landscape design that would attract songbirds is 23.___

A. tall trees with woodchip understory
B. tall trees with shrub understory
C. shrubs and small trees
D. tall trees with nesting hollows
E. small trees with grassy areas

24. The FIRST consideration in any urban redevelopment project is 24.___

A. the relationship of planned open space to the surrounding area
B. the width of the corridors
C. the presence of stress factors
D. public access
E. the home range of the desired species

25. Great care is needed in selecting, planting and caring for trees and shrubs in urban areas due to 25.___

A. the limited home range of the city environment
B. poor soils, pollution and heavy usage
C. the scarcity of wide corridors
D. vandalism
E. heavy use of insecticides

26. Natural meadows can be provided in urban parks by reducing the frequency of mowing to 26.___

A. once in early spring
B. once in late summer
C. once in early spring and once in early fall
D. three or four times a year
E. once in mid summer

27. The LEAST benefit derived from buffer strips along streams is the 27.____

A. prevention of erosion
B. preservation of the stream channel's integrity
C. prevention of storm damage
D. maintenance of suitable water temperature
E. provision of food

28. In a cold-water pond, the temperature is measured 28.____

I. 6" below the surface
II. during summer
III. after sunset
IV. during the early spring
V. before sunrise

The CORRECT answer is:

A. I, II, III
B. I, II, V
C. I, III
D. I, III, IV
E. I, IV, V

29. Impoundments designed to attract a broad variety of wildlife should 29.____

A. be shallow
B. have a high water level
C. have diversified margins
D. have gentle sloping margins
E. have steep margins

30. Wading birds or shorebirds will be attracted to areas 30.____

A. of mud, silt, and shallow water
B. dense vegetation
C. thin vegetation
D. where water temperatures fluctuate the least
E. of stormwater detention basins

31. Which of the following design features are recommended for the safety of children playing in the area of a wildlife impoundment? 31.____

I. Well vegetated
II. Thinly vegetated
III. Gently sloping banks
IV. Shallow margins
V. Steep margins

The CORRECT answer is:

A. I, III, IV
B. I, III, V
C. I, IV
D. II, III, IV
E. II, III, V

32. Sand, gravel pit, and stone quarries may be used for all the following EXCEPT 32.____

A. flood-water storage
B. desilting basins
C. recreation lakes
D. desalinization recharge basins
E. fish and wildlife enhancement

33. Which of the following will help reduce shock loads on waters receiving runoff from urban roadways? 33.___

    I. Intensifying street cleaning operations
    II. Utilizing low curbs where the road is adjacent to grass areas
    III. Using nonporous pavement
    IV. Selecting roadway sites less likely to drain directly into the receiving body of water
    V. Detaining storm runoff

    The CORRECT answer is:

    A. I, II, IV
    B. I, III, IV
    C. I, IV
    D. I, IV, V
    E. all of the above

34. After a few years of cessation of mowing, there will be a(n) 34.___

    A. decrease in variation of plant life
    B. reduction of nitrate levels in the soil
    C. growth of woody vegetation
    D. increase in the erosion of soil
    E. decrease in the number of habitats

35. For both nesting and escape cover, MOST songbirds require ______ height and ______ cover. 35.___

    A. medium, dense
    B. low, dense
    C. low, sparse
    D. high, sparse
    E. high, dense

36. Which of the following should be planned to be UNATTRACTIVE to wildlife? 36.___

    A. Cemeteries
    B. Golf courses
    C. Airports
    D. Highways
    E. School grounds

37. The type of habitat that should be AVOIDED in managing metropolitan watersheds for water supply is 37.___

    A. deciduous woodland plantations
    B. living fences of shrubs
    C. bush and tree fruits
    D. orchards
    E. dense pine plantations

38. The planner can have soil testing done at the 38.___

    A. U.S. Department of the Interior
    B. U.S. Soil Conservation Service
    C. U.S. Geological Survey Center
    D. U.S. Department of Agriculture
    E. U.S. Agricultural Extension Service

39. The marsh and aquatic plant that is of the GREATEST value throughout the United States is 39.____

A. water lily
B. cattail
C. bristle grass
D. ragweed
E. pondweed

40. Park maintenance should control woody vegetation 40.____

A. before the nesting season
B. at the beginning of the nesting season
C. at the peak of the nesting season
D. after the peak of the nesting season
E. at any time

41. Watersheds filter strips bordering tributaries in flat terrain should be ______ feet wide. 41.____

A. 10 B. 25 C. 50 D. 75 E. 100

42. Which of the following are better suited to a *warm* water pond? 42.____

I. Large mouth bass
II. Bluegills
III. Catfish
IV. Salmon
V. Greyling

The CORRECT answer is:

A. I, II, III
B. I, III
C. I, III, V
D. I, IV, V
E. II, III, V

43. The productivity of a pond would be affected by 43.____

A. siltation
B. evaporation
C. oxygen content
D. nutrient content
E. all of the above

44. The fish population of the wildlife impoundment can BEST be controlled by 44.____

A. reducing the home range
B. constructing islands
C. attracting natural predators
D. allowing recreational fishing
E. restricting access to nesting sites

45. The MINIMUM depth of a pond located in cold climates that will prevent fish kill is _______ feet. 45.____

A. 3 B. 6 C. 10 D. 15 E. 25

46. Storm detention ponds should be installed PRIOR to the grading of a development to 46.____

A. ensure a wetland habitat to the site
B. prevent spillways
C. minimize erosion
D. trap sediment generated by construction
E. satisfy safety requirements

47. The bird that would show the MOST striking increase after a development replaces farmland is the 47.____

A. mockingbird
B. mourning dove
C. bobtail quail
D. starling
E. song sparrow

48. What adverse effect do grey squirrels have on urban and suburban residents? 48.____

A. They transmit disease.
B. Their droppings are unsanitary.
C. They inflict serious wounds, particularly on children.
D. They attract parasites.
E. They damage buildings and property.

49. On institutional grounds, shrubbery should be placed 49.____

A. in clumps away from the buildings
B. in clumps near or against the buildings
C. in clean lines against the buildings
D. in clean lines around borders
E. singly and scattered

50. Which of the following has done the MOST to ensure wildlife considerations on a project-by-project basis? 50.____

A. Environmental impact statement requirements
B. Land development ordinances
C. The U.S. Environmental Protection Agency
D. Conservation easements
E. Use of severance tax

KEY (CORRECT ANSWERS)

1. B	11. B	21. D	31. A	41. C
2. E	12. A	22. B	32. D	42. A
3. B	13. D	23. B	33. D	43. E
4. B	14. C	24. A	34. C	44. E
5. A	15. E	25. B	35. A	45. D
6. B	16. D	26. B	36. C	46. D
7. A	17. C	27. C	37. E	47. D
8. B	18. B	28. B	38. E	48. E
9. A	19. E	29. D	39. E	49. A
10. D	20. D	30. A	40. D	50. A

EXAMINATION SECTION
TEST 1

DIRECTIONS: Each question or incomplete statement is followed by several suggested answers or completions. Select the one that BEST answers the question or completes the statement. *PRINT THE LETTER OF THE CORRECT ANSWER IN THE SPACE AT THE RIGHT.*

1. Each of the following is an example of a biome EXCEPT the 1.____

   A. North American prairie
   B. Grand Canyon
   C. tropical rain forest
   D. grasslands of the sub-Sahara

2. When an aquatic environment experiences an explosion in the population of microorganisms, the organisms later die and decompose, causing a chain reaction of death and decay until the body of water becomes marshy. 2.____
   This process is called

   A. eutrophication B. putrefaction
   C. aerobiosis D. biodegradation

3. The total weight of all the living organisms in any given system is called 3.____

   A. ecotone B. biomass
   C. demography D. census

4. What is the name for an organism, usually a mold or fungus, that consumes the tissue of dead plants or animals? 4.____

   A. Parasite B. Epiphyte
   C. Saprophyte D. Autotroph

5. The term for an arctic or mountainous area that is too cold to support trees and is vegetated with low mosses and grasses is 5.____

   A. savanna B. taiga C. steppe D. tundra

6. In a body of water, microscopic free-floating organisms that photosynthesize their own food are called 6.____

   A. krill B. zooplankton
   C. phytoplankton D. plasma

7. Animals that receive their energy from direct consumption of plant matter are called _______ consumers. 7.____

   A. primary B. secondary
   C. tertiary D. quaternary

8. Each of the following is one of the principal reasons, imposed by humans, for the extinction of modern species EXCEPT 8.____

   A. imposed breeding combinations
   B. destruction of habitat

C. introduction of foreign species
D. extermination of predators

9. When an ecosystem has reached a final stage of development in which it can only be changed by some outside agent, such as the introduction of another species, this is called a 9.____

A. critical level
B. climax community
C. saturation
D. plateau

10. Which of the following animals are MOST likely to exhibit territorial behaviors? 10.____

A. Large grazing mammals
B. Small predatory mammals
C. Fishes
D. Birds

11. Which of the types of associations below does NOT result in a positive effect for both species involved in the relationship? 11.____

A. Symbiosis
B. Commensalism
C. Parasitism
D. Mutualism

12. A plant (such as moss) that grows on another plant but does not use the host plant for food is called a(n) 12.____

A. osmotroph
B. epiphyte
C. fungus
D. phagocyte

13. What is the term for organic matter that is in the soil and is characterized by slow decomposition? 13.____

A. Topsoil
B. Substrate
C. Subsoil
D. Humus

14. Evolution involves changing gene frequencies resulting from each of the following EXCEPT 14.____

A. genetic drift
B. selection pressure from the environment and interacting species
C. learned survival behaviors
D. recurrent mutations

15. What is the name for a partially enclosed coastal body of shallow water that has a free connection with the open sea? 15.____

A. Delta
B. Estuary
C. Bay
D. Aquifer

16. Autotrophs are organisms that obtain their energy 16.____

A. directly from the sun
B. through the consumption of plant matter
C. through predation of other animals
D. from decomposing plant and animal tissues

17. When the common gene pool's genetic flow is interrupted by an isolating mechanism, resulting in species diversity or the formation of a new species, what natural selection process has occurred? 17.____

A. Mutation
B. Speciation
C. Character displacement
D. Gestation

18. The surface volume of water in the ocean or a large lake that receives enough light to support photosynthesis is called the ______ zone. 18.____

A. benthic
B. eukaryotic
C. littoral
D. euphotic

19. Which of the following is NOT capable of transforming molecular nitrogen into forms that are usable by living organisms? 19.____

A. Photochemical reactions
B. Lightning
C. Specialized bacteria and algae
D. Atmospheric pressure

20. What kind of ecosystems GENERALLY characterize temperate areas with low rainfall? 20.____

A. Desert
B. Prairie
C. Deciduous forest
D. Tundra

21. All the non-living organic matter in an ecosystem is known collectively as 21.____

A. ore
B. plankton
C. detritus
D. particulate

22. In regions where chemical air pollutants have darkened the surrounding trees, some species of moths adapt by shifting their population's coloring from light to dark. This adaptation is known as 22.____

A. industrial melanism
B. homeostasis
C. genetic osmosis
D. natural succession

23. In the United States, which of the following species has made the most successful adaptation to the growth and expansion of human populations? 23.____

A. Mountain lion
B. Bighorn sheep
C. Deer
D. Bison

24. The vertebrate animals that appear FIRST on the evolutionary record are 24.____

A. birds
B. fish
C. reptiles
D. mammals

25. All organisms that obtain their energy from sources other than sunlight are known collectively as 25.____

A. autotrophs
B. primary consumers
C. heterotrophs
D. omnivores

KEY (CORRECT ANSWERS)

1. B
2. A
3. B
4. C
5. D
6. C
7. A
8. A
9. B
10. D
11. C
12. B
13. D
14. C
15. B
16. A
17. B
18. D
19. D
20. B
21. C
22. A
23. C
24. B
25. C

TEST 2

DIRECTIONS: Each question or incomplete statement is followed by several suggested answers or completions. Select the one that BEST answers the question or completes the statement. *PRINT THE LETTER OF THE CORRECT ANSWER IN THE SPACE AT THE RIGHT.*

1. Dystrophic lakes are characterized by which of the following conditions? 1.____

   A. High concentrations of calcium and oxygen
   B. Inadequate decomposition of matter
   C. Lack of photosynthetic organisms
   D. Large number and variety of organisms

2. Which of the animals below is generally considered to have the LEAST complex social order among members of its species? 2.____

   A. African lion
   B. Honeybee
   C. North American alligator
   D. Canada goose

3. The taiga is the 3.____

   A. coniferous forest of the northern latitudes of North America
   B. scrub desert of Southwestern North America
   C. temperate deciduous forest of Eurasia
   D. subtropical grasslands of Africa

4. The uppermost trees on a mountain slope inhabit an area known as the 4.____

   A. Longren B. tundra C. humus D. Krummholz

5. Which of the following organisms is likely to be MORE abundant in a swiftly-moving stream than in a slow stream? 5.____

   A. Phytoplankton B. Fish
   C. Crayfish D. Zooplankton

6. A wheat field has an inherent ability to support more locusts than a short-grass prairie. Therefore, it is said to have a ______ for locusts. 6.____

   A. commensal requirement
   B. greater environmental resistance
   C. more limiting habitat
   D. larger carrying capacity

7. The place where wildlife lives is called 7.____

   A. habitat B. pasture C. home D. tundra

8. The unique function of a particular species, along with its habitat, are known together as its 8.____

   A. home range B. critical level
   C. ecotone D. ecological niche

9. Which of the types of wild species below probably has the LOWEST risk of extinction in the modern world? 9.____

   A. Highly specialized or immobile organisms
   B. Animals that aggregate and migrate in large groups
   C. Large grazing animals
   D. Large carnivorous predators

10. With what kind of species association do wild rose bushes and mountain lions interact? 10.____

   A. Competition
   B. Parasitism
   C. Neutralism
   D. Mutualism

11. Which of the bird species below is currently the LEAST endangered in the United States? 11.____

   A. Bald eagle
   B. Ivory-billed woodpecker
   C. California condor
   D. Whooping crane

12. When populations of differing species become dependent on each other for survival, the relationship is described as 12.____

   A. neutralism
   B. mutualism
   C. unibiosis
   D. parasitism

13. Which of the organisms below is an example of an ungulate? 13.____

   A. Rhesus monkey
   B. Kodiak bear
   C. Tule elk
   D. Cheetah

14. Large North American carnivores such as the timber wolf and the black bear generally prey upon the same types of animal species. Therefore, they are said to share the same 14.____

   A. habitat
   B. food chain
   C. ecological niche
   D. trophic level

15. Which is the LIKELIEST result of overcrowding on a species population? 15.____

   A. Immediate adaptation
   B. Forced migration
   C. An explosion in predation
   D. Reduced reproductive yield

16. Respiration that takes place without the presence of oxygen is described as 16.____

   A. antibiotic
   B. carbonic
   C. anaerobic
   D. unsaturated

17. Environmental resistance is the 17.____

   A. natural resilience of the environment to disturbances from outside sources
   B. tendency of ecosystems to remain the same over a period of time
   C. environmental interactions which collectively inhibit the growth of a species
   D. worldwide industrial practices that repeatedly damage the natural environment

18. Which of the animals below is characterized by a matriarchal social order? 18.____

A. African elephant
B. Mountain gorilla
C. Caribou
D. American bald eagle

19. In the months after lava flow has cooled and settle on a Hawaiian island, the area is gradually populated by ferns and lichens. 19.____
Which successional stage does this represent?

A. Primary
B. Secondary
C. Tertiary
D. Quaternary

20. With what kind of species association do intertidal barnacles and mussels interact? 20.____

A. Competition
B. Parasitism
C. Neutralism
D. Mutualism

21. Which of the following ecosystems below is an example of a climax system? 21.____
A(n)

A. woodland meadow
B. old-growth redwood forest
C. inland marsh
D. small wooded pond

22. In a climate that is milder than that of the coniferous forest, where rainfall is abundant relative to evaporation, what kind of ecological community would be MOST likely? 22.____

A. Tundra
B. Tallgrass prairie
C. Short-grass prairie
D. Deciduous forest

23. The middle waters of a lake, where oxygen content falls off rapidly with depth, are the 23.____

A. hypolimnion
B. benthic zone
C. thermocline
D. euphotic zone

24. The control mechanisms within an ecosystem that maintain constancy by resisting external stresses are known collectively as 24.____

A. homeostasis
B. contrapuntal mechanisms
C. environmental resistance
D. heterotrophic modulation

25. Biotic potential is the 25.____

A. largest possible size of an individual organism
B. range of adaptive flexibility for an organism in a given environment
C. maximum rate of growth for a species population
D. range of possibilities for an evolving ecosystem

KEY (CORRECT ANSWERS)

1. B
2. C
3. A
4. D
5. C

6. D
7. A
8. D
9. B
10. C

11. A
12. B
13. C
14. B
15. D

16. C
17. C
18. A
19. A
20. A

21. B
22. D
23. C
24. A
25. C

EXAMINATION SECTION
TEST 1

DIRECTIONS: Each question or incomplete statement is followed by several suggested answers or completions. Select the one that *BEST* answers the question or completes the statement. *PRINT THE LETTER OF THE CORRECT ANSWER IN THE SPACE AT THE RIGHT.*

1. The OLDEST living things are 1.____

   A. birds B. human beings C. trees
   D. insects E. elephants

2. The development of an egg without fertilization is known as 2.____

   A. meiosis B. oogenesis
   C. parthenogenesis D. gametogenesis

3. The process by which sugar is changed by yeast to alcohol and carbon dioxide is 3.____

   A. oxidation B. fertilization C. digestion
   D. assimilation E. fermentation

4. The HIGHEST plants from the standpoint of evolution are 4.____

   A. fungi B. spermatophytes C. algae
   D. diatoms E. ferns

5. A type of reproduction in which sexual reproduction is followed by asexual is 5.____

   A. budding B. grafting
   C. alternation of generations D. egg laying
   E. fission

6. The stages in complete metamorphosis are 6.____

   A. egg, larva, nymph B. nymph, larva, pupa
   C. egg, larva, pupa, adult D. adult, nymph, cocoon
   E. cocoon, pupa, nymph

7. An important cause of decay of organic matter is 7.____

   A. heat B. bacteria C. legumes
   D. rain E. air

8. The plan of planting sweet clover in a field one year then planting grain in the field the next year is 8.____

   A. strip farming B. contouring
   C. dry farming D. crop rotation
   E. terracing

9. The carrier of Texas cattle fever is 9.____

   A. lice B. boll weevils C. fleas
   D. flies E. ticks

10. The GREATEST destroyer of forests is 10.___

A. fire B. floods C. insects D. fungi

11. The national parks are managed by the Department of 11.___

A. State B. Interior C. Agriculture D. Labor

12. The quantity of heat energy required to raise the temperature (1000 grams) of water one degree centigrade is 12.___

A. calorie B. 10 calories C. kilocalorie
D. foot-pound E. all of the above

13. The MOST valuable source of proteins is 13.___

A. sugar B. potatoes C. lettuce
D. meat E. butter

14. The *islands of Langerhans* which control the amount of sugar used by the body are located in the 14.___

A. spleen B. kidney C. liver
D. throat E. pancreas

15. Sperm and eggs of the same species are *identical* in 15.___

A. size and number
B. shape and mobility
C. chromosome number
D. amount of cytoplasm

16. Cancer is caused by a 16.___

A. virus B. bacterium C. protozoan
D. fungus E. unknown

17. The FIRST stage of cell division is 17.___

A. anaphase B. metaphase C. prophase D. telophase

18. Bacteria are 18.___

A. algae B. protozoa C. fungi D. viruses

Questions: 19-33

DIRECTIONS: From the choices following each term in questions 19-33, pick the letter of the choice which is *most closely* associated with that term.

19. Association of disease with a specific organism 19.___

A. Darwin B. bacilli C. Koch
D. Goldberger E. cocci

20. Evolution 20.___

A. Darwin B. bacilli C. Koch
D. Goldberger E. cocci

21. Spherical bacteria 21._____

A. Darwin B. bacilli C. Koch
D. Goldberger E. cocci

22. Carries sleeping sickness germs 22._____

A. Vitamin A B. tsetse fly
C. Anopheles mosquito D. Rocky Mountain spotted fever
E. Vitamin C

23. Carried by ticks 23._____

A. Vitamin A B. tsetse fly
C. Anopheles mosquito D. Rocky Mountain spotted fever
E. Vitamin C

24. Prevents scurvy 24._____

A. Vitamin A B. tsetse fly
C. Anopheles mosquito D. Rocky Mountain spotted fever
E. Vitamin C

25. Time between fertilization and birth 25._____

A. paleontology B. loam C. nymph
D. gestation E. placenta

26. Study of fossils 26._____

A. paleontology B. loam C. nymph
D. gestation E. placenta

27. Young grasshopper 27._____

A. paleontology B. loam C. nymph
D. gestation E. placenta

28. A venereal disease 28._____

A. xylem B. phloem C. microorganism
D. tropism E. syphilis

29. Tiny organism 29._____

A. xylem B. phloem C. microorganism
D. tropism E. syphilis

30. Water conducting tubules 30._____

A. xylem B. phloem C. microorganism
D. tropism E. syphilis

31. Father of modern heredity 31._____

A. Hooke B. Roux C. Mendel
D. Goldberger E. Lamarck

32. Theory of inheritance of acquired traits 32.____

A. Hooke B. Roux C. Mendel
D. Goldberger E. Lamarck

33. Observed and described plants' cells 33.____

A. Hooke B. Roux C. Mendel
D. Goldberger E. Lamarck

Questions 34-50

DIRECTIONS: Each question or incomplete statement is followed by several suggested answers or completions. Select the one that *BEST* answers the question or completes the statement. *PRINT THE LETTER OF THE CORRECT ANSWER IN THE SPACE AT THE RIGHT.*

34. The ______ is *primarily* concerned with photosynthesis. 34.____

A. root B. stem C. leaf D. flower

35. Which part of the flower develops into the mature fruit? 35.____

A. Ovary B. Pistil C. Petal D. Receptacle

36. Which taxonomic category contains the LARGEST number of different kinds of organisms? 36.____

A. Class B. Species C. Genus D. Phylum

37. The MOST important role of plants in the environment involes the 37.____

A. production of wood
B. production of drugs
C. fixation of carbon dioxide
D. transpiration of water

38. Respiration and photosynthesis *differ* in that respiration requires 38.____

A. chlorophyll B. carbon dioxide
C. light D. oxygen

39. Algae, bacteria, fungi and protozoans still pose a taxonomic problem. 39.____
A solution that has gained support in recent years is to classify all these organisms as members of

A. one or more separate kingdoms
B. both the plant and animal kingdoms
C. the plant kingdom only
D. the animal kingdom only

40. ______ include the flowering plants. 40.____

A. Mosses B. Ferns
C. Gymnosperms D. Angiosperms

41. It has been observed that green plants bend toward a light source. What substance is responsible for this tropism? 41.____

A. Auxins
B. Chlorophyll
C. Glucose
D. Carbon dioxide

42. Two hundred pea seedlings were planted and grown in the dark. When observed a few days later, they all appeared to be albino. When placed in the light, *most* turned green. The albino appearance for those that turned green may be attributed to 42.____

A. environment
B. heredity
C. both environment and heredity
D. neither environment nor heredity

43. The ______ are organisms which contain chlorophyl. 43.____

A. amoeba
B. euglena
C. paramecium
D. plasmodium

44. Blue-green algae *differ* from bacteria in that blue-green algae are 44.____

A. primarily autotrophic
B. primarily heterotrophic
C. unicellular
D. eucaryotic

45. In an optimal environment, bacteria reproduce rapidly by 45.____

A. endospore formation
B. cyst formation
C. asexual means
D. sexual means

46. Identify the streptobacillus bacterial form. 46.____

A. B. C. D.

47. The modern horse is larger than its original ancestors. Which of these statements BEST describes this change based on Darwin's theory of natural selection? 47.____

A. Mutations account for the increased size.
B. Chromosomal aberrations account for the increased size.
C. Ancestors developed longer legs in order to run away from enemies.
D. Larger horses survived and reproduced, and smaller ones died, leaving *only* larger horses.

48. Examine the chromatographic separation shown below. What BEST represents the identity of unknown X? 48.____
A mixture of ______.

A. 1, 2 and 3
B. 1 and 2
C. 1 and 3
D. 2 and 3

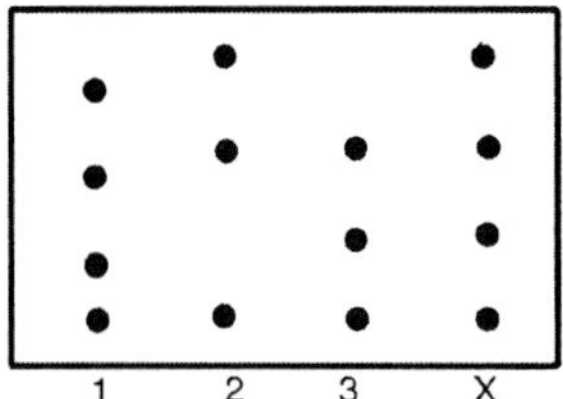

49. Identify the BEST experimental design for determining the effectiveness of a vaccine in preventing a bacterial infection in humans. 49.____

A. Expose 50 humans to the disease and then inoculate 25 with the vaccine.
B. Expose 50 humans to the disease and then inoculate all 50 with the vaccine.
C. Inoculate 25 humans with the vaccine and 25 with sterile saline and then expose *only* those inoculated with the vaccine to the disease.
D. Inoculate 25 humans with the vaccine and 25 with sterile saline and then expose all 50 to the disease.

50. The graph shown below illustrates cell population growth. The period of most rapid population growth occurs between ______ and ______ hours. 50.____

A. 4; 16 B. 12; 16 C. 16; 24 D. 24; 28

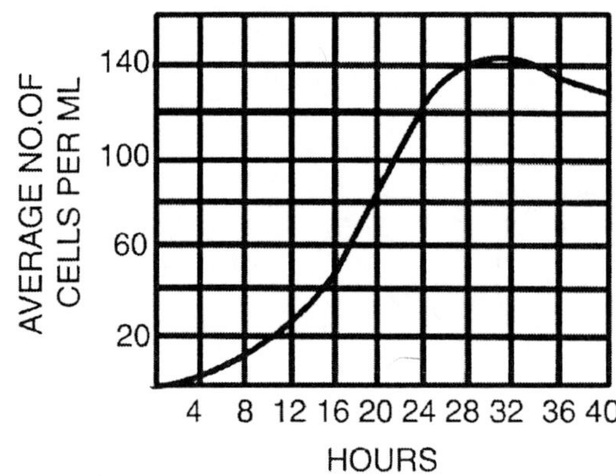

KEY (CORRECT ANSWERS)

1. C	11. B	21. E	31. C	41. A
2. C	12. A	22. B	32. E	42. A
3. E	13. D	23. D	33. A	43. B
4. B	14. E	24. E	34. C	44. A
5. C	15. C	25. D	35. A	45. C
6. C	16. E	26. A	36. D	46. B
7. B	17. C	27. C	37. C	47. D
8. D	18. C	28. E	38. D	48. D
9. E	19. C	29. C	39. A	49. D
10. A	20. A	30. A	40. D	50. C

TEST 2

DIRECTIONS: Each question or incomplete statement is followed by several suggested answers or completions. Select the one that *BEST* answers the question or completes the statement. *PRINT THE LETTER OF THE CORRECT ANSWER IN THE SPACE AT THE RIGHT.*

1. The FIRST item on the list of treatments of heart disease is 1.____
   A. relaxation B. diet
   C. sedatives D. change of climate

2. Something that causes an organism to react is a(n) 2.____
   A. response B. stimulus C. interjection D. enzyme

3. The substance that causes plants to grow towards light is 3.____
   A. enzyme B. stimulus C. hormone D. none of the above

4. End organs are 4.____
   A. reactors B. receptors C. activators D. simulators

5. Inborn behavior patterns are 5.____
   A. instincts B. conditioned reactions
   C. learned reactions D. acquired responses

6. A method of asexual reproduction in some plants is 6.____
   A. fusion B. budding C. grafting D. gametogenesis

7. Sex cells are 7.____
   A. spores B. zygotes C. gametes D. diatoms

8. The union of sperm and egg is 8.____
   A. fertilization B. sporulation C. conjugation D. budding

9. The twig that is to be grafted on to another plant is a(n) 9.____
   A. acion B. stock C. runner D. prothallium

10. The female part of a flower is a 10.____
    A. filament B. stigma C. petal D. pollen

11. The reserve food supply in a seed is 11.____
    A. starch B. plumule C. testa D. endosperm

12. The hollow ball stage of embryonic development is a(n) 12.____
    A. zygote B. gastrula C. blastula D. morula

13. The stage of mitosis in which the chromosomes line up at the equator is 13.____
    A. metaphase B. prophase C. anaphase D. telophase

14. The nerves develop from 14.___
    A. endoderm B. ectoderm C. mesoderm D. none of the above

15. Mutations can be induced by 15.___
    A. sudden jolts
    B. adverse temperature
    C. x-rays
    D. none of the above

16. A term applied to a gene that kills is 16.___
    A. epistatic B. recessive C. hybrid D. lethal

17. The science of improving genetics is 17.___
    A. euthenics B. eugenics C. genetics D. hemophilia

18. The study of the earth is 18.___
    A. evolution B. geography C. geology D. paleontology

19. Land plant life probably began ______ years ago 19.___
    A. five million
    B. fifty million
    C. five hundred million
    D. five billion

20. The study of cells is 20.___
    A. morphology B. taxonomy C. cytology D. ecology

21. The highest temperature at which any organism can grow is 21.___
    A. 140° F B. 148° F C. 170° F D. 212° F

22. The relationship of two organisms living together with mutual benefit is 22.___
    A. parasitism
    B. symbiosis
    C. microbiology
    D. equilibrium

23. Plant hormones are 23.___
    A. vitamins B. instincts C. auxins D. phagocytes

24. The nerve of the eye is the ______ nerve. 24.___
    A. auditory B. optic C. spinal D. vagus

25. A nerve cell is the 25.___
    A. dendrite B. axon C. neuron D. neutron

26. The part of the brain enabling man to talk is the 26.___
    A. cerebellum B. cerebrum C. medulla D. metencephalon

27. An electrical disturbance traveling along a nerve is a(n) 27.___
    A. impulse B. response C. sensation D. stimulus

28. The food MOST important for growth and repair of tissue is 28.___
    A. fat B. carbohydrate C. mineral D. protein

29. The metabolic activity unique to plants is 29._____

A. digestion B. assimilation
C. photosynthesis D. oxidation

30. Division of a fertilized egg is 30._____

A. fertilization B. fission C. pollination D. cleavage

31. The outside layer of cells of a leaf is 31._____

A. palisade B. spongy tissue
C. guard cells D. epidermis

32. A plant that lives only one season is 32._____

A. annual B. biannual C. biennial D. perennial

33. The substance that can assist in the change of the chemical composition of another substance without itself being changed is a(n) 33._____

A. enzyme B. Lubricant C. antitoxin D. hormone

34. The tissue covering the human cerebrum is 34._____

A. axon B. endoderm C. cortex D. periosteum

35. Insects breathe by means of 35._____

A. gills B. lungs C. muscles D. tracheae

36. An animal having gills in its adult stage is the 36._____

A. frog B. bass C. whale D. snake

37. A condition that makes cross-pollination necessary is the 37._____

A. stamens and pistils on separate plants
B. winged pollen
C. stocky stigma
D. brightly colored sepals

38. An animal having a four-chambered heart is the 38._____

A. catfish B. ant C. cow D. frog

39. An important process carried on by plants and NOT by animals is 39._____

A. assimilation B. photosynthesis
C. respiration D. oxidation

40. The simplest animal in which there is cellular division of labor is a(n) 40._____

A. moss B. liverwort C. sponge D. amoeba

KEY (CORRECT ANSWERS)

1.	A	11.	D	21.	C	31.	D
2.	B	12.	C	22.	B	32.	A
3.	C	13.	A	23.	C	33.	A
4.	B	14.	B	24.	B	34.	C
5.	A	15.	C	25.	C	35.	D
6.	B	16.	D	26.	B	36.	B
7.	C	17.	B	27.	A	37.	A
8.	A	18.	C	28.	D	38.	C
9.	A	19.	B	29.	B	39.	B
10.	B	20.	D	30.	D	40.	C

TEST 3

DIRECTIONS: Each question or incomplete statement is followed by several suggested answers or completions. Select the one that *BEST* answers the question or completes the statement. *PRINT THE LETTER OF THE CORRECT ANSWER IN THE SPACE AT THE RIGHT.*

1. The _______ is a predatory animal. 1.____

   A. chicken B. rodent C. rabbit D. hawk

2. The study of microscopic nongreen plants, some of which cause disease, is 2.____

   A. cytology B. bacteriology C. entomology
   D. parasitology E. taxonomy

3. In the human, the baby normally goes through embryonic development in the 3.____

   A. ovary B. vagina C. uterus
   D. oviduct E. marsupium

4. Protoplasm consists MOSTLY of 4.____

   A. proteins B. sugars C. fats
   D. mineral salts E. water

5. Any sex cell may be called a(n) 5.____

   A. gamete B. sperm C. ovum
   D. zygote E. gonad

6. Monocots are characterized by having their flower parts in 6.____

   A. ones B. threes C. fours
   D. fives E. various numbers, from one to many

7. Milk is *usually* freed of its most dangerous bacteria by a process called 7.____

   A. sterilization B. inoculation
   C. autoclaving D. pasteurization
   E. boiling

8. An animal, such as a deer, that feeds *primarily* upon plant material is called a(n) 8.____

   A. herbivore B. omnivore C. carnivore
   D. saprophyte E. autotroph

9. An organism that invades the bodies of plants and animals and takes its nourishment directly from living tissue is a 9.____

   A. saprophyte B. commensal C. mutual
   D. predator E. parasite

10. A single-celled, asexual reproductive body produced by fungi and ferns is a(n) 10.____

    A. sperm B. ovum C. zygote
    D. spore E. zygospore

11. Tube feet and a water vascular system are characteristic of a(n) 11.___

A. starfish B. snail C. jellyfish
D. octopus E. crayfish

12. A powerful insecticide that is used to control harmful insects is 12.___

A. 2-4D B. DDT C. ATP
D. DNA E. FSH

13. In the human body, muscle, bone, and other body cells reproduce by a process called 13.___

A. meiosis B. fission C. conjugation
D. mitosis E. fragmentation

14. The breakdown of complex food particles into simpler, soluble particles is termed 14.___

A. ingestion B. digestion C. egestion
D. assimilation E. oxidation

15. All organic compounds contain the element 15.___

A. phosphorus B. iron C. carbon
D. sulfur E. nitrogen

16. Mitochrondia have to do *primarily* with the process of 16.___

A. cell division B. respiration C. digestion
D. food manufacture E. growth

17. A group of similar cells performing a similar activity make up a(n) 17.___

A. tissue B. organism C. organ
D. system E. syncitium

18. The process by which water passes from the spongy areas of a leaf through the stomates and into the air as a vapor is 18.___

A. translocation B. guttation
C. transpiration D. capillary attraction
E. cohesion

19. The important organic catalyst that allows plants to carry on photosynthesis is 19.___

A. pepsin B. carotene C. xanthophyll
D. anthocyanin E. chlorophyll

20. A phylum of animals all of whose members are marine is 20.___

A. Echinodermata B. Porifera
C. Coelenterata D. Annelida
E. Mollusca

21. Breathing pores found in the bark of small twigs are called 21.___

A. stomata B. vascular bundles C. stipules
D. lenticels E. spiracles

22. If an animal has eight legs and two body regions, it is *most likely* a 22._____

A. June beetle B. centipede C. crayfish
D. spider E. mosquito

23. One of the essential parts of a flower is the 23._____

A. calyx B. corolla C. petal
D. sepal E. stamen

24. In a plant, the female sex calls are produced in the 24._____

A. stigma B. stamen C. receptacle
D. anther E. ovary

25. A seed is a ripened or matured 25._____

A. receptacle B. stigma C. ovule
D. ovary E. anther

26. A dicot stem increases in thickness because new cells are formed by the 26._____

A. cortex B. periderm C. endodermis
D. central cylinder E. cambium

27. The carrying away of the topsoil by wind and water is an example of 27._____

A. sublimation B. guttation
C. sedimentation D. erosion
E. translocation

28. Disease-producing bacteria are termed 28._____

A. antibodies B. symbionts C. pathogens,
D. commensals E. mutuals

29. The endocrine gland in the body which MOST influences the growth of a person is the 29._____

A. pancreas B. adrenal C. thymus
D. pituitary E. pineal

30. An example of an insect with biting or chewing mouthparts is a 30._____

A. flea B. beetle C. mosquito
D. housefly E. bedbug

31. Simplest independent plants of the following are the 31._____

A. algae B. ferns C. horsetails
D. fungi E. bacteria

32. Most plant cells have a wall around them composed of 32._____

A. protoplasm B. cellulose C. starch
D. sugar E. chitin

33. Humans *usually* get trichinosis from eating rare or under-cooked 33._____

A. steak B. wild game C. pork
D. fish E. vegetables

34. Traits like blue eyes and blond hair in humans are called 34.____

A. dominant
B. sex-linked
C. lethal
D. sex-limited
E. recessive

35. The earthworm takes in oxygen and gives off carbon dioxide through its 35.____

A. nephridia
B. gills
C. lungs
D. skin
E. mouth

36. In a cell, energy is released from the food by a process called 36.____

A. excretion
B. respiration
C. assimilation
D. digestion
E. secretion

37. The study of animals is 37.____

A. zoology
B. physiology
C. taxonomy
D. botany
E. herpetology

38. The one-celled animal, Paramecium, swims about by means of its 38.____

A. pellicle
B. tail
C. vacuole
D. cilia
E. flagella

39. A group of plants that are used as soil builders as they join with certain bacteria to enrich the nitrogen content of the soil is the 39.____

A. grasses
B. legumes
C. fungi
D. elms
E. mosses

40. The substance agar-agar, used in the laboratories as a base for the culture of bacteria, is made from 40.____

A. wheat flour
B. dried milk
C. lean meat
D. sugar
E. algae

KEY (CORRECT ANSWERS)

1. E	11. A	21. D	31. A
2. B	12. B	22. D	32. B
3. C	13. D	23. E	33. C
4. E	14. B	24. E	34. E
5. A	15. C	25. C	35. D
6. B	16. B	26. E	36. B
7. D	17. A	27. D	37. A
8. A	18. C	28. C	38. D
9. E	19. E	29. D	39. B
10. D	20. A	30. B	40. E

TEST 4

DIRECTIONS: Each question or incomplete statement is followed by several suggested answers or completions. Select the one that *BEST* answers the question or completes the statement. *PRINT THE LETTER OF THE CORRECT ANSWER IN THE SPACE AT THE RIGHT.*

1. In a flower, all of the petals together make up the 1.____

   A. calyx B. receptacle C. essential organs
   D. corolla E. peduncle

2. The automatic response of a plant or any of its parts toward or away from a stimulus is 2.____

   A. tropism B. impulse C. reflex
   D. instinct E. irritation

3. The absorption of large quantities of water by an organic substance such as starch, gelatin, wood, and seed coats, resulting in swelling is 3.____

   A. turgor B. plasmolysis C. imbibition
   D. guttation E. osmosis

4. The sum *total* of all the essential chemical processes that take place in an organism's body is 4.____

   A. catabolism B. metabolism
   C. anabolism D. symbiosis
   E. mastication

5. Pollen of a flowering plant is produced by the 5.____

   A. stamen B. pistil C. ovary
   D. stigma E. receptacle

6. The growing tip of a root, where new cells are formed, is the 6.____

   A. maturation region B. elongation region
   C. embryonic region D. root cap
   E. central cylinder

7. A fertilized egg cell is a(n) 7.____

   A. spore B. gamete C. gonad
   D. endosperm E. zygote

8. A plant tissue specialized to conduct water and dissolved material up the plant stem is the 8.____

   A. pericycle B. xylem C. phloem
   D. endodermis E. cortex

9. Cell division of body cells, involving the nucleus and chromosomes is called 9.____

   A. mitosis B. fission C. conjugation
   D. meiosis E. fragmentation

10. In the higher organisms, the uniting of the female and male sex cells is called 10.___

A. conjugation B. meiosis C. cleavage
D. fertilization E. gametogenesis

11. The MOST primitive vertebrate in the following list is the 11.___

A. monkey B. chicken C. rattlesnake
D. bullfrog E. catfish

12. An enlarged thyroid, called a goiter, is due to a diet deficient in the element 12.___

A. iron B. phosphorus C. copper
D. iodine E. calcium

13. Amino acids are the building blocks from which the body makes 13.___

A. glycogen B. fatty acids C. glucose
D. glycerin E. proteins

14. An example of an inorganic compound is 14.___

A. $C_6H_{12}O_6$ B. N_2 C. C
D. NaCL E. O_2

15. Genes are *most closely* associated with 15.___

A. chromosomes B. cytoplasm C. mitochondria
D. vacuoles E. centrioles

16. The GREATEST amount of food manufacture in a leaf takes place in the 16.___

A. cuticle B. palisade layer C. epidermis
D. stomata E. petiole

17. MOST of the dependent plants, such as the yeast, molds, mildews, and mushrooms, belong to the group known as 17.___

A. saprophytes B. parasites C. fungi
D. commensals E. symbionts

18. The earthworm contains both male and female reproductive organs, a condition called 18.___

A. parthenogenesis B. pedogenesis
C. dioecious D. metamorphosis
E. hermaphroditism

19. Tetanus, typhoid, and tuberculosis are diseases caused by parasitic 19.___

A. roundworms B. protozoans C. bacteria
D. insects E. viruses

20. The sexual union of cells of about the same size is called 20.___

A. fission B. fertilization
C. plasmolysis D. parthenogenesis
E. conjugation

21. Muscles arise from the embryonic tissue or layer called the 21.____

A. gastrula
B. endoderm
C. ectoderm
D. amnion
E. mesoderm

22. A form of respiration which does NOT involve the presence of atmospheric oxygen is called 22.____

A. pulmonary
B. cutaneous
C. branchial
D. aerobic
E. anaerobic

23. Blood is carried away from the heart by means of the 23.____

A. capillaries
B. lymph vessels
C. veins
D. arteries
E. sinuses

24. The CLOSEST relative of the tick in the following list is the 24.____

A. centipede
B. June beetle
C. spider
D. praying mantis
E. mosquito

25. The hookworm in the southern states *usually* enters the body 25.____

A. through the bite of a mosquito
B. through the thin skin of the hands and feet
C. through contaminated food and water
D. from eating rare or undercooked meat
E. directly from one infected person to another

26. The man who FIRST described and named cells is 26.____

A. Alfred Wallace
B. Charles Darwin
C. Theodore Schwann
D. Robert Hooke
E. Matthias Schleiden

27. A lichen is a biological partnership between ______ and 27.____

A. bacteria; clover
B. an alga; a fungus
C. roundworms; elm trees
D. a leech; its host
E. an insect; a bird

28. An insect that undergoes regular migration northward and southward is the 28.____

A. monarch butterfly
B. viceroy butterfly
C. honeybee
D. flying locust
E. periodic cicada

29. The order of insects containing flies and mosquitos may be distinguished from other orders by the possession of 29.____

A. compound eyes
B. three body regions
C. one pair of wings
D. three pairs of legs
E. an exoskeleton

30. Examples of plants having a fibrous type of root system are ______ and ______. 30.____

A. oak; elm trees
B. beets; carrots
C. beans; peas
D. roses; petunias
E. bluegrass; wheat

31. The carbohydrate foods enter the cells of organisms as 31.____

A. glucose
B. amino acids
C. fatty acids
D. glycogen
E. glycerin

32. The antibiotic penicillin is secured from a (the) 32.____

A. virus
B. mold
C. bodies of infected organisms
D. protozoan
E. glands of butchered animals

33. The branch of biology that has to do with the classification, or naming, of plants and animals is 33.____

A. ecology
B. entomology
C. taxonomy
D. ichthyology
E. ornithology

34. Decay, nitrogen-fixation, and fermentation may be caused by various forms of 34.____

A. viruses
B. bacteria
C. algae
D. ferns
E. seed-bearing plants

35. A common marsupial of the United States is the 35.____

A. coyote
B. raccoon
C. pocket gopher
D. kangaroo rat
E. opossum

36. In vertebrates, a larval stage is present in 36.____

A. opossums
B. rattlesnakes
C. tiger salamanders
D. robins
E. snapping turtles

37. MOST of the force for driving a fish through the water is applied by the ______ fin(s). 37.____

A. caudal
B. pectoral
C. pelvic
D. dorsal
E. anal

38. The part of the brain that controls the conscious, or voluntary actions, of an animal is the 38.____

A. cerebellum
B. cerebrum
C. medulla
D. olfactory lobes
E. spinal cord

39. A hereditary trait, such as freckles and skin color, is associated *most closely* with the 39.____

A. Golgi bodies
B. mitochondria
C. nucleus
D. cytoplasm
E. vacuoles

40. Digestion of protein begins in the 40.____

A. mouth
B. stomach
C. small intestine
D. pancreas
E. liver

41. The gradual changes of the plants and animals present in an area through the years after habitat disturbance are called 41.____

A. adaptation
B. climax
C. succession
D. biotic potential
E. estivation

42. The man who receives credit for starting our present-day system of naming plants and animals is 42.____

A. Charles Darwin
B. Louis Pasteur
C. Jean Lamarck
D. Carl Linnaeus
E. Alfred Wallace

43. The discredited theory that nonliving materials can change into living things is 43.____

A. spontaneous generation
B. biogenesis
C. continuity
D. vegetative propagation
E. reincarnation

44. An organic compound composed of carbon, hydrogen, and oxygen, in which the hydrogen and oxygen are present in the ratio of 2:1 is 44.____

A. water
B. carbohydrate
C. protein
D. amino acid
E. fat

45. Which of these plants is a hydrophyte? 45.____

A. Water lily
B. Cactus
C. Wheat
D. Oak tree
E. Bluegrass

KEY (CORRECT ANSWERS)

1.	D	11.	E	21.	E	31.	A	41.	C
2.	A	12.	D	22.	E	32.	B	42.	D
3.	C	13.	E	23.	D	33.	C	43.	A
4.	B	14.	D	24.	C	34.	B	44.	B
5.	A	15.	A	25.	B	35.	E	45.	A
6.	C	16.	B	26.	D	36.	C		
7.	E	17.	C	27.	B	37.	A		
8.	B	18.	E	28.	A	38.	B		
9.	A	19.	C	29.	C	39.	C		
10.	D	20.	E	30.	E	40.	B		

EXAMINATION SECTION
TEST 1

DIRECTIONS: Each question or incomplete statement is followed by several suggested answers or completions. Select the one that *BEST* answers the question or completes the statement. *PRINT THE LETTER OF THE CORRECT ANSWER IN THE SPACE AT THE RIGHT.*

1. When 60,987 is added to 27,835, the result is 1.____
   A. 80,712 B. 80,822 C. 87,712 D. 88,822

2. The sum of 693 + 787 + 946 + 355 + 731 is 2.____
   A. 3,512 B. 3,502 C. 3,412 D. 3,402

3. When 2,586 is subtracted from 3,003, the result is 3.____
   A. 417 B. 527 C. 1,417 D. 1,527

4. When 1.32 is subtracted from 52.6, the result is 4.____
   A. 3.94 B. 5.128 C. 39.4 D. 51.28

5. When 56 is multiplied by 438, the result is 5.____
   A. 840 B. 4,818 C. 24,528 D. 48,180

6. When 8.7 is multiplied by .34, the result is, most nearly, 6.____
   A. 2.9 B. 3.0 C. 29.5 D. 29.6

7. When 1/2 is divided by 2/3, the result is 7.____
   A. 1/3 B. 3/4 C. 1 1/3 D. 3

8. When 8,340 is divided by 38, the result is, most nearly 8.____
   A. 210 B. 218 C. 219 D. 220

Questions 9-11.

DIRECTIONS: Questions 9 to 11 inclusive are to be answered *SOLELY* on the basis of the information given below.

Assume that a certain water treatment plant has consumed quantities of chemicals E and F over a five-week period, as indicated in the following table:

Time Period	Number of 100-pound sacks consumed	
	Chemical E	Chemical F
Week 1	5	4
Week 2	7	5
Week 3	6	5
Week 4	8	6
Week 5	6	4

9. The *total* number of pounds of chemical E consumed at the end of the first three weeks is 9.____

A. 180 B. 320 C. 1,400 D. 1,800

10. According to the table, the week in which the *most* chemicals were consumed was 10.____

A. week 2 B. week 3 C. week 4 D. week 5

11. According to the table, the *average* number of sacks of chemical F consumed over the first four weeks was 11.____

A. 4 B. 5 C. 6 D. 7

12. Of the following actions, the *best* one to take *FIRST* after smoke is seen coming from an electric control device is to 12.____

A. shut off the power to it
B. call the main office for advice
C. look for a wiring diagram
D. throw water on it

13. Of the following items, the one which would *LEAST* likely be included on a memorandum is the 13.____

A. home address of the writer of the memorandum
B. name of the writer of the memorandum
C. subject of the memorandum
D. names or titles of the person who will receive the memorandum

14. When testing joints for leaks in pipe lines containing natural gas, it is *BEST* to use 14.____

A. water in the lines under pressure
B. a lighted candle
C. an aquastat
D. soapy water

Questions 15-17.

DIRECTIONS: Questions 15 to 17 inclusive are to be answered *SOLELY* on the basis of the information given below.

Assume that at various hours of a typical day the amounts of chlorine residual in parts per million (ppm) at a certain water treatment plant are as shown in the following graph:

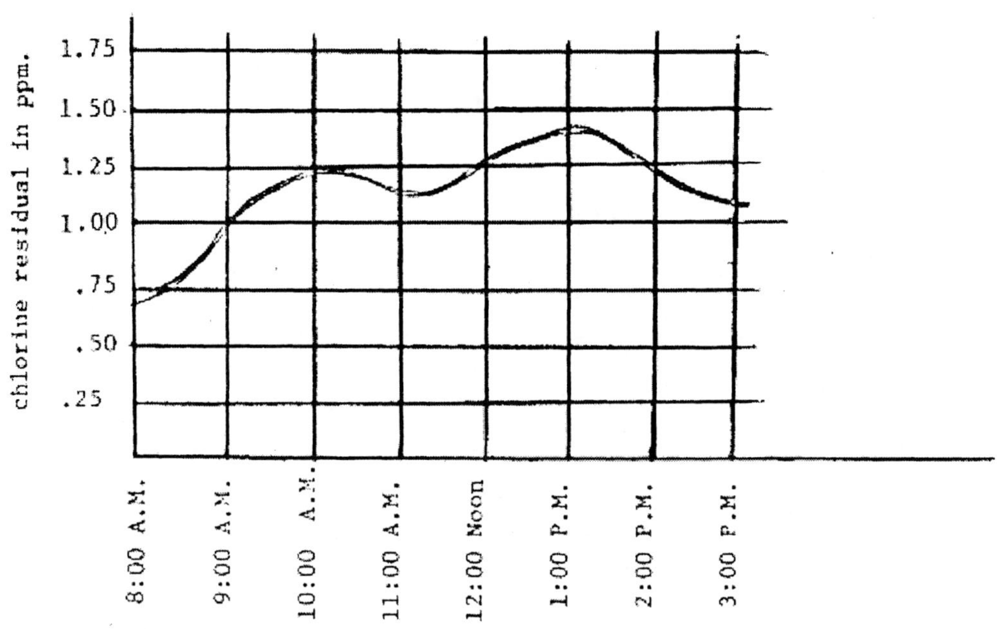

15. According to the graph, the chlorine residual measured in ppm at 9:00 A.M. was, most nearly, 15.____

A. .70 B. .75 C. 1.00 D. 1.25

16. The maximum chlorine residual between 8:00 A.M. and 3:00 P.M. was, most nearly, 16.____

A. .68 ppm B. 1.10 ppm C. 1.25 ppm D. 1.37 ppm

17. According to the graph, between the hour of 12:00 Noon and 1:00 P.M., the chlorine residual was 17.____

A. always increasing
B. always decreasing
C. increasing, then decreasing
D. decreasing, then increasing

18. Of the following statements concerning the use and care of wooden ladders, the *one* which is *TRUE* is that 18.____

A. a light oil should be applied to the rungs to preserve the wood
B. each rung should be sharply struck with a metal hammer to test its soundness before using it
C. ladders should be stored in a warm damp area to prevent the wood from getting brittle
D. tops of ordinary stepladders should not be used as steps

19. It is *poor* practice to use gasoline to clean metal parts that are coated with grease *PRIMARILY* because gasoline 19.____

A. contains lead which is harmful to the user
B. is a poor solvent for grease
C. corrodes metal
D. vapors ignite easily

Questions 20-21.

DIRECTIONS Questions 20 and 21 are to be answered *SOLELY* on the basis of the information given in the tables below.

Inventory of 100 pound bags on hand as of 1-1	
Chemical X	16 1/2
Chemical Y	12

Date	Chemical	Number of 100 pound bags used	Number of 100 pound bags received
1-5	X	8 1/2	
1-9	X	3 1/2	
1-9	Y	5	
1-14	X		8
1-18	Y	2 1/2	
1-23	X	3	
1-27	Y	4 1/2	
1-30	X		2
1-31	X	1	

Inventory of 100 pound bags on hand as of 1-31	
Chemical X	
Chemical Y	

J. Doe
Operator

2-2

20. According to the information given in the table, the number of 100-pound bags of chemical Y *on hand* as of 1-31 is 20.___

A. 0 B. 1/2 C. 1 D. 1 1/2

21. According to the information in the table, the *total* number of pounds of chemical X consumed in the month was, most nearly, 21.___

A. 500 B. 1,600 C. 1,800 D. 2,800

Questions 22-27.

DIRECTIONS: Questions 22 to 27 inclusive are to be answered *SOLELY* on the basis of the paragraph below.

FIRST AID INSTRUCTIONS

The main purpose of first aid is to put the injured person in the best possible position until medical help arrives. This includes the performance of emergency treatment for the purpose of saving a life if a doctor is not present. When a person is hurt, a crowd usually gathers around the victim. If nobody uses his head, the injured person fails to get the care he needs. You must stay calm and, most important, it is your duty to take charge at an accident. The first thing for you to do is to see, as best you can, what is wrong with the injured person. Leave the victim where he is until the nature and extent of his injury are determined. If he is unconscious he should not be moved except to lay him flat on his back if he is in some other position. Loosen the clothing of any seriously hurt person and make him as comfortable as possible. Medical help should be called as soon as possible. You should remain with the injured person and send someone else to call the doctor. You should try to make sure that the one who calls for a doctor is able to give correct information as to the location of the injured person. In order to help the physician to know what equipment may be needed in each particular case, the person making the call should give the doctor as much information about the injury as possible.

22. If nobody uses his head at the scene of an accident, there is danger that 22.____

A. no one will get the names of all the witnesses
B. a large crowd will gather
C. the victim will not get the care he needs
D. the victim will blame the City for negligence

23. When an accident occurs, the *FIRST* thing you should do is 23.____

A. call a doctor
B. loosen the clothing of the injured person
C. notify the victim's family
D. try to find out what is wrong with the injured person

24. If you do *NOT* know the extent and nature of the victim's injuries, you should 24.____

A. let the injured person lie where he is
B. immediately take the victim to a hospital yourself
C. help the injured person to his feet to see if he can walk
D. have the injured person sit up on the ground while you examine him

25. If the injured person is breathing and unconscious, you should 25.____

A. get some hot liquid such as coffee or tea in to him
B. give him artificial respiration
C. lift up his head to try to stimulate blood circulation
D. see that he lies flat on his back

26. If it is necessary to call a doctor, you should 26.___

A. go and make the call yourself since you have all the information
B. find out who the victim's family doctor is before making the call
C. have someone else make the call who knows the location of the victim
D. find out which doctor the victim can afford

27. It is important for the caller to give the doctor as much information as is available regarding the injury so that the doctor 27.___

A. can bring the necessary equipment
B. can make out an accident report
C. will be responsible for any malpractice resulting from the first aid treatment
D. can inform his nurse on how long he will be in the field

Questions 28-29.

DIRECTIONS: Questions 28 and 29 are to be answered *SOLELY* on the basis of the paragraph below.

When a written report must be submitted by an operator to his supervisor, the best rule is "the briefer the better." Obviously, this can be carried to extremes, since all necessary information must be included. However, the ability to write a satisfactory one-page report is an important communication skill. There are several different kinds of reports in common use. One is the form report, which is printed and merely requires the operator to fill in blanks. The greatest problems faced in completion of this report are accuracy and thoroughness. Another type of report is one that must be submitted regularly and systematically. This type of report is known as the periodic report.

28. According to the passage above, accuracy and thoroughness are the *GREATEST* problems in the completion of 28.___

A. one-page reports
B. form reports
C. periodic reports
D. long reports

29. According to the passage above, a good written report from an operator to his supervisor should be 29.___

A. printed
B. formal
C. periodic
D. brief

Question 30.

DIRECTIONS: The sketches below show 150-lb. chlorine cylinders stored in three different ways:

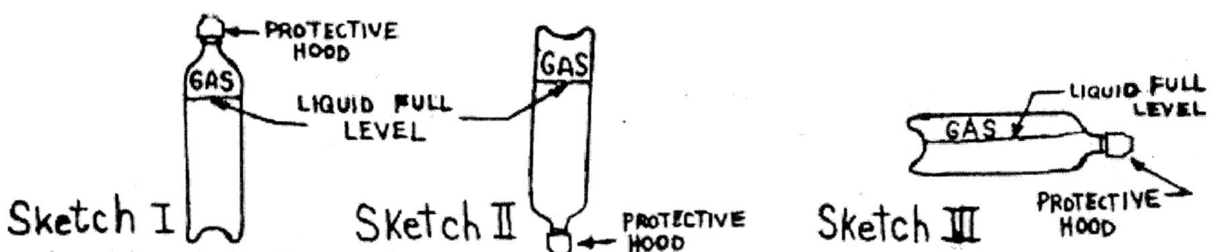

30. *Recommended* practice is to store a 150-lb. chlorine cylinder as shown in 30.____

A. Sketch I *only*
B. Sketch II *only*
C. Sketch III *only*
D. Sketches II and III

31. Of the following, the *MOST* serious defect in the installation shown below is that 31.____

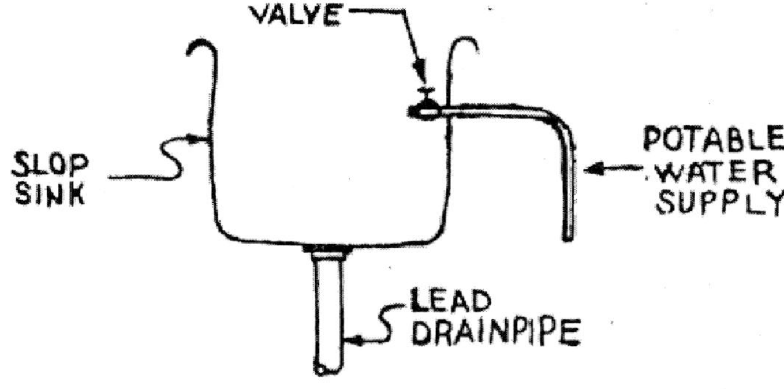

A. the water supply should be directed downward to prevent excessive splashing over the rim
B. the above installation may allow backflow of waste water into the water supply line
C. lead pipes should not be used on drains from fixtures connected to the potable water supply
D. excessive corrosion will occur on the valve if it becomes submerged

32. Of the following, the distance "x" which would be *SAFEST* when using the extension ladder shown in the sketch below is 32.____

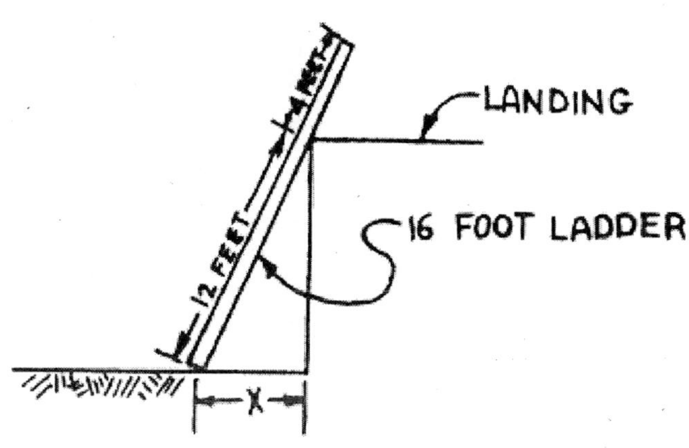

A. 1 foot
B. 3 feet
C. 5 feet
D. 7 fee

33. Of the following statements regarding safe procedures for lifting a heavy object by yourself from the floor, the one which is *FALSE* is that 33.____

   A. you should keep your back as straight as possible
   B. you should bend your knees
   C. you should mainly use your back muscles in lifting
   D. your feet should be kept clear in case the object is dropped

34. It is generally not considered to be good practice to paint wood ladders. Of the following, the *best* reason for *NOT* painting wood ladders is that 34.____

   A. it may hide defects in the wood
   B. the rungs become slippery
   C. the hardware on the ladder becomes unworkable
   D. it would rub off on the surfaces against which it is resting

35. A rip saw would *MOST* likely be used to cut 35.____

   A. wood B. steel C. copper D. aluminum

Questions 36-37.

DIRECTIONS: Questions 36 and 37 are to be answered *SOLELY* on the basis of the paragraph below.

NATURAL LAKES

Large lakes may yield water of exceptionally fine quality except near the shore line and in the vicinity of sewer outlets or near outlets of large streams. Therefore, minimum treatment is required. The availability of practically unlimited quantities of water is also a decided advantage. Unfortunately, however, the sewage from a city is often discharged into the same lake from which the water supply is taken. Great care must be taken in locating both the water intake and the sewer outlet so that the pollution handled by the water treatment plant is a minimum.

Sometimes the distance from the shore where dependable, satisfactory water can be found is so great that the cost of water intake facilities is prohibitive for a small municipality. In such cases, another supply must be found, or water must be obtained from a neighboring large city. Lake water is usually uniform in quality from day to day and does not vary in temperature as much as water from a river or small impounding reservoir.

36. A disadvantage of drawing a water supply from a large lake is that 36.____

   A. expensive treatment is required
   B. a limited quantity of water is available
   C. nearby cities may dump sewage into the lake
   D. the water is too cold.

37. An advantage of drawing a water supply from a large lake is that the 37.____

   A. water is uniform in quality
   B. water varies in temperature
   C. intake is distant from the shore
   D. intake may be near a sewer outlet

38. The *BEST* type of wrench to use to tighten a pipe without marring the pipe surface is 38.____

A. pipe wrench
B. strap wrench
C. spanner wrench
D. box wrench

39. Of the following statements concerning the use and care of files, the *one* which is *FALSE* is that 39.____

A. files should have tight-fitting handles
B. rasps are generally used on wood
C. files should be protected by a light coating of oil when cutting metal
D. files should be given a quick blow on a wood block to unclog teeth

40. A device which permits flow of a fluid in a pipe in one direction only is known as 40.____

A. diode
B. curb box
C. gooseneck
D. check valve

KEY (CORRECT ANSWERS)

1.	D	11.	B	21.	B	31.	B
2.	A	12.	A	22.	C	32.	B
3.	A	13.	A	23.	D	33.	C
4.	D	14.	D	24.	A	34.	A
5.	C	15.	C	25.	D	35.	A
6.	B	16.	D	26.	C	36.	C
7.	B	17.	A	27.	A	37.	A
8.	C	18.	D	28.	B	38.	B
9.	D	19.	D	29.	D	39.	C
10.	C	20.	A	30.	A	40.	D

TEST 2

DIRECTIONS: Each question or incomplete statement is followed by several suggested answers or completions. Select the one that *BEST* answers the question or completes the statement. *PRINT THE LETTER OF THE CORRECT ANSWER IN THE SPACE AT THE RIGHT.*

Questions 1-2.

DIRECTIONS: Questions 1 and 2 are to be answered *SOLELY* on the basis of the paragraph below.

PRECIPITATION AND RUNOFF

In the United States, the average annual precipitation is about 30 inches, of which about 21 inches is lost to the atmosphere by evaporation and transpiration. The remaining 9 inches becomes runoff into rivers and lakes. Both the precipitation and runoff vary greatly with geography and season. Annual precipitation varies from more than 100 inches in parts of the northwest to only 2 or 3 inches in parts of the southwest. In the northeastern part of the country, including New York State, the annual average precipitation is about 45 inches, of which about 22 inches becomes runoff. Even in New York State, there is some variation from place to place and considerable variation from time to time. During extremely dry years, the precipitation may be as low as 30 inches and the runoff below 10 inches. In general, there are greater variations in runoff rates from smaller watersheds. A critical water supply situation occurs when there are three or four abnormally dry years in succession.

Precipitation over the state is measured and recorded by a net- work of stations operated by the U. S. Weather Bureau. All of the precipitation records and other data such as temperature, humidity and evaporation rates are published monthly by the Weather Bureau in "Climatological Data." Runoff rates at more than 200 stream-gauging stations in the state are measured and recorded by the U. S. Geological Survey in cooperation with various state agencies. Records of the daily average flows are published annually by the U. S. Geological Survey in "Surface Water Records of New York." Copies may be obtained by writing to the Water Resources Division, United States Geological Survey, Albany, New York 23301.

1. From the above paragraphs it is *appropriate* to conclude that 1.____

   A. critical supply situations do not occur
   B. the greater the rainfall, the greater the runoff
   C. there are greater variations in runoff from larger watersheds
   D. the rainfall in the southwest is greater than the average in the country

2. From the above paragraphs, it is appropriate to conclude that 2.____

   A. an annual rainfall of about 50 inches does not occur in New York State
   B. the U. S. Weather Bureau is only interested in rainfall
   C. runoff is equal to rainfall less losses to the atmosphere
   D. information about rainfall and runoff in New York State is unavailable to the public

3. The following are diagrams of various types of bolt heads. 3.____

A B C D

The *one* of the above which is a Phillips head type is the one labelled
A. A B. B C. C D. D

4. The appearance of frost on the outer surface of a chlorine cylinder which has been placed in service would *MOST* likely indicate that 4.____

A. the cylinder is empty
B. the gas is escaping too quickly from the cylinder
C. there is too much pressure in the cylinder
D. the humidity of the storage area is too high

5. One of the outer belts of a matched set of three V-belts becomes badly frayed. Of the following, the *BEST* course of action to take is to 5.____

A. replace only the worn belt
B. replace only the worn belt but put the new belt in the middle
C. remove the worn belt, put the center belt on the end and continue running the machine
D. replace the whole set of belts even if the other two belts show no signs of wear\

6. Of the following, the *BEST* type of valve to use for throttling or when the valve must be opened and closed frequently is a 6.____

A. check valve
B. globe valve
C. butterfly valve
D. pop valve

7. Of the following, the device which is used to measure *both* pressure and vacuum is the 7.____

A. compound gage
B. aquastat
C. pyrometer
D. thermocouple

8. Electrical energy is consumed and paid for in units of 8.____

A. voltage
B. ampere-hours
C. kilowatt-hours
D. watts

9. A “governor” on an engine is used to control the engine’s 9.____

A. speed
B. temperature
C. interval of operation
D. engaging and disengaging the “load”

10. Pressure *below* that of the atmospheric pressure is usually expressed in 10.____

A. vacuum inches of mercury
B. inches of pressure absolute
C. BTU’s
D. gallons per minute

11. A short piece of pipe with outside threads at both ends is called a 11.___

A. union B. nipple C. tee D. sleeve

12. Of the following, which device would *MOST* likely produce water hammer in a plumbing installation? A(n) 12.___

A. relief valve
B. air chamber
C. surge tank
D. quick-closing valve

13. Some portable electric tools have a third conductor in the line cord which is electrically connected to the receptacle box. The reason for this is to 13.___

A. have a spare wire in case one power wire breaks
B. protect the user of the tool from electrical shock
C. strengthen the power lead so that it cannot be easily damaged
D. allow use of the tool for extended periods of time without overheating

14. Of the following, the device which is usually used to measure the rate of flow of water in a pipe is a 14.___

A. pressure gage
B. Bourden gage
C. manometer
D. velocity meter

15. Acid, rosin fluid, or paste applied to metal surfaces to remove oxide film in preparation for soldering is known as 15.___

A. grout B. lampblack C. plumber's soil D. flux

16. In plumbing work, a coil spring which is inserted into a drain to facilitate cleaning of the drain is known as a 16.___

A. pipe reamer B. snake C. plunger D. spigot

17. Of the following, a pneumatic device is one that is driven or powered by 17.___

A. air pressure
B. oil pressure
C. water pressure
D. steam pressure

18. Of the following metals, the one which would *MOST* likely be used for an electric motor shaft is 18.___

A. wrought iron
B. hard bronze
C. steel
D. bras

19. Of the following, a rotary gear pump is *BEST* suited for pumping 19.___

A. #6 fuel oil B. hot water C. sewage D. kerosene

20. The *MAIN* reason for using a flexible coupling to join the shafts of two pieces of machinery together is that a flexible coupling 20.___

A. allows for slight misalignment of the two shafts
B. can be immediately disengaged in an emergency
C. will automatically slip when overloaded thus protecting the driver machinery
D. allows the driven load shaft to continue rotating under its own momentum, when the driver shaft is stopped

21. Of the following, the *MAIN* purpose of a house trap is to 21.____

A. provide the house drain with a cleanout
B. prevent gases from the public sewer from entering the house plumbing system
C. trap articles of value that are accidentally dropped into the drainage pipes
D. eliminate the necessity for traps under all other plumbing fixtures

22. Of the following, the *MAIN* reason for sometimes applying bituminous coating to the interiors of steel and cast-iron pipe is that this coating 22.____

A. increases the tensile strength of the pipe
B. increases the shock resistance of the pipe
C. removes any objectionable taste from the water imparted by the pipe walls
D. protects the pipe walls from corrosion

23. The one of the following electrical devices which is most likely to be used to raise or lower A.C. voltages is a 23.____

A. resistor B. thermistor C. transformer D. circuit-breaker

24. When a metal is galvanized, it is given a coating of 24.____

A. nickel B. tin C. oxide D. zinc

25. A conduit hickey is used to 25.____

A. measure conduit pipe
B. bend conduit pipe
C. thread conduit pipe
D. cut conduit pipe

Questions 26-27.

DIRECTIONS: Questions 26 and 27 are to be answered *SOLELY* on the basis of the electrical circuit shown below.

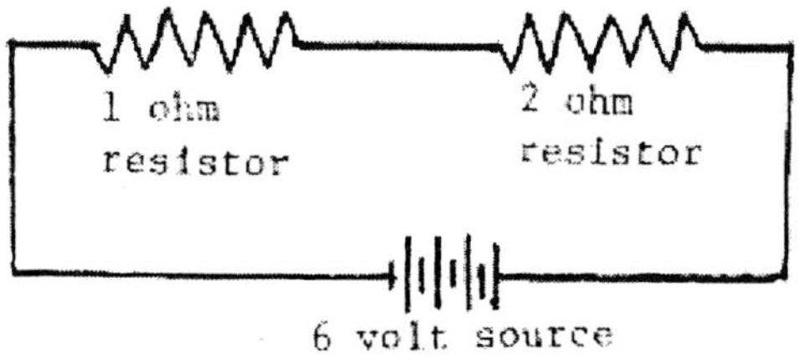

1 ohm resistor
2 ohm resistor
6 volt source

26. The circuit above is commonly known as a 26.____

A. series circuit
B. parallel circuit
C. short circuit
D. circuit breaker

27. The current flowing in the circuit above is 27.____

A. 1 amp B. 2 amps C. 3 amps D. 6 amps

Questions 28-30.

DIRECTIONS: Questions 28 to 30 inclusive are to be answered *SOLELY* on the basis of the sketches shown below.

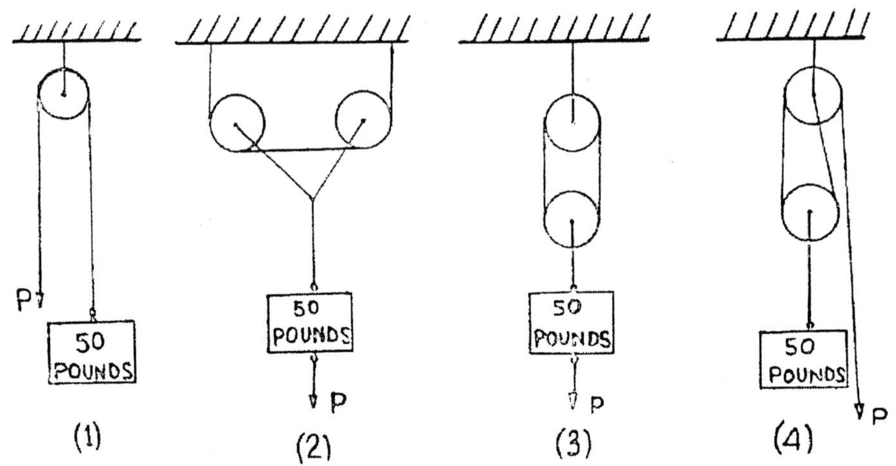

28. The two arrangements in the above diagrams which *CANNOT* be used to raise the load at all by applying a pull "p" as shown are setups 28.____

A. 1 and 2 B. 2 and 3 C. 3 and 4 D. 1 and 4

29. The arrangement in the diagram above which requires the *LEAST* effort "p" to move the 50-pound weight is setup 29.____

A. 1 B. 2 C. 3 D. 4

30. The effort required to hold the 50-pound weight at rest off the ground in setup (1) in the diagram above is 30.____

A. 10 pounds B. 25 pounds C. 50 pounds D. 100 pounds

31. Of the following formulas, the one which *CORRECTLY* shows the relationship between gage pressure and absolute pressure is 31.____

A. Absolute pressure = gage pressure / atmospheric pressure
B. Absolute pressure + gage pressure = atmospheric pressure
C. Absolute pressure = gage pressure + atmospheric pressure
D. Absolute pressure + atmospheric pressure = gage pressure

32. The weight of a gallon of water is, most nearly, 32.____

A. 8.3 pounds B. 16.6 pounds C. 24.9 pounds D. 33.2 pounds

33. Solenoid valves are usually operated 33.____

A. thermally B. manually C. hydraulically D. electrically

34. A 1/2-inch, 8-32 round-head machine screw has 34.____

A. a diameter of 1/2 inch
B. a length of 8 inches
C. 8 threads per inch
D. 32 threads per inch

35. The *MAIN* purpose for the stuffing usually found in centrifugal pump stuffing boxes is 35.____

A. supporting the shaft
B. controlling the rate of discharge
C. preventing fluid leakage
D. compensating for shaft misalignment

36. The *BEST* wrench to use on screwed valves and fittings having hexagonal shape connections is the 36.____

A. chain wrench
B. open-end wrench
C. pipe wrench
D. strap wrench

37. A tap is a tool commonly used to 37.____

A. remove broken screws
B. flare pipe ends
C. cut external threads
D. cut internal threads

38. A thread chaser is *MOST* likely to be used to 38.____

A. rethread damaged threads
B. remove broken taps
C. flare tubing
D. adjust diestocks

39. If an air-conditioning unit shorted out and caught fire, the *BEST* fire extinguisher to use would be a 39.____

A. water extinguisher
B. foam extinguisher
C. carbon dioxide extinguisher
D. soda acid extinguisher

40. Of the following, the *best* action to take to help someone whose eyes have been splashed with lye is to *FIRST* 40.____

A. wash out the eyes with clean water
B. wash out the eyes with a salt water solution
C. apply a sterile dressing over the eyes
D. do nothing to the eyes, but telephone for medical help

KEY (CORRECT ANSWERS)

1. B	11. B	21. B	31. C
2. C	12. D	22. D	32. A
3. C	13. B	23. C	33. D
4. B	14. D	24. D	34. D
5. D	15. D	25. B	35. C
6. B	16. B	26. A	36. B
7. A	17. A	27. B	37. D
8. C	18. C	28. B	38. A
9. A	19. A	29. D	39. C
10. A	20. A	30. C	40. A

MECHANICAL APTITUDE

EXAMINATION SECTION
TEST 1

MECHANICAL COMPREHENSION

DIRECTIONS: Questions 1 to 4 test your ability to understand general mechanical devices. Pictures are shown and questions asked about the mechanical devices shown in the picture. Read each question and study the picture. Each question is followed by four choices. For each question, choose the one BEST answer (A, B, C, or D). Then *PRINT THE LETTER OF THE CORRECT ANSWER IN THE SPACE AT THE RIGHT.*

1. The reason for crossing the belt connecting these wheels is to 1.____

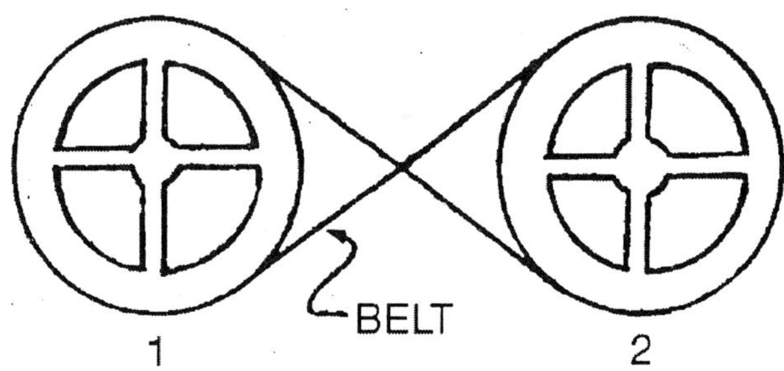

A. make the wheels turn in opposite directions
B. make wheel 2 turn faster than wheel 1
C. save wear on the belt
D. take up slack in the belt

2. The purpose of the small gear between the two large gears is to 2.____

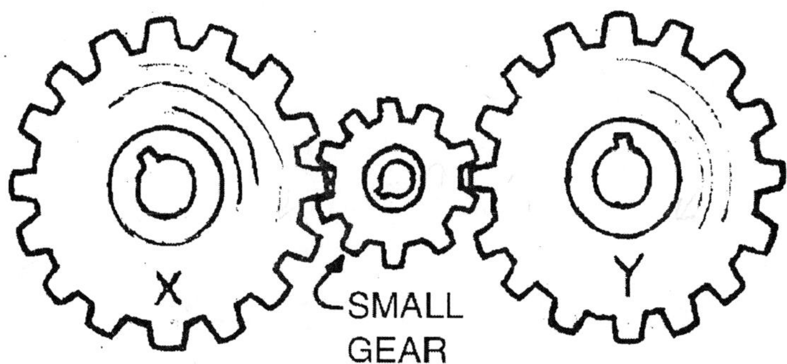

A. increase the speed of the larger gears
B. allow the larger gears to turn in different directions
C. decrease the speed of the larger gears
D. make the larger gears turn in the same direction

3. Each of these three-foot-high water cans have a bottom with an area of-one square foot. The pressure on the bottom of the cans is 3.___

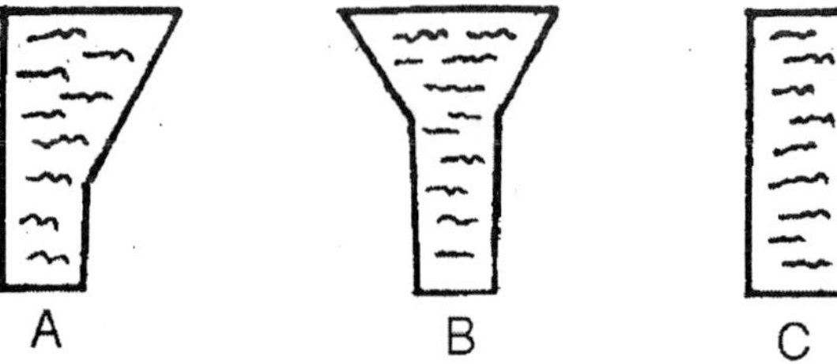

A. least in A
B. least in B
C. least in C
D. the same in all

4. The reading on the scale should be 4.___

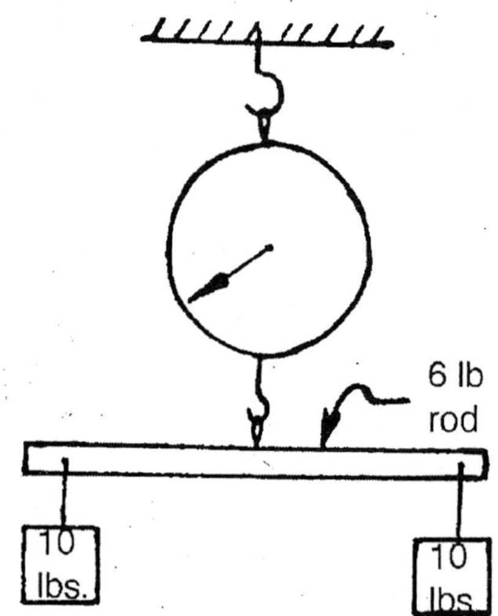

A. zero
B. 10 pounds
C. 13 pounds
D. 26 pounds

KEY (CORRECT ANSWERS)

1. A
2. D
3. D
4. D

TEST 2

DIRECTIONS: Questions 1 to 6 test knowledge of tools and how to use them. For each question, decide which one of the four things shown in the boxes labeled A, B, C, or D normally is used with or goes best with the thing in the picture on the left. Then *PRINT THE LETTER OF THE CORRECT ANSWER IN THE SPACE AT THE RIGHT.*

NOTE: All tools are NOT drawn to the same scale.

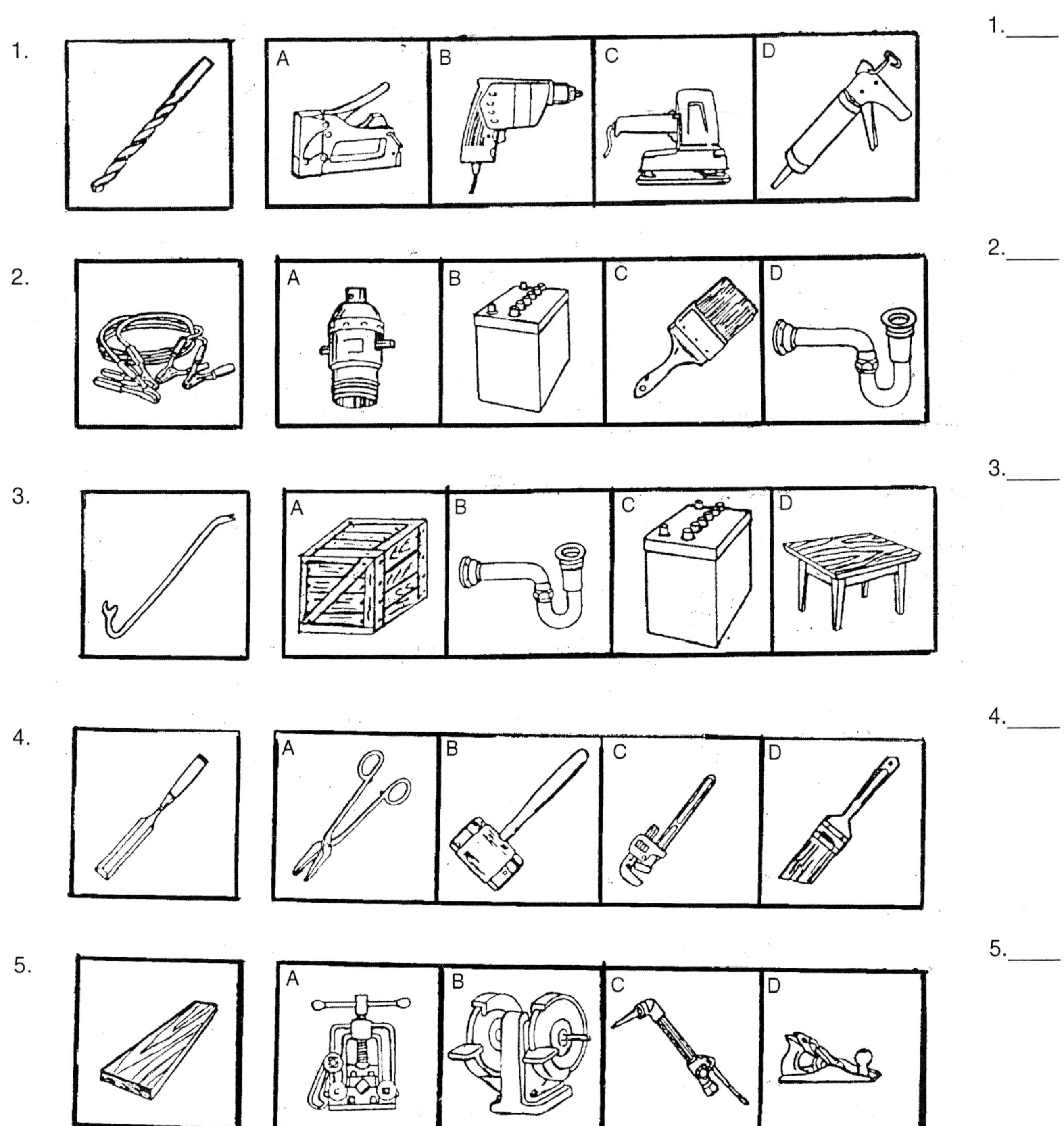

1.____

2.____

3.____

4.____

5.____

6.  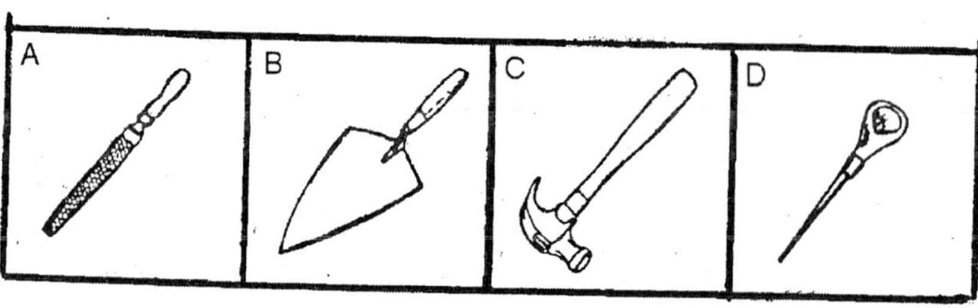

6.__

KEY (CORRECT ANSWERS)

1. B
2. B
3. A
4. B
5. D
6. B

RECORD KEEPING
EXAMINATION SECTION
TEST 1

DIRECTIONS: Each question or incomplete statement is followed by several suggested answers or completions. Select the one that BEST answers the question or completes the statement. *PRINT THE LETTER OF THE CORRECT ANSWER IN THE SPACE AT THE RIGHT.*

Questions 1-15.

DIRECTIONS: Questions 1 through 15 are to be answered on the basis of the following list of company names below. Arrange a file alphabetically, word-by-word, disregarding punctuation, conjunctions, and apostrophes. Then answer the questions.

A Bee C Reading Materials
ABCO Parts
A Better Course for Test Preparation
AAA Auto Parts Co.
A-Z Auto Parts, Inc.
Aabar Books
Abbey, Joanne
Boman-Sylvan Law Firm
BMW Autowerks
C Q Service Company
Chappell-Murray, Inc.
E&E Life Insurance
Emcrisco
Gigi Arts
Gordon, Jon & Associates
SOS Plumbing
Schmidt, J.B. Co.

1. Which of these files should appear FIRST? 1.____

   A. ABCO Parts
   B. A Bee C Reading Materials
   C. A Better Course for Test Preparation
   D. AAA Auto Parts Co.

2. Which of these files should appear SECOND? 2.____

   A. A-Z Auto Parts, Inc.
   B. A Bee C Reading Materials
   C. A Better Course for Test Preparation
   D. AAA Auto Parts Co.

3. Which of these files should appear THIRD? 3.____

   A. ABCO Parts
   B. A Bee C Reading Materials
   C. Aabar Books
   D. AAA Auto Parts Co.

4. Which of these files should appear FOURTH? 4.___

   A. Aabar Books
   B. ABCO Parts
   C. Abbey, Joanne
   D. AAA Auto Parts Co.

5. Which of these files should appear LAST? 5.___

   A. Gordon, Jon & Associates
   B. Gigi Arts
   C. Schmidt, J.B. Co.
   D. SOS Plumbing

6. Which of these files should appear between A-Z Auto Parts, Inc. and Abbey, Joanne? 6.___

   A. A Bee C Reading Materials
   B. AAA Auto Parts Co.
   C. ABCO Parts
   D. A Better Course for Test Preparation

7. Which of these files should appear between ABCO Parts and Aabar Books? 7.___

   A. A Bee C Reading Materials
   B. Abbey, Joanne
   C. Aabar Books
   D. A-Z Auto Parts

8. Which of these files should appear between Abbey, Joanne and Boman-Sylvan Law Firm? 8.___

   A. A Better Course for Test Preparation
   B. BMW Autowerks
   C. Chappell-Murray, Inc.
   D. Aabar Books

9. Which of these files should appear between Abbey, Joanne and C Q Service? 9.___

   A. A-Z Auto Parts,Inc.
   B. BMW Autowerks
   C. Choices A and B
   D. Chappell-Murray, Inc.

10. Which of these files should appear between C Q Service Company and Emcrisco? 10.___

   A. Chappell-Murray, Inc.
   B. E&E Life Insurance
   C. Gigi Arts
   D. Choices A and B

11. Which of these files should NOT appear between C Q Service Company and E&E Life Insurance? 11.___

   A. Gordon, Jon & Associates
   B. Emcrisco
   C. Gigi Arts
   D. All of the above

12. Which of these files should appear between Chappell-Murray Inc., and Gigi Arts? 12.____

    A. CQ Service Inc. E&E Life Insurance, and Emcrisco
    B. Emcrisco, E&E Life Insurance, and Gordon, Jon & Associates
    C. E&E Life Insurance and Emcrisco
    D. Emcrisco and Gordon, Jon & Associates

13. Which of these files should appear between Gordon, Jon & Associates and SOS Plumbing? 13.____

    A. Gigi Arts
    B. Schmidt, J.B. Co.
    C. Choices A and B
    D. None of the above

14. Each of the choices lists the four files in their proper alphabetical order except 14.____

    A. E&E Life Insurance; Gigi Arts; Gordon, Jon & Associates; SOS Plumbing
    B. E&E Life Insurance; Emcrisco; Gigi Arts; SOS Plumbing
    C. Emcrisco; Gordon, Jon & Associates; SOS Plumbing; Schmidt, J.B. Co.
    D. Emcrisco; Gigi Arts; Gordon, Jon & Associates; SOS Plumbing

15. Which of the choices lists the four files in their proper alphabetical order? 15.____

    A. Gigi Arts; Gordon, Jon & Associates; SOS Plumbing; Schmidt, J.B. Co.
    B. Gordon, Jon & Associates; Gigi Arts; Schmidt, J.B. Co.; SOS Plumbing
    C. Gordon, Jon & Associates; Gigi Arts; SOS Plumbing; Schmidt, J.B. Co.
    D. Gigi Arts; Gordon, Jon & Associates; Schmidt, J.B. Co.; SOS Plumbing

16. The alphabetical filing order of two businesses with identical names is determined by the 16.____

    A. length of time each business has been operating
    B. addresses of the businesses
    C. last name of the company president
    D. none of the above

17. In an alphabetical filing system, if a business name includes a number, it should be 17.____

    A. disregarded
    B. considered a number and placed at the end of an alphabetical section
    C. treated as though it were written in words and alphabetized accordingly
    D. considered a number and placed at the beginning of an alphabetical section

18. If a business name includes a contraction (such as *don't* or *it's*), how should that word be treated in an alphabetical filing system? 18.____

    A. Divide the word into its separate parts and treat it as two words.
    B. Ignore the letters that come after the apostrophe.
    C. Ignore the word that contains the contraction.
    D. Ignore the apostrophe and consider all letters in the contraction.

19. In what order should the parts of an address be considered when using an alphabetical filing system? 19.____

    A. City or town; state; street name; house or building number
    B. State; city or town; street name; house or building number
    C. House or building number; street name; city or town; state
    D. Street name; city or town; state

20. A business record should be cross-referenced when a(n) 20.__

A. organization is known by an abbreviated name
B. business has a name change because of a sale, incorporation, or other reason
C. business is known by a *coined* or common name which differs from a dictionary spelling
D. all of the above

21. A geographical filing system is MOST effective when 21.__

A. location is more important than name
B. many names or titles sound alike
C. dealing with companies who have offices all over the world
D. filing personal and business files

Questions 22-25.

DIRECTIONS: Questions 22 through 25 are to be answered on the basis of the list of items below, which are to be filed geographically. Organize the items geographically and then answer the questions.

1. University Press at Berkeley, U.S.
2. Maria Sanchez, Mexico City, Mexico
3. Great Expectations Ltd. in London, England
4. Justice League, Cape Town, South Africa, Africa
5. Crown Pearls Ltd. in London, England
6. Joseph Prasad in London, England

22. Which of the following arrangements of the items is composed according to the policy of: *Continent, Country, City, Firm or Individual Name?* 22.__

A. 5, 3, 4, 6, 2, 1
B. 4, 5, 3, 6, 2, 1
C. 1, 4, 5, 3, 6, 2
D. 4, 5, 3, 6, 1, 2

23. Which of the following files is arranged according to the policy of: *Continent, Country, City, Firm or Individual Name?* 23.__

A. South Africa. Africa. Cape Town. Justice League
B. Mexico. Mexico City, Maria Sanchez
C. North America. United States. Berkeley. University Press
D. England. Europe. London. Prasad, Joseph

24. Which of the following arrangements of the items is composed according to the policy of: *Country, City, Firm or Individual Name*? 24.__

A. 5, 6, 3, 2, 4, 1
B. 1, 5, 6, 3, 2, 4
C. 6, 5, 3, 2, 4, 1
D. 5, 3, 6, 2, 4, 1

25. Which of the following files is arranged according to a policy of: *Country, City, Firm or Individual Name*? 25.__

A. England. London. Crown Pearls Ltd.
B. North America. United States. Berkeley. University Press
C. Africa. Cape Town. Justice League
D. Mexico City. Mexico. Maria Sanchez

26. Under which of the following circumstances would a phonetic filing system be MOST effective? 26.____

    A. When the person in charge of filing can't spell very well
    B. With large files with names that sound alike
    C. With large files with names that are spelled alike
    D. All of the above

Questions 27-29.

DIRECTIONS: Questions 27 through 29 are to be answered on the basis of the following list of numerical files.

1. 391-023-100
2. 361-132-170
3. 385-732-200
4. 381-432-150
5. 391-632-387
6. 361-423-303
7. 391-123-271

27. Which of the following arrangements of the files follows a consecutive-digit system? 27.____

    A. 2, 3, 4, 1
    B. 1, 5, 7, 3
    C. 2, 4, 3, 1
    D. 3, 1, 5, 7

28. Which of the following arrangements follows a terminal-digit system? 28.____

    A. 1, 7, 2, 4, 3
    B. 2, 1, 4, 5, 7
    C. 7, 6, 5, 4, 3
    D. 1, 4, 2, 3, 7

29. Which of the following lists follows a middle-digit system? 29.____

    A. 1, 7, 2, 6, 4, 5, 3
    B. 1, 2, 7, 4, 6, 5, 3
    C. 7, 2, 1, 3, 5, 6, 4
    D. 7, 1, 2, 4, 6, 5, 3

Questions 30-31.

DIRECTIONS: Questions 30 and 31 are to be answered on the basis of the following information.

1. Reconfirm Laura Bates appointment with James Caldecort on December 12 at 9:30 A.M.
2. Laurence Kinder contact Julia Lucas on August 3 and set up a meeting for week of September 23 at 4 P.M.
3. John Lutz contact Larry Waverly on August 3 and set up appointment for September 23 at 9:30 A.M.
4. Call for tickets for Gerry Stanton August 21 for New Jersey on September 23, flight 143 at 4:43 P.M.

30. A chronological file for the above information would be 30.____

A. 4, 3, 2, 1
B. 3, 2, 4, 1
C. 4, 2, 3, 1
D. 3, 1, 2, 4

31. Using the above information, a chronological file for the date of September 23 would be 31.____

A. 2, 3, 4 B. 3, 1, 4 C. 3, 2, 4 D. 4, 3, 2

Questions 32-34.

DIRECTIONS: Questions 32 through 34 are to be answered on the basis of the following information.

1. Call Roger Epstein, Ashoke Naipaul, Jon Anderson, and Sarah Washington on April 19 at 1:00 P.M. to set up meeting with Alika D'Ornay for June 6 in New York.
2. Call Martin Ames before noon on April 19 to confirm afternoon meeting with Bob Greenwood on April 20th
3. Set up meeting room at noon for 2:30 P.M. meeting on April 19th;
4. Ashley Stanton contact Bob Greenwood at 9:00 A.M. on April 20 and set up meeting for June 6 at 8:30 A.M.
5. Carol Guiland contact Shelby Van Ness during afternoon of April 20 and set up meeting for June 6 at 10:00 A.M.
6. Call airline and reserve tickets on June 6 for Roger Epstein trip *to* Denver on July 8
7. Meeting at 2:30 P.M. on April 19th

32. A chronological file for all of the above information would be 32.____

A. 2, 1, 3, 7, 5, 4, 6
B. 3, 7, 2, 1, 4, 5, 6
C. 3, 7, 1, 2, 5, 4, 6
D. 2, 3, 1, 7, 4, 5, 6

33. A chronological file for the date of April 19th would be 33.____

A. 2, 3, 7, 1
B. 2, 3, 1, 7
C. 7, 1, 3, 2
D. 3, 7, 1, 2

34. Add the following information to the file, and then create a chronological file for April 20th: 34.____
8. April 20: 3:00 P.M. meeting between Bob Greenwood and Martin Ames.

A. 4, 5, 8 B. 4, 8, 5 C. 8, 5, 4 D. 5, 4, 8

35. The PRIMARY advantage of computer records filing over a manual system is 35.____

A. speed of retrieval
B. accuracy
C. cost
D. potential file loss

KEY (CORRECT ANSWERS)

1. B
2. C
3. D
4. A
5. D

6. C
7. B
8. B
9. C
10. D

11. D
12. C
13. B
14. C
15. D

16. B
17. C
18. D
19. A
20. D

21. A
22. B
23. C
24. D
25. A

26. B
27. C
28. D
29. A
30. B

31. C
32. D
33. B
34. A
35. A

ARITHMETICAL COMPUTATION AND REASONING
EXAMINATION SECTION
TEST 1

DIRECTIONS: Each question or incomplete statement is followed by several suggested answers or completions. Select the one that BEST answers the question or completes the statement. *PRINT THE LETTER OF THE CORRECT ANSWER IN THE SPACE AT THE RIGHT.*

1. 3/8 less than $40 is 1.____

   A. $25 B. $65 C. $15 D. $55

2. 27/64 expressed as a percent is 2.____

   A. 40.625% B. 42.188% C. 43.750% D. 45.313%

3. 1/6 more than 36 gross is ______ gross. 3.____

   A. 6 B. 48 C. 30 D. 42

4. 15 is 20% of 4.____

5. The number which when increased by 1/3 of itself equals 96 is 5.____

   A. 128 B. 72 C. 64 D. 32

6. 0.16 3/4 written as percent is 6.____

   A. 16 3/4% B. 16.3/4% C. .016 3/4% D. .0016 3/4%

7. 55% of 15 is 7.____

   A. 82.5 B. 0.825 C. 0.0825 D. 8.25

8. The number which when decreased by 1/3 of itself equals 96 is 8.____

   A. 64 B. 32 C. 128 D. 144

9. A carpenter used a board 15 3/4 ft. long from which 3 footstools were made with sufficient lumber left over for half of another footstool. 9.____
   If the lumber cost 24 1/2¢ per foot, the cost of EACH footstool was

   A. $1.54 B. $3.86 C. $1.10 D. $1.08

10. In one year, a luncheonette purchased 1231 gallons of milk for $907.99. 10.____
    The AVERAGE cost per half pint was

    A. $0.046 B. $0.045 C. $0.047 D. $0.044

11. The product of 23 and 9 3/4 is 11.____

    A. 191 2/3 B. 224 1/4 C. 213 3/4 D. 32 3/4

12. An order for 345 machine bolts at $4.15 per hundred will cost 12.____

    A. $0.1432 B. $1.1432 C. $14.32 D. $143.20

13. The fractional equivalent of .0625 is 13.___

A. 1/16 B. 1/15 C. 1/14 D. 1/13

14. The number 0.03125 equals 14.___

A. 3/64 B. 1/16 C. 1/64 D. 1/32

15. 21.70 divided by 1.75 equals 15.___

A. 124 B. 12.4 C. 1.24 D. .124

16. The average cost of school lunches for 100 children varied as follows: Monday, $0.285; Tuesday, $0.237; Wednesday, $0.264; Thursday, $0.276; Friday, $0.292. The AVERAGE lunch cost 16.___

A. $0.136 B. $0.270 C. $0.135 D. $0.271

17. The cost of 5 dozen eggs at $8.52 per gross is 17.___

A. $3.50 B. $42.60 C. $3.55 D. $3.74

18. 410.07 less 38.49 equals 18.___

A. 372.58 B. 371.58 C. 381.58 D. 382.68

19. The cost of 7 3/4 tons of coal at $20.16 per ton is 19.___

A. $15.12 B. $151.20 C. $141.12 D. $156.24

20. The sum of 90.79, 79.09, 97.90, and 9.97 is 20.___

A. 277.75 B. 278.56 C. 276.94 D. 277.93

KEY (CORRECT ANSWERS)

1.	A	11.	B
2.	B	12.	C
3.	D	13.	A
4.	C	14.	D
5.	B	15.	B
6.	A	16.	D
7.	D	17.	C
8.	D	18.	B
9.	C	19.	D
10.	A	20.	A

SOLUTIONS TO PROBLEMS

1. ($40)(5/8) = $25

2. 27/64 = .421875 ≈ 42.188%

3. (36)(1 1/6) = 42

4. Let x = missing number. Then, 15 = .20x. Solving, x = 75

5. Let x = missing number. Then, x + 1/3 x = 96. Simplifying, 4/3 x = 96. Solving, x = 96 ÷ 4/3 = 72

6. .16 3/4 = 16 3/4% by simply moving the decimal point two places to the right.

7. (.55)(15) = 8.25

8. Let x = missing number. Then, x - 1/3 x = 96. Simplifying, 2/3 x = 96. Solving, x = 96 ÷ 2/3 = 144

9. 15 3/4 ÷ 3 1/2 = 4.5 feet per footstool. The cost of one footstool is ($.245)(4.5) = $1.1025 ≈ $1.10

10. $907.99 ÷ 1231 = $.7376 per gallon. Since there are 16 half-pints in a gallon, the average cost per half-pint is $.7376 ÷ 16 ≈ $.046

11. (23)(9 3/4) = (23)(9.75) = 224.25 or 224 1/4

12. ($4.15)(3.45) = $14.3175 = $14.32

13. .0625 = 625/10,000 = 1/16

14. .03125 = 3125/100,000 = 1/32

15. 21.70 ÷ 1.75 = 12.4

16. The sum of these lunches is $1.354. Then, $1.354 ÷ 5 = $.2708 = $.271

17. $8.52 ÷ 12 = $.71 per dozen. Then, the cost of 5 dozen is ($.71)(5) = $3.55

18. 410.07 - 38.49 = 371.58

19. ($20.16)(7.75) = $156.24

20. 90.79 + 79.09 + 97.90 + 9.97 = 277.75

TEST 2

DIRECTIONS: Each question or incomplete statement is followed by several suggested answers or completions. Select the one that BEST answers the question or completes the statement. *PRINT THE LETTER OF THE CORRECT ANSWER IN THE SPACE AT THE RIGHT.*

1. 1600 is 40% of what number? 1.___

   A. 6400 B. 3200 C. 4000 D. 5600

2. An executive's time card reads: Arrived 9:15 A.M., Left 2:05 P.M. 2.___
   How many hours was he in the office? ______ hours ______ minutes.

   A. 5; 10 B. 4; 50 C. 4; 10 D. 5; 50

3. .4266 times .3333 will have the following number of decimals in the product: 3.___

   A. 8 B. 4 C. 1 D. None of these

4. An office floor is 25 ft. wide by 36 ft. long. 4.___
   To cover this floor with carpet will require ______ square yards.

   A. 100 B. 300 C. 900 D. 25

5. 1/8 of 1% expressed as a decimal is 5.___

   A. .125 B. .0125 C. 1.25 D. .00125

6. $\frac{6 \div 4}{6 \times 4}$ equals 6x4 6.___

   A. 1/16 B. 1 C. 1/6 D. 1/4

7. 1/25 of 230 equals 7.___

   A. 92.0 B. 9.20 C. .920 D. 920

8. 4 times 3/8 equals 8.___

   A. 1 3/8 B. 3/32 C. 12.125 D. 1.5

9. 3/4 divided by 4 equals 9.___

   A. 3 B. 3/16 C. 16/3 D. 16

10. 6/7 divided by 2/7 equals 10.___

    A. 6 B. 12/49 C. 3 D. 21

11. The interest on $240 for 90 days ' 6% is 11.___

    A. $4.80 B. $3.40 C. $4.20 D. $3.60

12. 16 2/3% of 1728 is 12.___

    A. 91 B. 288 C. 282 D. 280

13. 6 1/4% of 6400 is 13.____

A. 2500 B. 410 C. 108 D. 400

14. 12 1/2% of 560 is 14.____

A. 65 B. 40 C. 50 D. 70

15. 2 yards divided by 3 equals 15.____

A. 2 feet B. 1/2 yard C. 3 yards D. 3 feet

16. A school has 540 pupils. 45% are boys. How many girls are there in this school? 16.____

A. 243 B. 297 C. 493 D. 394

17. .1875 is equivalent to 17.____

A. 18 3/4 B. 75/18 C. 18/75 D. 3/16

18. A kitchen cabinet listed at $42 is sold for $33.60. The discount allowed is 18.____

A. 10% B. 15% C. 20% D. 30%

19. 3 6/8 divided by 8 1/4 equals 19.____

A. 9 1/8 B. 12 C. 5/11 D. 243.16

20. An agent sold goods to the amount of $1480. His commission at 5 1/2% was 20.____

A. $37.50 B. $81.40 C. 76.70 D. $81.10

KEY (CORRECT ANSWERS

1.	C	11.	D
2.	B	12.	B
3.	A	13.	D
4.	A	14.	D
5.	D	15.	A
6.	A	16.	B
7.	B	17.	D
8.	D	18.	C
9.	B	19.	C
10.	C	20.	B

SOLUTIONS TO PROBLEMS

1. Let x = missing number. Then, 1600 = .40x. Solving, x = 4000
2. 2:05 PM - 9:15 AM = 4 hours 50 minutes
3. The product of two 4-decimal numbers is an 8-decimal number.
4. (25 ft)(36 ft) = 900 sq.ft. = 100 sq.yds.
5. (1/8)(1%) = (.125)(.01) = .00125
6. (6 ÷ 4) ÷ (6 x 4) = 3/2 ÷ 24 = (3/2)(1/24)= (1/16)
7. (1/25)(230) = 9.20
8. (4)(3/8) = 12/8 = 1.5
9. 3/4 ÷ 4 = (3/4)(1/4) = 3/16
10. 6/7 / 2/7 = (6/7)(7/2) = 3
11. ($240)(.06)(90/360) = $3.60
12. (16 2/3%)(1728) = (1/6)(1728) = 288
13. (6 1/4%)(6400) = (1/16)(6400) = 400
14. (12 1/2%)(560) = (1/8)(560) = 70
15. 2 yds ÷ 3 = 2/3 yds = (2/3)(3) = 2 ft.
16. If 45% are boys, then 55% are girls. Thus, (540)(.55) = 297
17. .1875 = 1875/10,000 = 3/16
18. $42 - $33.60 = $8.40.
    The discount is $8.40 ÷ $42 = .20 = 20%
19. 3 6/8 - 8 1/4 = (30/8)(4/33) = 5/11
20. ($1480)(.055) = $81.40

TEST 3

DIRECTIONS: Each question or incomplete statement is followed by several suggested answers or completions. Select the one that BEST answers the question or completes the statement. *PRINT THE LETTER OF THE CORRECT ANSWER IN THE SPACE AT THE RIGHT.*

1. 93.648 divided by 0.4 is 1.____

   A. 23.412 B. 234.12 C. 2.3412 D. 2341.2

2. Add 4.3682, .0028, 34., 9.92, and from the sum subtract 1.992. The remainder is 2.____

   A. .46299 B. 4.6299 C. 462.99 D. 46.299

3. At $2.88 per gross, three dozen will cost 3.____

   A. $8.64 B. $0.96 C. $0.72 D. $11.52

4. 13 times 2.39 times 0.024 equals 4.____

   A. 745.68 B. 74.568 C. 7.4568 D. .74568

5. A living room suite is marked $64 less 25 percent. A cash discount of 10 percent is allowed.
   The cash price is 5.____

   A. $53.20 B. $47.80 C. $36.00 D. $43.20

6. 1/8 of 1 percent expressed as a decimal is 6.____

   A. .125 B. .0125 C. 1.25 D. .00125

7. 16 percent of 482.11 equals 7.____

   A. 77.1376 B. 771.4240 C. 7714.2400 D. 7.71424

8. A merchant sold a chair for $60. This was at a profit of 25 percent of what it cost him. The chair cost him 8.____

   A. $48 B. $45 C. $15 D. $75

9. Add 5 hours 13 minutes, 3 hours 49 minutes, and 14 minutes. The sum is ______ hours ______ minutes. 9.____

   A. 9; 16 B. 9;76 C. 8;16 D. 8;6

10. 89 percent of $482 is 10.____

    A. $428.98 B. $472.36 C. $42.90 D. $47.24

11. 200 percent of 800 is 11.____

    A. 16 B. 1600 C. 2500 D. 4

12. Add 2 feet 3 inches, 4 feet 11 inches, 8 inches, 6 feet 6 inches. The sum is ______ feet ______ inches. 12.____

    A. 12; 4 B. 12; 14 C. 14; 4 D. 14; 28

13. A merchant bought dresses at $15 each and sold them at $20 each. His overhead expenses are 20 percent of cost. His net profit on each dress is 13.___

A. $1 B. $2 C. $3 D. $4

14. 0.0325 expressed as a percent is 14.___

A. 325% B. 3 1/4% C. 32 1/2% D. 32.5%

15. Add 3/4, 1/8, 1/32, 1/2; and from the sum subtract 4/8. The remainder is 15.___

A. 2/32 B. 7/8 C. 29/32 D. 3/4

16. A salesman gets a commission of 4 percent on his sales. If he wants his commission to amount to $40, he will have to sell merchandise totaling 16.___

A. $160 B. $10 C. $1,000 D. $100

17. Jones borrowed $225,000 for five years at 3 1/2 percent. The annual interest charge was 17.___

A. $1,575 B. $1,555 C. $7,875 D. $39,375

18. A kitchen cabinet listed at $42 is sold for $33.60. The discount allowed is ______ percent. 18.___

A. 10 B. 15 C. 20 D. 30

19. The exact number of days from May 5, 2007 to July 1, 2007 is ______ days. 19.___

A. 59 B. 58 C. 56 D. 57

20. A dealer sells an article at a loss of 50% of the cost. Based on the selling price, the loss is 20.___

A. 25% B. 50% C. 100% D. none of these

KEY (CORRECT ANSWERS)

1. B
2. D
3. C
4. D
5. D

6. D
7. A
8. A
9. A
10. A

11. B
12. C
13. B
14. B
15. C

16. C
17. C
18. C
19. D
20. C

SOLUTIONS TO PROBLEMS

1. 93.648 ÷ .4 = 234.12
2. 4.368 + .0028 + 34 + 9.92 - 1.992 = 48.291 - 1.992 = 46.299
3. $2.88 for 12 dozen means $.24 per dozen. Three dozen will cost (3)($.24) = $.72
4. (13)(2.39)(.024) = .74568
5. ($64)(.75)(.90) = $43.20
6. (1/8)(1%) = (.125)(.01) = .00125
7. (.16)(482.11) = 77.1376
8. Let x = cost. Then, 1.25x = $60. Solving, x = $48
9. 5 hrs. 13 min. + 3 hrs. 49 min. + 14 min = 8 hrs. 76 min.
10. (.89)($482) = $428.98
11. 200% = 2. So, (200%)(800) = (2)(800) = 1600
12. 2 ft. 3 in. + 4 ft. 11 in. + 8 in. + 6 ft. 6 in. + 12 ft. 28 in. = 14 ft. 4 in.
13. Overhead is (.20)($15) = $3. The net profit is $20 - $15 - $3 = $2
14. .0325 = 3.25% = 3 1/4%
15. 3/4 + 1/8 + 1/32 + 1/2 - 4/8 = 45/32 - 4/8 = 29/32
16. Let x = sales. Then, $40 = .04x. Solving, x = $1000
17. Annual interest is ($225,000)(.035) x 1 = 7875
18. $42 - $33.60 = $8.40. Then, $8.40 ÷ $42 = .20 = 20%
19. The number of days left for May, June, July is 26, 30, and 1. Thus, 26 + 30 + 1 = 57
20. Let x = cost, so that .50x = selling price. The loss is represented by .50x ÷ .50x = 1 = 100% on the selling price. (Note: The loss in dollars is x - .50x = .50x)

EXAMINATION SECTION
TEST 1

DIRECTIONS: Each question or incomplete statement is followed by several suggested answers or completions. Select the one that BEST answers the question or completes the statement. *PRINT THE LETTER OF THE CORRECT ANSWER IN THE SPACE AT THE RIGHT.*

1. A *basic* method of operation that a *good* supervisor should follow is to 1.____

   A. check the work of subordinates constantly to make sure they are not making exceptions to the rules
   B. train subordinates so they can handle problems that come up regularly themselves and come to him only with special cases
   C. delegate to subordinates only those duties which he cannot do himself
   D. issue directions to subordinates only on special matters

2. To do a *good* job of performance evaluation, it is BEST for a supervisor to 2.____

   A. compare the employee's performance to that of another employee doing similar work
   B. give greatest weight to instances of unusually good or unusually poor performance
   C. leave out any consideration of the employee's personal traits
   D. measure the employee's performance against standard performance requirements

3. Of the following, the MOST important reason for a supervisor to have private face to face discussions with subordinates about their performance is to 3.____

   A. help employees improve their work
   B. give special praise to employees who perform well
   C. encourage the employees to compete for higher performance ratings
   D. discipline employees who perform poorly

4. Of the following, the CHIEF purpose of a probationary period for a new employee is to allow time for 4.____

   A. finding out whether the selection processes are satisfactory
   B. the employee to make adjustments in his home circumstances made necessary by the job
   C. the employee to decide whether he wants a permanent appointment
   D. determining the fitness of the employee to continue in the job

5. When a subordinate resigns his job, it is MOST important to conduct an exit interview in order to 5.____

   A. try to get the employee to remain on the job
   B. learn the true reasons for the employee's resignation
   C. see that the employee leaves with a good opinion of the agency
   D. ask the employee if he would consider a transfer

6. Chronic lateness of employees is generally LEAST likely to be due to 6.____

   A. distance of job location from home
   B. poor personnel administration
   C. unexpressed employee grievances
   D. low morale

7. Of the following, the LEAST effective stimulus for motivating employees toward inproved performance over a long-range period is 7.____

   A. their sense of achievement
   B. their feeling of recognition
   C. opportunity for their self-development
   D. an increase in salary

8. Suppose that NOT ONE of a group of employees has turned in an idea to the employees suggestion system during the past year. 8.____
   The *most probable* reason for this situation is that the

   A. money awards given for suggestions used are not high enough to make employees interested
   B. employees in this group are not able to develop any good ideas
   C. supervisor of these employees is not doing enough to encourage them to take part in the program
   D. methods and procedures of operation do not need improvement

9. A subordinate tells you that he is having trouble concentrating on his work due to a personal problem at home. 9.____
   Of the following, it would be BEST for you to

   A. refer him to a community service agency
   B. listen quietly to the story because he may just need a sympathetic ear
   C. tell him that you cannot help him because the problem is not job related
   D. ask him questions about the nature of the problem and tell him how you would handle it

10. For you as a supervisor to give each of your subordinates *exactly* the same type of supervision is 10.____

   A. *advisable,* because doing this insures fair and impartial treatment of each individual
   B. *not advisable,* because individuals like to think that they are receiving better treatment than others
   C. *advisable,* because once a supervisor learns how to deal with a subordinate who brings a problem to him, he can handle another subordinate with this problem in the same way
   D. *not advisable,* because each person is different and there is no one supervisory procedure for dealing with individuals that applies in every case

11. A senior employee under your supervision tells you that he is reluctant to speak to one of his subordinates about his poor work habits, because this worker is "strong-willed" and he does not want to antagonize him. 11.____
   For you to offer to speak to the subordinate about this matter yourself would be

   A. *advisable,* since you are in a position of greater authority
   B. *inadvisable,* since handling this problem is a basic supervisory responsibility of the senior employee
   C. *advisable,* since the senior employee must work more closely with the worker than you do
   D. *inadvisable,* since you should not risk antagonizing the employee yourself

12. Some of your subordinates have been coming to you with complaints you feel are unimportant. For you to hear their stories out is 12.____

    A. *poor practice,* you should spend your time on more important matters
    B. *good practice,* this will increase your popularity with your subordinates
    C. *poor practice,* subordinates should learn to come to you only with major grievances
    D. *good practice,* it may prevent minor complaints from developing into major grievances

13. Assume that an agency has an established procedure for handling employee grievances. An employee in this agency, comes to his immediate supervisor with a grievance. The supervisor investigates the matter and makes a decision. 13.____
    However, the employee is not satisfied with the decision made by the supervisor. The BEST action for the supervisor to take is to

    A. tell the employee he will review the matter further
    B. remind the employee that he is the supervisor and the employee must act in accordance with his decision
    C. explain to the employee how he can carry his complaint forward to the next step in the grievance procedure
    D. tell the employee he will consult with his own superiors on the matter

14. Subordinate employees and senior employees often must make quick decisions while in the field. The supervisor can BEST help subordinates meet such situations by 14.____

    A. training them in the appropriate action to take for every problem that may come up
    B. limiting the areas in which they are permitted to make decisions
    C. making certain they understand clearly the basic policies of the bureau and the department
    D. delegating authority to make such decisions to only a few subordinates on each level

15. Studies have shown that the CHIEF cause of failure to achieve success as a supervisor is 15.____

    A. an unwillingness to delegate authority to subordinates
    B. the establishment of high performance standards for subordinates
    C. the use of discipline that is too strict
    D. showing too much leniency to poor workers

16. When a supervisor delegates to a subordinate certain work that he normally does himself, it is MOST important that he give the subordinate 16.____

    A. responsibility for also setting the standards for the work to be done
    B. sufficient authority to be able to carry out the assignment
    C. written, step-by-step instructions for doing the work
    D. an explanation of one part of the task at a time

17. It is particularly important that disciplinary actions be equitable as between individuals. This statement *implies* that 17.____

    A. punishment applied in disciplinary actions should be lenient
    B. proposed disciplinary actions should be reviewed by higher authority
    C. subordinates should have an opportunity to present their stories before penalties are applied
    D. penalties for violations of the rules should be standardized and consistently applied

18. You discover that from time to time a number of false rumors circulate among your subordinates.
Of the following, the BEST way for you to handle this situation is to 18.____

    A. ignore the rumors since rumors circulate in every office and can never be eliminated
    B. attempt to find those responsible for the rumors and reprimand them
    C. make sure that your employees are informed as soon as possible about all matters that affect them
    D. inform your superior about the rumors and let him deal with the matter

19. Supervisors who allow the "halo effect" to influence their evaluations of subordinates are *most likely* to 19.____

    A. give more lenient ratings to older employees who have longer service
    B. let one highly favorable or unfavorable trait unduly affect their judgment of an employee
    C. evaluate all employees on one trait before considering a second
    D. give high evaluations in order to avoid antagonizing their subordinates

20. For a supervisor to keep records of reprimands to subordinates about infractions of the rules is 20.____

    A. *good practice,* because these records are valuable to support disciplinary actions recommended or taken
    B. *poor practice,* because such records are evidence of the supervisor's inability to maintain discipline
    C. *good practice,* because such records indicate that the supervisor is doing a good job
    D. *poor practice,* because the best way to correct subordinates is to give them more training

21. When a new departmental policy has been established, it would be MOST advisable for you, as a supervisor, to 21.____

    A. distribute a memo which states the new policy and instruct your subordinates to read it
    B. explain specifically to your subordinates how the policy is going to affect them
    C. make sure your subordinates understand that you are not responsible for setting the policy
    D. tell your subordinates whether you agree or disagree with the policy

22. As a supervisor, you receive several complaints about the rude conduct of a subordinate. The FIRST action you should take is to 22.____

A. request his transfer to another office
B. prepare a charge sheet for disciplinary action
C. assign a senior employee to work with him for a week
D. interview the employee to determine possible reason, and warn that correction is necessary

23. A supervisor is *most likely* to get subordinates to work cooperatively toward accomplishing bureau goals if he 23.____

A. creates an atmosphere that contributes to their feeling of security
B. backs up subordinates even when they occasionally disobey regulations
C. shows interest in subordinates by helping them solve their personal problems
D. uses an authoritarian or "bossy" approach to supervision

24. A supervisor is holding a staff meeting with his senior employees to try to find an acceptable solution to a problem that has come up. 24.____
Of the following, the CHIEF role of the supervisor at this meeting should be to

A. see that every member of the group contributes at least one suggestions
B. act as chairman of the meeting, but take no other active part to avoid influencing the senior employees
C. keep the participants from wandering off into discussions of irrelevant matters
D. make certain the participants hear his views on the matter at the beginning of the meeting

25. An employee shows you a certificate that he has just received for completing two years of study in conversational Spanish. As his supervisor, it would be BEST for you to 25.____

A. put a note about this accomplishment in his personnel folder
B. assign him to areas in which people of Spanish origin live
C. congratulate him on this accomplishment, but tell him frankly that you doubt this is likely to have any direct bearing on his work
D. encourage him to continue his studies and become thoroughly fluent in speaking the language

---

KEY (CORRECT ANSWERS)

1. B
2. D
3. A
4. D
5. B

6. A
7. D
8. C
9. B
10. D

11. B
12. D
13. C
14. C
15. A

16. B
17. D
18. C
19. B
20. A

21. B
22. D
23. A
24. C
25. A

TEST 2

DIRECTIONS: Each question or incomplete statement is followed by several suggested answers or completions. Select the one that BEST answers the question or completes the statement. *PRINT THE LETTER OF THE CORRECT ANSWER IN THE SPACE AT THE RIGHT.*

1. Of the following, the factor affecting employee morale which the immediate supervisor is LEAST able to control is 1._____

   A. handling of grievances
   B. fair and impartial treatment of subordinates
   C. general presonnel rules and regulations
   D. accident prevention

2. When one of your workers does outstanding work, you should 2._____

   A. explain to your other employees that you expect the same kind of work of them
   B. praise him for his work so that he will know it is appreciated
   C. say nothing, because other employees may think you are showing favoritism
   D. show him how his work can be improved still more so that he will not sit back

3. For you as a supervisor to consider a suggestion from a probationary worker for improving a procedure would be 3._____

   A. *poor practice,* because this employee is too new on the job to know much about it
   B. *good practice,* because you may be able to share credit for the suggestion
   C. *poor practice,* because it may hurt the morale of the older employees
   D. *good practice,* because the suggestion may be worthwhile

4. If you find you must criticize the work of one of your workers, it would be BEST for you to 4._____

   A. mention the good points in his work as well as the faults
   B. caution him that he will receive an unsatisfactory performance report unless his work improves
   C. compare his work to that of the other agents you supervise
   D. apologize for making the criticism

5. As a senior employee which one of the following matters would it be BEST for you to talk over with your supervisor before you take final action? 5._____

   A. One of the workers you supervise continues to disregard your instructions repeatedly in spite of repeated warnings
   B. One of your workers tells you he wants to discuss a personal problem
   C. A probationary employee tells you he does not understand a procedure
   D. One of your workers tells you he disagrees with the way you rate his work

6. If one of your subordinates asks you a question about a department rule and you do not know the answer, you should tell him that 6._____

   A. he should try to get the information himself
   B. you do not have the answer, but you will get it for him as soon as you can
   C. he should ask you the question again a week from now
   D. he should put the question in writing

7. If, as a supervisor, you realize that you have been unfair in criticizing one of your subordinates, the BEST action for you to take is to 7.____

   A. say nothing, but overlook some error made by this employee in the future
   B. be frank and tell the employee that you are sorry for the mistake you made
   C. let the employee know in some indirect way without admitting your mistake, that you realize he was not at fault
   D. say nothing, but be more careful about criticizing subordinates in the future

8. Of the following, the MOST important reason for a supervisor to write an accident report as soon as possible after an accident has happened is to 8.____

   A. make sure that important facts about the accident are not forgotten
   B. avoid delay in getting compensation for the injured person
   C. get adequate medical treatment for the injured person
   D. keep department accident statistics up to date

9. In any matter which may require disciplinary action, the FIRST responsibility of the supervisor is to 9.____

   A. decide what penalty should be applied for the offense
   B. refer the matter to a higher authority for complete investigation
   C. place the interests of the department above those of the employee
   D. investigate the matter fully to get all the facts

10. Suppose you find it necessary to criticize one of the subordinates you supervise. You should 10.____

   A. send an official letter to his home
   B. speak to him about the matter privately
   C. speak to him at a staff meeting
   D. ask another worker who is friendly with him to talk to him about the matter

11. Some of your subordinates have been coming to you with complaints you feel are unimportant. For you to hear their stories out is 11.____

   A. *poor practice,* you should spend your time on more important matters
   B. *good practice,* this will increase your popularity with your subordinates
   C. *poor practice,* subordinates should learn to come to you only with major grievances
   D. *good practice,* it may prevent minor complaints from developing into major grievances

12. Suppose that NOT ONE of a group of employees has turned in an idea to the employees' suggestion system during the past year. The *most probable* reason for this situation is that the 12.____

   A. supervisor of these employees is not doing enough to encourage them to take part in this program
   B. employees in this group are not able to develop any good ideas
   C. money awards given for suggestions used are not high enough to make employees interested
   D. methods and procedures of operation do not need improvement

13. For you as a supervisor to give each of your subordinates *exactly* the same type of supervision is 13.____

   A. *advisable,* because doing this insures fair and impartial treatment of each individual
   B. *not advisable,* because each person is different and there is no one supervisory procedure for dealing with individuals that applies in every case
   C. *advisable,* because once a supervisor learns how to deal with a subordinate who brings a problem to him, he can handle another subordinate with this problem in the same way
   D. *not advisable,* because individuals like to think that they are receiving better treatment than others

14. In evaluating personnel, a supervisor should keep in mind that the MOST important objective of performance evaluations is to 14.____

   A. encourage employees to compete for higher performance ratings
   B. give recognition to employees who perform well
   C. help employees improve their work
   D. discipline employees who perform poorly

15. A subordinate tells you that he is having trouble concentrating on his work due to a personal problem at home. Of the following, it would be BEST for you to 15.____

   A. refer him to a community service agency
   B. listen quietly to the story because he may just need a sympathetic ear
   C. tell him that you cannot help him because the problem is not job-related
   D. ask him some questions about the nature of the problem and tell him how you would handle it

16. To do a good job of performance evaluation, it is BEST for a supervisor to 16.____

   A. measure the employee's performance against standard performance requirements
   B. compare the employee's performance to that of another employee doing similar work
   C. leave out any consideration of the employee's personal traits
   D. give greatest weight to instances of unusually good or unusually poor performance

17. It is particularly important that disciplinary actions be equitable as between individuals. This statement *implies* that 17.____

   A. punishment applied in disciplinary actions should be lenient
   B. proposed disciplinary actions should be reviewed by higher authority
   C. subordinates should have an opportunity to present their stories before penalties are applied
   D. penalties for violations of the rules should be standardized and consistently applied

18. Assume that an agency has an established procedure for handling employee grievances. An employee in this agency comes to his immediate supervisor with a grievance. The supervisor investigates the matter and makes a decision. However, the employee is not satisfied with the decision made by the supervisor. 18.____
The BEST action for the supervisor to take is to

A. tell the employee he will review the matter further
B. remind the employee that he is the supervisor and the employee must act in accordance with his decision
C. explain to the employee how he can carry his complaint forward to the next step in the grievance procedure
D. tell the employee he will consult with his own superiors on the matter

19. Of the following, the CHIEF purpose of a probationary period for a new employee is to allow time for 19.____

A. finding out whether the selection processes are satisfactory
B. determining the fitness of the employee to continue in the job
C. the employee to decide whether he wants a permanent appointment
D. the employee to make adjustments in his home circumstances made necessary by the job

20. Of the following, the subject that would be MOST important to include in a "break-in" program for new employees is 20.____

A. explanation of rules, regulations and policies of the agency
B. Instruction in the agency's history and programs
C. explanation of the importance of the new employees' own particular job
D. explanation of the duties and responsibilities of the employee

21. Suppose a new employee under your supervision seems slow to learn and is making mistakes in performing his duties. Your FIRST action should be to 21.____

A. pass this information on to the bureau director
B. reprimand the worker so he will not repeat these mistakes
C. find out whether this worker understands your instructions
D. note these facts for future reference when writing up the monthly performance evaluation

22. In training new employees to do a certain job it would be LEAST desirable for you to 22.____

A. demonstrate how the job is done, step by step
B. encourage the workers to ask questions if they aren't clear about any point
C. tell them about the various mistakes other agents have made in doing this job
D. have the workers do the job, explaining to you what they are doing and why

23. One of the workers under your supervision is resentful when you ask her to remove her jangling bracelets before she starts her tour of duty. 23.____
Of the following, the BEST explanation you can give her for the rule against wearing such jewelry while on duty is that

A. the jewelry may create a safety hazard
B. employees must give up certain personal liberties if they want to keep their jobs
C. workers cannot perform their duties as efficiently if they wear distracting jewelry
D. citizens may receive an unfavorable impression of the department

24. Of the following, the LEAST important reason for having a department handbook and a bureau standard operating procedure is to 24.____

 A. help in training new employees
 B. provide a source of reference for department and bureau rules and procedures
 C. prevent errors in work by providing clear guidelines
 D. make the supervisor's job easy

25. On inspecting your squad prior to their tour of duty, you note an employee improperly and unacceptably dressed. 25.____
The FIRST action you should take is to

 A. call the employee aside and insist on immediate correction if possible
 B. notify the district commander right away
 C. have the employee submit a memorandum explaining the reason for the improper uniform
 D. permit the employee to proceed on duty but warn him not to let this happen again

---

KEY (CORRECT ANSWERS)

1. C
2. B
3. D
4. A
5. A
6. B
7. B
8. A
9. D
10. B
11. D
12. A
13. B
14. C
15. B
16. A
17. D
18. C
19. B
20. D
21. C
22. C
23. D
24. D
25. A

SUPERVISION STUDY GUIDE

Social science has developed information about groups and leadership in general and supervisor-employee relationships in particular. Since organizational effectiveness is closely linked to the ability of supervisors to direct the activities of employees, these findings are important to executives everywhere.

IS A SUPERVISOR A LEADER?

First-line supervisors are found in all large business and government organizations. They are the men at the base of an organizational hierarchy. Decisions made by the head of the organization reach them through a network of intermediate positions. They are frequently referred to as part of the management team, but their duties seldom seem to support this description.

A supervisor of clerks, tax collectors, meat inspectors, or securities analysts is not charged with budget preparation. He cannot hire or fire the employees in his own unit on his say-so. He does not administer programs which require great planning, coordinating, or decision making.

Then what is he? He is the man who is directly in charge of a group of employees doing productive work for a business or government agency. If the work requires the use of machines, the men he supervises operate them. If the work requires the writing of reports, the men he supervises write them. He is expected to maintain a productive flow of work without creating problems which higher levels of management must solve. But is he a leader?

To carry out a specific part of an agency's mission, management creates a unit, staffs it with a group of employees and designates a supervisor to take charge of them. Management directs what this unit shall do, from time to time changes directions, and often indicates what the group should not do. Management presumably creates status for the supervisor by giving him more pay, a title, and special priviledges.

Management asks a supervisor to get his workers to attain organizational goals, including the desired quantity and quality of production. Supposedly, he has authority to enable him to achieve this objective. Management at least assumes that by establishing the status of the supervisor's position it has created sufficient authority to enable him to achieve these goals -- not his goals, nor necessarily the group's, but management's goals.

In addition, supervision includes writing reports, keeping records of membership in a higher-level administrative group, industrial engineering, safety engineering, editorial duties, housekeeping duties, etc. The supervisor as a member of an organizational network, must be responsible to the changing demands of the management above him. At the same time, he must be responsive to the demands of the work group of which he is a member. He is placed in the difficult position of communicating and implementing new decisions, changed programs and revised production quotas for his work group, although he may have had little part in developing them.

It follows, then, that supervision has a special characteristic: achievement of goals, previously set by management, through the efforts of others. It is in this feature of the supervisor's job that we find the role of a leader in the sense of the following definition: *A leader is that person who <u>most</u> effectively influences group activities toward goal setting and goal achievements.*

This definition is broad. It covers both leaders in groups that come together voluntarily and in those brought together through a work assignment in a factory, store, or government agency. In the natural group, the authority necessary to attain goals is determined by the group membership and is granted by them. In the working group, it is apparent that the establishment of a supervisory position creates a predisposition on the part of employees to accept the authority of the occupant of that position. We cannot, however, assume that mere occupancy confers authority sufficient to assure the accomplishment of an organization's goals.

Supervision is different, then, from leadership. The supervisor is expected to fulfill the role of leader but without obtaining a grant of authority from the group he supervises. The supervisor is expected to influence the group in the achieving of goals but is often handicapped by having little influence on the organizational process by which goals are set. The supervisor, because he works in an organizational setting, has the burdens of additional organizational duties and restrictions and requirements arising out of the fact that his position is subordinate to a hierarchy of higher-level supervisors. These differences between leadership and supervision are reflected in our definition: *Supervision is basically a leadership role, in a formal organization, which has as its objective the effective influencing of other employees.*

Even though these differences between supervision and leadership exist, a significant finding of experimenters in this field is that supervisors <u>must</u> be leaders to be successful.

The problem is: How can a supervisor exercise leadership in an organizational setting? We might say that the supervisor is expected to be a natural leader in a situation which does not come about naturally. His situation becomes really difficult in an organization which is more eager to make its supervisors into followers rather than leaders.

LEADERSHIP: NATURAL AND ORGANIZATIONAL

Leadership, in its usual sense of *natural* leadership, and supervision are not the same. In some cases, leadership embraces broader powers and functions than supervision; in other cases, supervision embraces more than leadership. This is true both because of the organization and technical aspects of the supervisor's job and because of the relatively freer setting and inherent authority of the natural leader.

The natural leader usually has much more authority and influence than the supervisor. Group members not only follow his command but prefer it that way. The employee, however, can appeal the supervisor's commands to his union or to the supervisor's superior or to the personnel office. These intercessors represent restrictions on the supervisor's power to lead.

The natural leader can gain greater membership involvement in the group's objectives, and he can change the objectives of the group. The supervisor can attempt to gain employee support only for management's objectives; he cannot set other objectives. In these instances leadership is broader than supervision.

The natural leader must depend upon whatever skills are available when seeking to attain objectives. The supervisor is trained in the administrative skills necessary to achieve management's goals. If he does not possess the requisite skills, however, he can call upon management's technicians.

A natural leader can maintain his leadership, in certain groups, merely by satisfying members' need for group affilation. The supervisor must maintain his leadership by directing and organizing his group to achieve specific organizational goals set for him and his group by management. He must have a technical competence and a kind of coordinating ability which is not needed by many natural leaders.

A natural leader is responsible only to his group which grants him authority. The supervisor is responsible to management, which employs him, and, also, to the work group of which he is a member. The supervisor has the exceedingly difficult job of reconciling the demands of two groups frequently in conflict. He is often placed in the untenable position of trying to play two antagonisic roles. In the above instances, supervision is broader than leadership.

ORGANIZATIONAL INFLUENCES ON LEADERSHIP

The supervisor is both a product and a prisoner of the organization wherein we find him. The organization which creates the supervisor's position also obstructs, restricts, and channelizes the exercise of his duties. These influences extend beyond prescribed functional relationships to specific supervisory behavior. For example, even in a face-to-face situation involving one of his subordinates, the supervisor's actions are controlled to a great extent by his organization. His behavior must conform to the organization policy on human relations, rules which dictate personnel procedures, specific prohibitions governing conduct, the attitudes of his own superior, etc. He is not a free agent operating within the limits of his work group. His freedom of action is much more circumscribed than is generally admitted. The organizational influences which limit his leadership actions can be classified as structure, prescriptions, and proscriptions.

The organizational structure places each supervisor's position in context with other designated positions. It determines the relationships between his position and specific positions which impinge on his. The structure of the organization designates a certain position to which he looks for orders and information about his work. It gives a particular status to his position within a pattern of statuses from which he perceives that (1) certain positions are on a par, organizationally, with his, (2) other positions are subordinate, and (3) still others are superior. The organizational structure determines those positions to which he should look for advice and assistance, and those positions to which he should give advice and assistance.

For instance, the organizational structure has predetermined that the supervisor of a clerical processing unit shall report to a supervisory position in a higher echelon. He shall have certain relationships with the supervisors of the work units which transmit work to and receive work from his unit. He shall discuss changes and clarification of procedures with certain staff units, such as organization and methods, cost accounting, and personnel. He shall consult supervisors of units which provide or receive special work assignments.

The organizational structure, however, establishes patterns other than those of the relationships of positions. These are the patterns of responsibility, authority, and expectations.

The supervisor is responsible for certain activities or results; he is presumably invested with the authority to achieve these. His set of authority and responsibility is interwoven with other sets to the end that all goals and functions of the organization are parceled out in small, manageable lots. This, of course, establishes a series of expectations: a single supervisor can perform his particular set of duties only upon the assumption that preceding or contiguous sets of duties have been, or are being, carried out. At the same time, he is aware of the expectations of others that he will fulfill his functional role.

The structure of an organization establishes relationships between specified positions and specific expectations for these positions. The fact that these relationships and expectations are established is one thing; whether or not they are met is another.

PRESCRIPTIONS AND PROSCRIPTIONS

But let us return to the organizational influences which act to restrict the supervisor's exercise of leadership. These are the prescriptions and proscriptions generally in effect in all organizations, and those peculiar to a single organization. In brief these are the *thous shalt's* and the *thou shalt not's.*

Organizations not only prescribe certain duties for individual supervisory positions, they also prescribe specific methods and means of carrying out these duties and maintaining management-employee relations. These include rules, regulations, policy, and. tradition. It does no good for the supervisor to say, *This seems to be the best way to handle such-and such,* if the organization has established a routine for dealing with problems. For good or bad, there are rules that state that firings shall be executed in such a manner, accompanied by a certain notification; that training shall be conducted, and in this manner. Proscriptions are merely negative prescriptions: you may not discriminate against any employee because of politics or race; you shall not suspend any employee without following certain procedures and obtaining certain approvals.

Most of these prohibitions and rules apply to the area of interpersonal relations, precisely the area which is now arousing most interest on the part of administrators and managers. We have become concerned about the contrast between formally prescribed relationships and interpersonal relationships, and this brings us to the often discussed informal organization.

FORMAL AND INFORMAL ORGANIZATIONS

As we well know, the functions and activities of any organization are broken down into individual units of work called positions. Administrators must establish a pattern which will link these positions to each other and relate them to a system of authority and responsibility. Man-to-man are spelled out as plainly as possible for all to understand. Managers, then, build an official structure which we call the formal organization.

In these same organizations employees react individually and in groups to institutionally determined roles. John, a worker, rides in the same car pool as Joe, a foreman. An unplanned communication develops. Harry, a machinist, knows more about highspeed machining than his foreman or anyone else in his shop. An unofficial tool boss comes into being. Mary, who fought with Jane is promoted over her. Jane now ignores Mary's directions. A planned relationship fails to develop. The employees have built a structure which we call the informal organization.

Formal organization is a system of management-prescribed relations between positions in an organization.

Informal organization is a network of unofficial relations between people in an organization.

These definitions might lead us to the absurd conclusion that positions carry out formal activities and that employees spend their time in unofficial activities. We must recognize that organizational activities are in all cases carried out by people. The formal structure provides a needed framework within which interpersonal relations occur. What we call informal organization is the complex of normal, natural relations among employees. These personal relationships may be negative or positive. That is, they may impede or aid the achievement of organizational, goals. For example, friendship between two supervisors greatly increases the probability of good cooperation and coordination between their sections. On the other hand, *buck passing* nullifies the formal structure by failure to meet a prescribed and expected responsibility.

It is improbable that an ideal organization exists where all activities are acarried out in strict conformity to a formally prescribed pattern of functional roles. Informal organization arises because of the incompleteness and ambiguities in the network of formally prescribed relationships, or in response to the needs or inadequacies of supervisors or managers who hold prescribed functional roles in an organization. Many of these relationships are not prescribed by the organizational pattern; many cannot be prescribed; many should not be prescribed.

Management faces the problem of keeping the informal organization in harmony with the mission of the agency. One way to do this is to make sure that all employees have a clear understanding of and are sympathetic with that mission. The issuance of organizational charts, procedural manuals, and functional descriptions of the work to be done by divisions and sections helps communicate management's plans and goals. Issuances alone, of course, cannot do the whole job. They should be accompanied by oral discussion and explanation. Management must ensure that there is mutual understanding and acceptance of charts and procedures. More important is that management acquaint itself with the attitudes, activities, and peculiar brands of logic which govern the informal organization. Only through this type of knowledge can they and supervisors keep informal goals consistent with the agency mission.

SUPERVISION, STATUS, AND FUNCTIONAL ROLE

A well-established supervisor is respected by the employees who work with him. They defer to his wishes. It is clear that a superior-subordinate relationship has been established. That is, status of the supervisor has been established in relation to other employees of the same work group. This same supervisor gains the respect of employees when he behaves in a certain manner. He will be expected generally, to follow the customs of the group in such matters as dress, recreation, and manner of speaking. The group has a set of expectations as to his behavior. His position is a functional role which carries with it a collection of rights and obligations.

The position of supervisor usually has a status distinct from the individual who occupies it: it is much like a position description which exists whether or not there is an incumbent. The status of a supervisory position is valued higher than that of an employee position both because of the functional role of leadership which is assigned to it and because of the status symbols of titles, rights, and privileges which go with it.

Social ranking, or status, is not simple because it involves both the position and the man. An individual may be ranked higher than others because of his education, social background, perceived leadership ability, or conformity to group customs and ideals. If such a man is ranked higher by the members of a work group than their supervisor, the supervisor's effectiveness may be seriously undermined.

If the organization does not build and reinforce a supervisor's status, his position can be undermined in a different way. This will happen when managers go around rather than through the supervisor or designate him as a straw boss, acting boss, or otherwise not a real boss.

Let us clarify this last point. A role, and corresponding status, establishes a set of expectations. Employees expect their supervisor to do certain things and to act in certain ways. They are prepared to respond to that expected behavior. When the supervisor's behavior does not conform to their expectations, they are surprised, confused, and ill-at-ease. It becomes necessary for them to resolve their confusion, if they can. They might do this by turning to one of their own members for leadership. If the confusion continues, or their attempted solutions are not satisfactory, they will probably become a poorly motivated, non-cohesive group which cannot function very well.

COMMUNICATION AND THE SUPERVISOR

In a recent survey railroad workers reported that they rarely look to their supervisors for information about the company. This is startling, at least to us, because we ordinarily think of the supervisor as the link between management and worker. We expect the supervisor to be the prime source of information about the company. Actually, the railroad workers listed the supervisor next to last in the order of their sources of information. Most suprising of all, the supervisors, themselves, stated that rumor and unofficial contacts were their principal sources of information. Here we see one of the reasons why supervisors may not be as effective as management desires.

The supervisor is not only being bypassed by his work group, he is being ignored, and his position weakened, by the very organization which is holding him responsible for the activities of his workers. If he is management's representative to the employee, then management has an obligation to keep him informed of its activities. This is necessary if he is to carry out his functions efficiently and maintain his leadership in the work group. The supervisor is expected to be a source of information; when he is not, his status is not clear, and employees are dissatisfied because he has not lived up to expectations.

By providing information to the supervisor to pass along to employees, we can strengthen his position as leader of the group, and increase satisfaction and cohesion within the group. Because he has more information than the other members, receives information sooner, and passes it along at the proper times, members turn to him as a source and also provide him with information in the hope of receiving some in return. From this we can see an increase in group cohesiveness because:

- o Employees are bound closer to their supervisor because he is *in the know*
- o there is less need to go outside the group for answers
- o employees will more quickly turn to the supervisor for enlightenment.

The fact that he has the answers will also enhance the supervisor's standing in the eyes of his men. This increased sta,tus will serve to bolster his authority and control of the group and will probably result in improved morale and productivity.

The foregoing, of course, does not mean that all management information should be given out. There are obviously certain policy determinations and discussions which need not or cannot be transmitted to all supervisors. However, the supervisor must be kept as fully informed as possible so that he can answer questions when asked and can allay needless fears and anxieties. Further, the supervisor has the responsibility of encouraging employee questions and submissions of information. He must be able to present information to employees so that it is clearly understood and accepted. His attitude and manner should make it clear that he believes in what he is saying, that the information is necessary or desirable to the group, and that he is prepared to act on the basis of the information.

SUPERVISION AND JOB PERFORMANCE

The productivity of work groups is a product; employees' efforts are multiplied by the supervision they receive. Many investigators have analyzed this relationship and have discovered elements of supervision which differentiate high and low production groups. These researchers have identified certain types of supervisory practices which they classify as *employee-centered* and other types which they classify as *production centered.*

The difference between these two kinds of supervision lies not in specific practices but in the approach or orientation to supervision. The employee-centered supervisor directs most of his efforts toward increasing employee motivation. He is concerned more with realizing the potential energy of persons than with administrative and technological methods of increasing efficiency and productivity. He is the man who finds ways of causing employees to want to work harder with the same tools. These supervisors emphasize the personal relations between their employees and themselves.

Now, obviously, these pictures are overdrawn. No one supervisor has all the virtues of the ideal type of employee-centered supervisor. And, fortunately, no one supervisor has all the bad traits found in many production-centered supervisors. We should remember that the various practices that researchers have found which distinguish these two kinds of supervision represent the many practices and methods of supervisors of all gradations between these extremes. We should be careful, too, of the implications of the labels attached to the two types. For instance, being production-centered is not necessarily bad, since the principal responsibility of any supervisor is maintaining the production level that is expected of his work group. Being employee-centered may not necessarily be good, if the only result is a happy, chuckling crew of loafers. To return to the researchers's findings, employee-centered supervisors:

- Recommend promotions, transfers, pay increases
- Inform men about what is happening in the company
- Keep men posted on how well they are doing
- Hear complaints and grievances sympathetically
- Speak up for subordinates

Production-centered supervisors, on the other hand, don't do those things. They check on employees more frequently, give more detailed and frequent instructions, don't give reasons for changes, and are more punitive when mistakes are made. Employee-centered supervisors were reported to contribute to high morale and high production, whereas production-centered supervision was associated with lower morale and less production.

More recent findings, however, show that the relationship between supervision and productivity is not this simple. Investigators now report that high production is more frequently associated with supervisory practices which combine employee-centered behavior with concern for production. (This concern is not the same, however, as anxiety about production, which is the hallmark of our production-centered supervisor.) Let us examine these apparently contradictory findings and the premises from which they are derived.

SUPERVISION AND MORALE

Why do supervisory activities cause high or low production? As the name implies, the activities of the employee-centered supervisor tend to relate him more closely and satisfactorily to his workers. The production-centered supervisor's practices tend to separate him from his group and to foster antagonism. An analysis of this difference may answer our question.

Earlier, we pointed out that the supervisor is a type of leader and that leadership is intimately related to the group in which it occurs. We discover, now, that an employee-centered supervisor's primary activities are concerned with both his leadership and his group membership. Such a supervisor is a member of a group and occupies a leadership role in that group.

These facts are sometimes obscured when we speak of the supervisor as management's representative, or as the organizational link between management and the employee, or as the end of the chain of command. If we really want to understand what it is we expect of the supervisor, we must remember that he is the designated leader of a group of employees to whom he is bound by interaction and interdependence.

Most of his actions are aimed, consciously or unconsciously, at strengthening membership ties in the group. This includes both making members more conscious that he is a member of their grout) and causing members to identify themselves more closely with the group. These ends are accomplished by:

making the group more attractive to the worker: they
find satisfaction of their needs for recognition,
friendship, enjoyable work, etc.;

maintaining open communication: employees can express
their views and obtain information about the organization.

giving assistance: members can seek advice on
personal problems as well as their work; and

acting as a buffer between the group and management:
he speaks up for his men and explains the reasons
for management's decisions.

Such actions both strengthen group cohesiveness and solidarity and affirm the supervisor's leadership position in the group.

DEFINING MORALE

This brings us back to a point mentioned earlier. We had said that employee-centered supervisors contribute to high morale as well as to high production. But how can we explain units which have low morale and high productivity, or vice versa? Usually production and morale are considered separately, partly because they are measured against different criteria and partly because, in some instances, they seem to be independent of each other.

Some of this difficulty may stem from confusion over definitions of morale. Morale has been defined as, or measured by, absences from work, satisfaction with job or company, dissension among members of work groups, productivity, apathy or lack of interest, readiness to help others, and a general aura of happiness as rated by observers. Some of these criteria of morale are not subject to the influence of the supervisor, and some of them are not clearly related to productivity. Definitions like these invite findings of low morale coupled with high production.

Both productivity and morale can be influenced by environmental factors not under the control of group members or supervisors. Such things as plant layout, organizational structure and goals, lighting, ventilation, communications, and management planning may have an adverse or desirable effect.

We might resolve the dilemma by defining morale on the basis of our understanding of the supervisor as leader of a group; morale is the degree of satisfaction of group members with their leadership. In this light, the supervisor's employee-centered activities bear a clear relation to morale. His efforts to increase employee identification with the group and to strengthen his leadership lead to greater satisfaction with that leadership. By increasing group cohesiveness and by demonstrating that his influence and power can aid the group, he is able to enhance his leadership status and afford satisfaction to the group.

SUPERVISION, PRODUCTION, AND MORALE

There are factors within the organization itself which determine whether increased production is possible:

Are production goals expressed in terms understandable to employees and are they realistic?

Do supervisors responsible for production respect the agency mission and production goals?

If employees do not know how to do the job well, does management provide a trainer--often the supervisor--who can teach efficient work methods?

There are other factors within the work group which determine whether increased production will be attained:

Is leadership present which can bring about the desired level of production?

Are production goals accepted by employees as reasonable and attainable?

If group effort is involved, are members able to coordinate their efforts?

Research findings confirm the view that an employee-centered supervisor can achieve higher morale than a production-centered supervisor. Managers may well ask what is the relationship between this and production?

Supervision is production-oriented to the extent that it focuses attention on achieving organizational goals, and plans and devises methods for attaining them; it is employee-centered to the extent that it focuses attention on employee attitudes toward those goals, and plans and works toward maintenance of employee satisfaction.

High productivity and low morale result when a supervisor plans and organizes work efficiently but cannot achieve high membership satisfaction. Low production and high morale result when a supervisor, though keeping members satisfied with his leadership, either has not gained acceptance of organizational goals or does not have the technical competence to achieve them.

The relationship between supervision, morale, and productivity is an interdependent one, with the supervisor playing an integrating role due to his ability to influence productivity and morale independently of each other.

A supervisor who can plan his work well has good technical knowledge, and who can install better production methods can raise production without necessarily increasing group satisfaction. On the other hand, a supervisor who can motivate his employees and keep them satisfied with his leadership can gain high production in spite of technical difficulties and environmental obstacles.

CLIMATE AND SUPERVISION

Climate, the intangible environment of an organization made up of attitudes, beliefs, and traditions, plays a large part in morale, productivity, and supervision. Usually when we speak of climate and its relationship to morale and productivity, we talk about the merits of *democratic* versus *authoritarian* climate. Employees seem to produce more and have higher morale in a democratic climate, whereas in an authoritarian climate, the reverse seems to be true or so the researchers tell us. We would do well to determine what these terms mean to supervision.

Perhaps most of our difficulty in understanding and applying these concepts comes from our emotional reactions to the words themselves. For example, authoritarian climate is usually painted as the very blackest kind of dictatorship. This not surprising, because we are usually expected to believe that it is invariably bad. Conversely, democratic climate is drawn to make the driven snow look impure by comparison.

Now these descriptions are most probably true when we talk about our political processes, or town meetings, or freedom of speech. However the same labels have been used by social scientists in other contexts and have also been applied to government and business organizations, without, it seems, any recognition that the meanings and their social values may have changed somewhat .

For example, these labels were used in experiments conducted in an informal class room setting using 11 year old boys as subjects. The descriptive labels applied to the climate of the setting as well as the type of leadership practiced. When these labels were transferred to a management setting it seems that many presumed that they principally meant the king of leadership rather than climate. We can see that there is a great difference between the experimental and management settings and that leadership practices for one might be inappropriate for the other.

It is doubtful that formal work organizations can be anything but authoritarian, in that goals are set by management and a hierarchy exists through which decisions and orders from the top are transmitted downward. Organizations are authoritarian by structure and need: direction and control are placed in the hands of a few in order to gain fast and efficient decision making. Now this does not mean to describe a dictatorship. It is merely the recognition of the fact that direction of organizational affairs comes from above. It should be noted that leadership in some natural groups is, in this sense, authoritarian.

Granting that formal organizations have this kind of authoritarian leadership, can there be a democratic climate? Certainly there can be, but we would want to define and delimit this term. A more realistic meaning of democratic climate in organizations is, the use of permissive and participatory methods in management-employee relations. That is, a mutual exchange of information and explanation with the granting of individual freedom within certain restricted and defined limits. However, it is not our purpose to debate the merits of authoritarianism versus democracy. We recognize that within the small work group there is a need for freedom from constraint and an increase in participation in order to achieve organizational goals within the framework of the organizational environment.

Another aspect of climate is best expressed by this familiar, and true saying: actions speak louder than words. Of particular concern to us is this effect of management climate on the behavior of supervisors, particularly in employee-centered activities.

There have been reports of disappointment with efforts to make supervisors more employee-centered. Managers state that, since research has shown ways of improving human relations, supervisors should begin to practice these methods. Usually a training course in human relations is established, and supervisors are given this training. Managers then sit back and wait for the expected improvements, only to find that there are none.

If we wish to produce changes in the supervisor's behavior,the climate must be made appropriate and rewarding to the changed behavior. This means that top-level attitudes and behavior cannot deny or contradict the change we are attempting to effect. Basic changes in organizational behavior cannot be made with any permanence, unless we provide an environment that is receptive to the changes and rewards those persons who do change.

IMPROVING SUPERVISION

Anyone who has read this far might expect to find *A Dozen Rules for Dealing With Employees* or *29 Steps to Supervisory Success.* We will not provide such a list.

Simple rules suffer from their simplicity. They ignore the complexities of human behavior. Reliance upon rules may cause supervisors to concentrate on superficial aspects of their relations with employees. It may preclude genuine understanding.

The supervisor who relies on a list of rules tends to think of people in mechanistic terms. In a certain situation, he uses *Rule No. 3.* Employees are not treated as thinking and feeling persons, but rather as figures in a formula: Rule 3 applied to employee X = Production.

Employees usually recognize mechanical manipulation and become dissatisfied and resentful. They lose faith in, and respect for, their supervisor, and this may be reflected in lower morale and productivity.

We do not mean that supervisors must become social science experts if they wish to improve. Reports of current research indicate that there are two major parts of their job which can be strengthened through self-improvement: (1) Work planning, including technical skills. (2) Motivation of employees.

The most effective supervisors combine excellence in the administrative and technical aspects of their work with friendly and considerate personal relations with their employees.

CRITICAL PERSONAL RELATIONS

Later in this chaper we shall talk about administrative aspects of supervision, but first let us comment on *friendly and considerate personal relations.* We have discussed this subject throughout the preceding chapters, but we want to review some of the critical supervisory influences on personal relations.

Closeness of Supervision

The closeness of supervision has an important effect on productivity and morale. Mann and Dent found that supervisors of low-producing units supervise very closely, while high-producing supervisors exercise only general supervision. It was found that the low-producing supervisors:

- o check on employees more frequently
- o give more detailed and frequent instructions
- o limit employee's freedom to do job in own way.

Workers who felt less closely supervised reported that they were better satisfied with their jobs and the company. We should note that the manner or attitude of the supervisor has an important bearing on whether employees perceive supervision as being close or general.

These findings are another way of saying that supervision does not mean standing over the employee and telling him what to do and when and how to do it. The more effective supervisor tells his employees what is required, giving general instructions.

COMMUNICATION

Supervisors of high-production units consider communication as one of the most important aspects of their job. Effective communication is used by these supervisors to achieve better interpersonal relations and improved employee motivation. Low-production supervisors do not rate communication as highly important.

High-producing supervisors find that an important aid to more effective communication is listening. They are ready to listen to both personal problems or interests and questions about the work. This does not mean that they are *nosey* or meddle in their employees' personal lives, but rather that they show a willingness to listen, and do listen, if their employees wish to discuss problems.

These supervisors inform employees about forthcoming changes in work; they discuss agency policy with employees; and they make sure that each employee knows how well he is doing. What these supervisors do is use two-way communication effectively. Unless the supervisor freely imparts information, he will not receive information in return.

Attitudes and perception are frequently affected by communication or the lack of it. Research surveys reveal that many supervisors are not aware of their employees' attitudes, nor do they know what personal reactions their supervision arouses. Through frank discussions with employees, they have been surprised to discover employee beliefs about which they were ignorant. Discussion sometimes reveals that the supervisor and his employees have totally different impressions about the same event. The supervisor should be constantly on the alert for misconceptions about his words and deeds. He must remember that, although his actions are perfectly clear to himself, they may be, and frequently are, viewed differently by employees.

Failure to communicate information results in misconceptions and false assumptions. What you say and how you say it will strongly affect your employees' attitudes and perceptions. By giving them available information you can prevent misconceptions; by discussion, you may be able to change attitudes; by questioning; you can discover what the perceptions and assumptions really are. And it need hardly be added that actions should conform very closely to words.

If we were to attempt to reduce the above discussion on communication to rules, we would have a long list which would be based on one cardinal principle: Don't make assumptions!

- o Don't assume that your employees know; tell them.
- o Don't assume that you know how they feel; find out.
- o Don't assume that they understand; clarify.

20 SUPERVISORY HINTS

1. Avoid inconsistency.
2. Always give employees a chance to explain their actions before taking disciplinary action. Don't allow too much time for a "cooling off" period before disciplining an employee.
3. Be specific in your criticisms.
4. Delegate responsibility wisely.
5. Do not argue or lose your temper, and avoid being impatient.
6. Promote mutual respect and be fair, impartial and open-minded.
7. Keep in mind that asking for employees' advice and input can be helpful in decision making.
8. If you make promises, keep them.
9. Always keep the feelings, abilities, dignity and motives of your staff in mind.
10. Remain loyal to your employees' interests.
11. Never criticize employees in front of others, or treat employees like children.
12. Admit mistakes. Don't place blame on your employees, or make excuses.
13. Be reasonable in your expectations, give complete instructions, and establish well-planned goals.
14. Be knowledgeable about office details and procedures, but avoid becoming bogged down in details.
15. Avoid supervising too closely or too loosely. Employees should also view you as an approachable supervisor.
16. Remember that employees' personal problems may affect job performance, but become involved only when appropriate.
17. Work to develop workers, and to instill a feeling of cooperation while working toward mutual goals.
18. Do not overpraise or underpraise, be properly appreciative.
19. Never ask an employee to discipline someone for you.
20. A complaint, even if unjustified, should be taken seriously.

BASIC PRINCIPLES OF UNDERSTANDING WILDLIFE

CONTENTS

Introduction 1

Basic Principles for Understanding Wildlife 3
- Habitat 4
- Interspersion 4
- Niche 5
- Territory 5
- Limiting Factor 5
- Population Dynamics 6

Project Activities 7
- Record Keeping 7
- Observing Wildlife 7

Habitat Improvement 9
- Planting 9
- Fence Row Planting 10
- Where to Get Shrubs and Trees 11
- Improvement of Existing Habitat 11
- Brush Piles and Rock Dens 12
- Water Holes and Ponds 13

Building Houses, Feeders, and Baths 13
- Houses 13
- Bird Feeders 18
- Sheet Metal Predator Guards 21

Squirrel, Raccoon, and Goose Nests 22

Preserving Animal Sign 24

Photography 26
- General Suggestions 26
- Photographs of Animals 27

Mapping 28

Census Methods 30
- Map Census 32
- Strip Census 32
- Drive Census 33
- Special Census Techniques 33
- Marked Animals 33

Additional Activities 34

Introduction

This project describes some basic principles of wildlife and some things you can do to study it.

What is wildlife? Most people think only of furred and feathered creatures when "wildlife" is mentioned. But in fact all creatures not tamed or domesticated are wildlife. This includes reptiles, amphibians, crustaceans, insects, spiders, and fish, as well as birds and mammals. The same ecological principles apply to all, so in learning about one animal we may come to understand many.

For many years man's interest in wildlife was limited to those animals he killed for food or clothing, to protect himself, or for recreation. We now recognize that all wild creatures have value.

Wildlife can be found everywhere; you do not need a forest or a marsh. "Waste" areas are often very rich in wildlife. The best place to begin the study of wildlife is any place convenient enough for you to go there often. When you have developed your skills and understanding in places near your home, you will be able to make the most of a field trip to woods or marsh.

If the activities in this project do not describe exactly the kinds of wildlife you would like to study, you can adapt the procedures to suit your needs. Also, most of the references mentioned in the project contain a wealth of detailed information or additional activities.

Left, chipmunks become accustomed to humans and can be studied at close range. Middle, the frog can be found nearly everywhere; study species convenient to you. Right, nesting studies must be done carefully to avoid driving the birds away.

ENVIRONMENTAL AWARENESS:

Wildlife

Basic Principles for Understanding Wildlife

All wildlife species must have certain basic things, and they must have them all year around. They need food to eat, water to drink, and cover or shelter to protect them from weather and from enemies. They also need a certain amount of living space.

This living space, which you may think of as "elbow room" or "personal space" is an area in which an animal will tolerate few if any animals of its own kind.

This area may be a few square feet for a field mouse, or a few thousand acres for a bear. Requirements for each species will be different, but whatever the requirements are for a certain species, **all four** must be met in an area or the species will not exist in that area.

To use a simple example: even if there were more than enough water, living space, and shelter you wouldn't expect to find deer living in an area that had no food. Many wildlife species have special ways of meeting their four basic needs. For example, in order to avoid a winter scarcity of food, some animals hibernate, others migrate to where there is enough food, and others store food. Some are independent of ponds and streams because they get enough water from dew or from their food.

Wildlife habitat is an area that provides the food, water, shelter and living space necessary to sustain a population of any wildlife species.

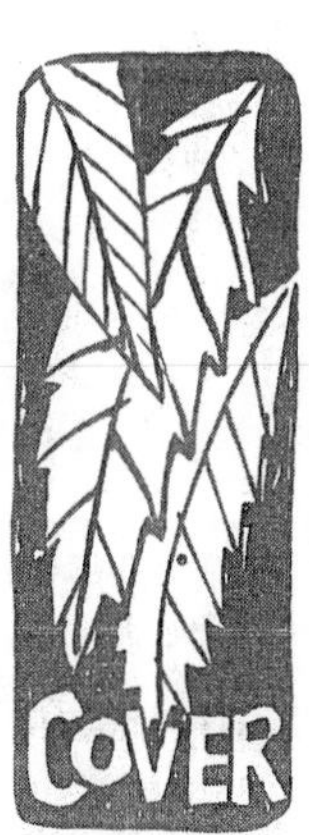

An edge between the field and forest.
Edges support high populations of wildlife species.

vegetation, such as trees taking over what was an open field, is an example of changing habitat. Natural changes affect carrying capacity the same as do changes made by man. If the population is greater than the carrying capacity, the excess animals will die or leave.

NICHE

Each species fills a slightly different place in nature, or "niche" (rhymes with "ditch"). Even though a chipmunk and a cottontail rabbit live on the same plot of ground, they don't eat the same foods, and therefore occupy different niches. Any difference in food, nesting behavior, etc. means the niche is different. Niches of two species may be similar, but are hardly ever the same.

TERRITORY

Many animals "own" a territory at certain times. This is an area, usually right around the home or nest, which the animal will defend against members of its own species and, occasionally, other species. Many birds share the tree in which they nest with birds of other species, but chase off any of their own kind. If a male pheasant defends a territory of three acres and you have a six acre field, you will have only two male pheasants no matter how much food, water, and shelter are available. In this case, living space is the limiting factor.

LIMITING FACTOR

The need — food, water, shelter or living space — that is in shortest supply and therefore prevents the wildlife population from getting larger is the **limiting factor.** In our example of deer, food was the limiting factor on the deer population. If a large farm has grain crops (food), ponds (water) plenty of space, but no hedgerows or other "waste" areas, what is the limiting factor on the pheasant population? Shelter, (cover) of course, since there are few hiding places. In this case the population will be kept on a low level because few young will hatch (few places to nest) and there will be increased mortality (death) from predators and bad weather.

Limiting factors are very important to wildlife management. If you want to increase the pheasant population, you have to know what is holding the population down. If it is lack of shelter, providing more food won't help.

Sometimes the population is below carrying capacity because of reasons that are difficult to discover: disease, parasites, excessive rainfall, etc.

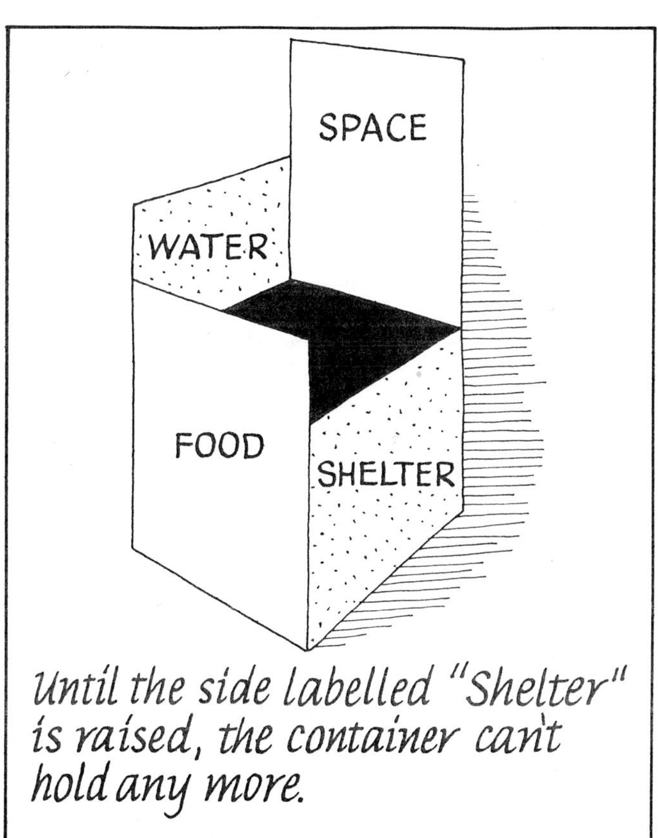

Until the side labelled "Shelter" is raised, the container can't hold any more.

Project Activities

There are a great many activities for you in a wildlife project. You can improve habitat, observe wildlife, make maps, take photographs, preserve animal sign, do research on a specific animal, conduct a community campaign to benefit wildlife, teach people about wildlife, or many other things. Only a few of these things are described in this project booklet. Read through the activities described in the following pages and choose the ones you like. If you need other activities, use your imagination to adapt these activities to meet your needs.

RECORD-KEEPING

Regardless of what activities you choose, you should keep a record of everything you do. **Don't** wait until you're finished with an activity before you sit down to write about it! A good field ecologist (a wildlife student like yourself is a field ecologist) always records observations as they are made. Best for this purpose is a pocket-sized, bound notebook; and a pen with waterproof ink, carried with you and **used** every time you go to the field or work on your project indoors. A loose-leaf notebook written in pencil will be satisfactory, but you will be tempted to make changes in what you've written. **Never** change field notes; if you change your mind, make an additional entry but leave the original.

This project has no forms or blanks to be filled in as you proceed. At some time in the future you will probably want to write a report on your project, either for a school science project, for a 4-H award trip, or for some other purpose. If you don't have good records you'll wish you did, so start your records when you start your project. Your records needn't be complicated; think of them as a scientific diary. Make them clear, concise, and to the point, and they will be useful to you later.

OBSERVING WILDLIFE

Observing wildlife is more than just looking at animals: observing means perceiving, noticing, or watching. You are observing wildlife when you use your ears or nose to determine something about an animal and, strictly speaking, you are observing wildlife when you perceive by interpreting animal sign.

Practice and experience will make you more skillful at observation, just as practice and experience make you better at basketball or playing the piano. This section of the Wildlife Project contains suggestions that will make your wildlife observation easier and more successful.

Keep the following points in mind when observing wildlife:

Use your knowledge of wildlife to assist you. If you're trying to observe a particular species, learn all you can about it before you go afield, then concentrate on the most likely places. If you're out to observe wildlife in general, remember that during the reduced light of dawn and dusk more species are active than during midday. Also, remember that increased animal populations occur around edges where food, water, and shelter are nearby.

Be safe. Tell someone where you will be and when you plan to return. If in an unfamiliar area carry a U.S.G.S. map and a compass and learn to use them both. During hunting season wear a bright orange jacket and hat.

Be inconspicuous — wear dull-colored clothing (except in hunting season). Don't make more noise or movement than necessary.

Be patient. Look carefully for animal sign as well as for animals.

Be comfortable. Apply and carry insect repellent. Proper clothing is important. If you plan to be sitting still in cool or cold weather, wear extra warm clothing. Durable shoes or boots and denim or similar clothing can ward off the effects of rocky terrain and thick underbrush. Use adequate rain-gear—being soaked is no fun.

Keep checking wind direction. Animals downwind are more likely to detect you; they will do their best to remain unseen.

Remember that nearly everything out doors is a home for something. If you lift a rock to look for a salamander, replace it exactly as it was. Never disrupt or destroy anything needlessly.

Use binoculars if possible. With them you won't need to get as close and risk scaring the animal away.

Habitat Improvement

Habitat improvement can be anything from building birdhouses for a yard or park to planting shrubs and building ponds on a farm or other large area. Remember limiting factors. Try to provide what is in short supply in the area you are improving. Make a plan or map of your habitat improvement activities.

PLANTING

Planting of trees, shrubs, and herbaceous (non woody) plants is one of the best ways to improve wildlife habitat because plants, carefully selected with wildlife in mind, provide food, shelter, and resting places year after year with no further assistance from you. To find out what species will grow in the climate of your region, contact the Soil Conservation Service office in your area.

HOUSE LOT PLANTING. Owners of suburban house lots frequently can devote a back corner to wildlife plantings with spectacular results. Some (but unfortunately not many) people plan the landscaping of their entire lot with both wildlife and appearance in mind. The illustration shows one example of the many types of trees, shrubs, and annuals that may be used. Incidentally, lawn grass alone is useful to almost no wildlife species.

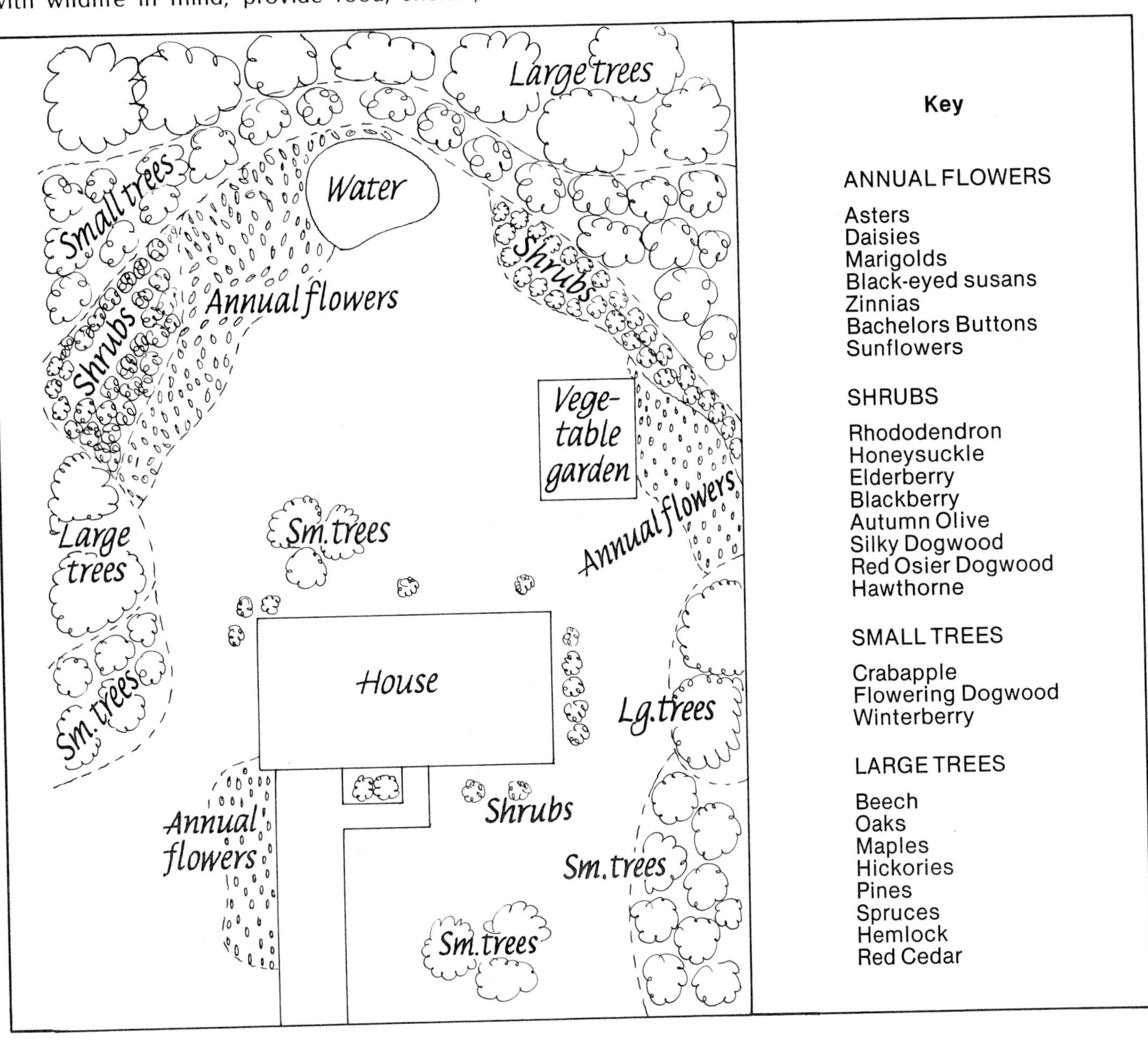

Key

ANNUAL FLOWERS

Asters
Daisies
Marigolds
Black-eyed susans
Zinnias
Bachelors Buttons
Sunflowers

SHRUBS

Rhododendron
Honeysuckle
Elderberry
Blackberry
Autumn Olive
Silky Dogwood
Red Osier Dogwood
Hawthorne

SMALL TREES

Crabapple
Flowering Dogwood
Winterberry

LARGE TREES

Beech
Oaks
Maples
Hickories
Pines
Spruces
Hemlock
Red Cedar

WHERE TO GET SHRUBS AND TREES

You can purchase plants from garden stores or nurseries, but there are less expensive sources. Shrubs and trees for wildlife are available at a very low cost from many state conservation departments. Normally they must be ordered several months in advance and picked up in spring for planting. For information on this program contact the Soil Conservation Service Office or conservation department office in your area.

You can propagate your own shrubs by layering, grafting, or making cuttings from existing shrubs. Some shrubs can be raised from seed. Your Cooperative Extension Service office should be able to provide information on this subject.

Shrubs can be transplanted. Be sure you don't destroy the habitat in one area to improve another. Dig shrubs only from an area of plentiful shrubbery where natural reproduction is occurring.

PLANTING TECHNIQUES. There is more to transplanting than digging them up in one place and putting them in a hole somewhere else. Following are general guidelines. For further information ask at your area Cooperative Extension Service office.

1. Transplant only small trees and shrubs. bigger transplants suffer from root injury and even if they survive may take a long time to recover.
2. Transplant in spring before the buds start to grow. If you must transplant in fall, wait until leaves have fallen, and protect transplanted shrubs from winter winds. Evergreens can be transplanted earlier in fall and later in spring than deciduous shrubs (shrubs that lose their leaves in winter).
3. Always keep the roots moist.
4. Evergreen plants require a ball of earth around the roots when you move them. Deciduous plants can be transplanted without a root ball ("bare root"), but if possible you should let some soil cling to roots.

The following recommendations apply to planting shrubs and trees only a few inches tall, which is what you will have if you grow your own from seed or from cuttings, or if you order from your state conservation department. Planting large shrubs takes time and is more difficult but results are seen sooner. You may wish to intersperse a few larger shrubs with your planting of seedling shrubs.

For small transplants it is especially important to remove sod, grass, and weeds within a foot of where you will put each plant. This allows the new shrub to get a head start without being crowded.

Plant the shrubs very soon after receiving them or if you grew your own, very soon after digging them. If you are unable to do this, find a shady place to "heel them in". This is done by digging a trench deep enough to cover the roots of the plants and temporarily planting the whole bunch together to ensure that the roots will not dry out. Planting can then be done as time becomes available. When planting, use the following steps:

1. Space shrubs two feet apart, trees and autumn olive, six feet.
2. Strike blade of mattock or grub hoe full depth into the ground.
3. Open slit or hole.
4. Place plant with roots spread into hole and tamp firmly with heel.

If a mattock or grub hoe is not available, use a shovel or spade. It is important that the roots be covered before they dry out and also that earth be packed firmly around them. Carrying the seedlings from hole to hole in a pail of water will keep the roots from drying out.

Apply fertilizer in a ring around each shrub or tree. Do not over-fertilize, and be sure that you do not fertilize the weeds surrounding the plant. If possible, water each transplant soon after planting.

IMPROVEMENT OF EXISTING HABITAT

Often there is a great deal that can be done with the vegetation already existing on the land.

In nature, vegetation goes through a process called succession. For example, a bare field soon grows up with grass and weeds. This is followed in a few years by shrubs, then a few (perhaps many) years later by trees, and then perhaps many decades later by a different kind of tree. By controlling this process of succession you can benefit wildlife. This is because one stage of succession may be better for wildlife than the stage that follows it.

SLASH CUTTING. Deer normally are browsers: they eat twigs and buds from shrubs and trees. In the winter this is nearly 100% of their diet.

Thus deer need an early successional stage,

ile. Small branches should be laid on last.

"Living brush piles" can be created by cutting unwanted trees or large bushes halfway through, then pulling them down in a crisscross fashion. If a strip of bark remains on at least one side of each tree, it will continue to live, and grow into a tangle, providing much shelter.

Rock dens are simply rock piles carefully constructed to provide shelter. Use larger rocks to shape tunnels and interior chambers, then pile smaller rocks and sod or brush over the top. Keep in mind the principle of interspersion; these dens will be most useful if they are near food and water.

WATER HOLES AND PONDS

Most animals need water at least once a day. If they must travel very far, the population will remain small — in this case water is the limiting factor.

You can get advice on building ponds from the Soil Conservation Service office in your county. Usually some expense is involved, but you may be able to build a small water hole for very little if you have a low, soggy area on your property.

Larger ponds provide swimming, fishing, and boating as well as nesting sites for wildlife, so the investment may be worthwhile.

Building Houses, Feeders, and Baths

You can improve wildlife habitat by building nesting or den sites, watering places, and feeding places. In addition to helping animals and birds, you may cause them to come near enough to watch from your window.

The instructions on the following pages will give you some ideas. Other plans and descriptions can be found in books and publications available from the Cooperative Extension Service, The Audubon Society, your library, and other organizations.

Most popular are bird houses, feeders, or baths. The principles of bird house construction can be applied to den sites for squirrels, raccoons, or other hole-inhabitating animals. And, when you build a bird feeder or bird bath you will probably be feeding and watering other animals as well as birds.

HOUSES

Don't forget that when you build a bird house you are providing a nesting site only for birds that nest in holes. Most birds need shrubs, trees, or fields to nest; good wildlife habitat has places for many kinds of animals.

A well-built house for birds should be durable, rainproof, cool, and readily accessible for cleaning. Wood is the best building material. Sawmill waste (rough slabs with bark on) is cheap and satisfactory for most purposes.

Bird houses will last much longer if they are painted. Dark green, brown, gray, or other dull colors are best. Do not paint the inside, and avoid painting the inside of the entrance hole. Roofs should have enough slant to make water run off quickly.

Since entrance holes for bird houses are usually made near the top, the inside of the house should be roughened, grooved, or cleated to assist the young in climbing to the opening. A perch at the en-

Small clumps of shrubs can produce a substantial increase in wildlife populations.

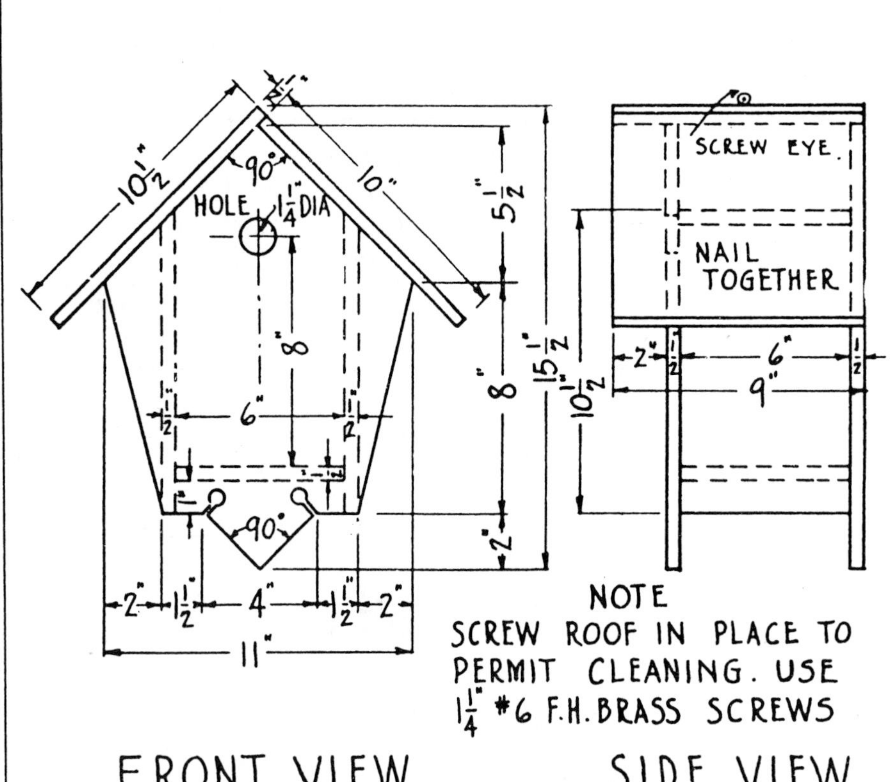

FOR BLUE BIRD

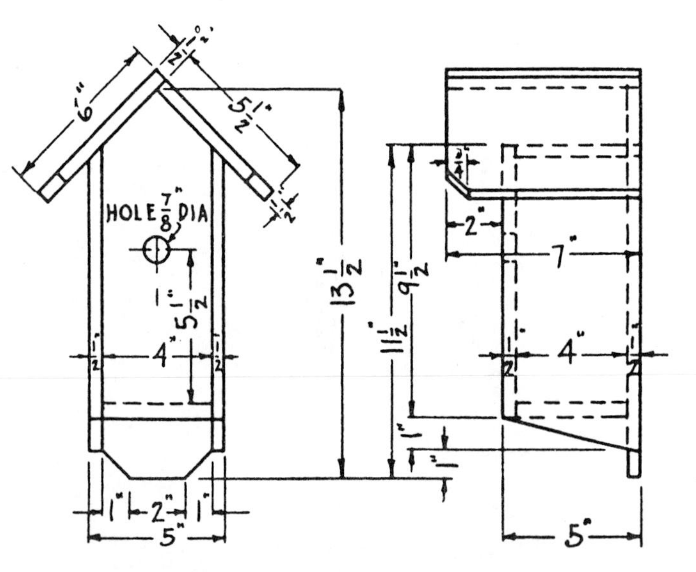

WREN HOUSE

IRD FEEDERS

ome bird feeders are merely board platforms ·here foods are placed and others are fancy, deluxe 1odels. Some type between these extremes is pro-ably best. In any case there are certain rules which 1ould be followed with any feeding station.

1. For best results it should be set up in the fall before cold weather sets in. Feeding stations are most effective and most used in winter months.
2. Once established, you should keep food available at all times and never let the food supply run out until spring. Birds will depend on it after they have been using it for only a short time.
3. Any platform type feeder where you are offering seeds and grains should be roofed and protected from rain and snow so that the food will stay dry and not spoil.
4. A feeding station should be made cat-proof if it is on a post, pole, or tree.
5. The station should be fairly close to the house, so you can enjoy watching the birds and also keep a check on the food supply.
6. It will be more effective if it is located near some kind of escape cover such as bushes or shrubs.

These same brushes and shrubs, however, will llow cats to hide near the feeder and easily kill nany birds that come to the ground. To avoid this, lace a wire screen fence around the base of any earby shrub that could provide concealment for a at.

There are a great many foods which birds will at from your feeding station. A wide variety of oods will get you a greater variety of birds. Mix-ures of cracked corn, millet, wheat, and sunflower eeds are always acceptable. Add to this some neats of walnuts or hickory nuts, peanuts or peanut utter, some raisins or cut up apples. Left over corn-read is an excellent and attractive food for most vintering birds. Avoid feeding anything spoiled. If ood becomes moldy or rotten, take it out of the eeder.

In the same feeder or a nearby, separate eeder, offer sand or other gritty materials to the irds. Birds have no teeth and use sand in their stomachs to grind food. Many birds killed by cars in winter were forced to go to the roads for sand.

Placing food under or near a platform feeder will attract some species of birds which will not use the elevated feeding station. Doves appreciate an offering of this type and will be joined at times by birds which normally don't feed on the ground.

Probably the easiest established and certainly one of the most effective bird feeding stations is a suet feeder. Beef suet (similar to but not the same as fat) can be attached to the trunk or low limb of a tree and will provide much needed energy-producing food during the cold of winter. It is attractive to woodpeckers, titmice, nuthatches, and many other birds. A large chunk of suet wrapped in one inch-mesh wire and firmly attached to a tree trunk makes a good bird feeder. The wire mesh will deter cats and raccoons — animals which will completely destroy a less sturdy suet feeder.

If left up during the summer, you may be treated to the sight of a brood of young birds brought there by their parents. In summer, however, suet may smell bad and you may have to move the feeder away from the house.

Hummingbirds drink nectar and eat small insects they find in flowers. They migrate south in winter, but a special feeder set up in the spring may attract them through the entire summer.

Hummingbird feeders and food tablets may be purchased at many garden supply or other stores. Homemade feeders and food mixtures work just as well. To make a food mixture, dissolve one tablespoon of sugar or honey in two tablespoons of water. **Never** make it too strong, as this may kill the birds. If you mix a larger batch in the 1:2 ratio and store it for later use, be sure to keep it in the refrigerator.

An easy feeder to make is simply a small pill bottle or vial fastened at an angle to a small pole or hung from a bush 2-5 feet from the ground. Red is attractive to hummingbirds, so cut a red "flower" from such material as an old plastic detergent bottle and place it around the opening of the vial. Fill the vial with the solution, and change it periodically to keep it from spoiling. Whether you use a commercial feeder or a homemade feeder you may need to place a ring of petroleum jelly around the pole to keep the ants away. Frequent cleaning may be necessary for any hummingbird feeder, especially in hot weather.

The plans on the following pages will give you further ideas on building feeders.

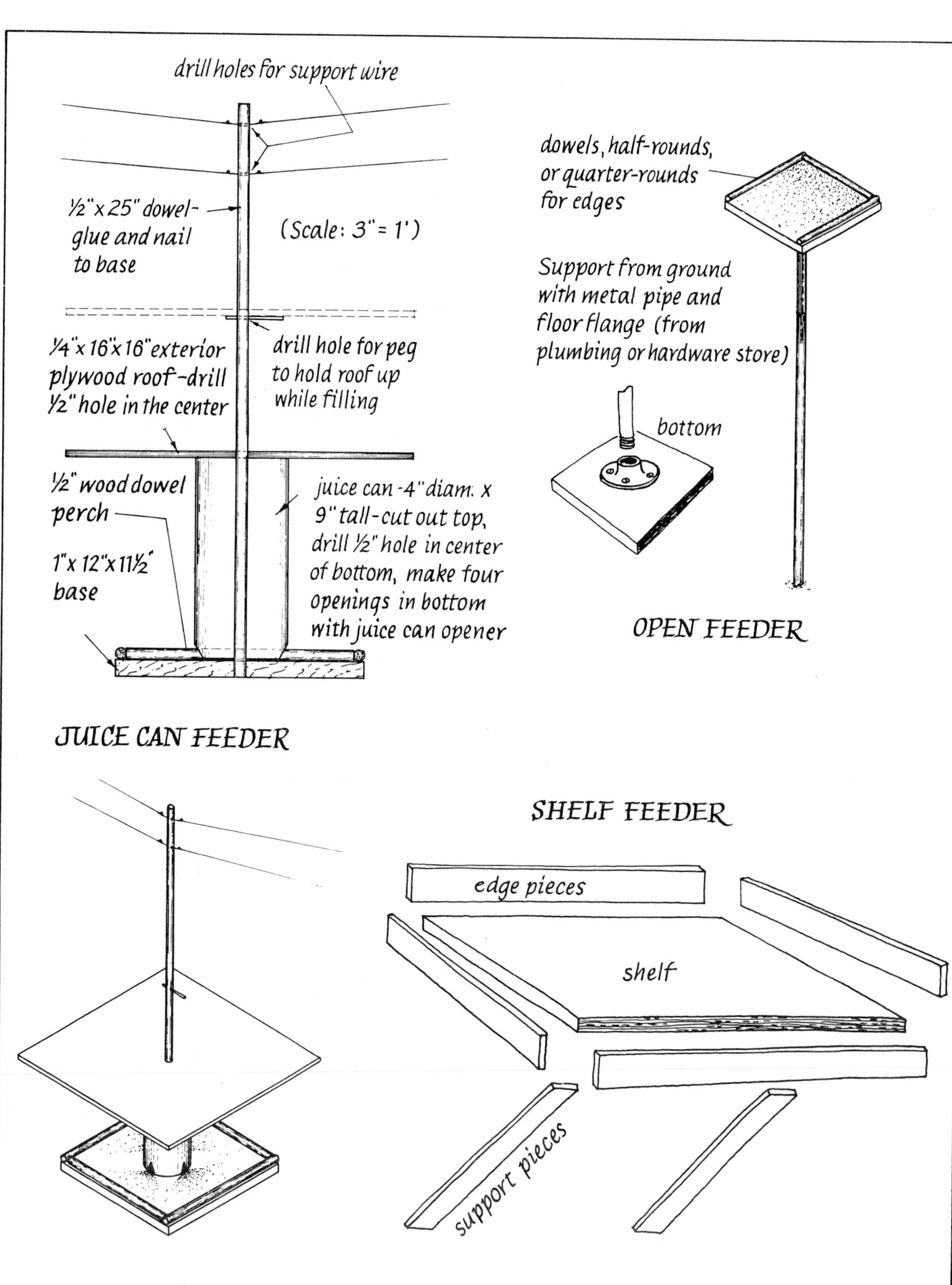
drill holes for support wire
½"x 25" dowel-
glue and nail
to base
(Scale: 3" = 1')
¼"x 16"x 16" exterior
plywood roof-drill
½" hole in the center
drill hole for peg
to hold roof up
while filling
½" wood dowel
perch
1"x 12"x 11½"
base
juice can-4" diam. x
9" tall-cut out top,
drill ½" hole in center
of bottom, make four
openings in bottom
with juice can opener
JUICE CAN FEEDER
dowels, half-rounds,
or quarter-rounds
for edges
Support from ground
with metal pipe and
floor flange (from
plumbing or hardware store)
bottom
OPEN FEEDER
SHELF FEEDER
edge pieces
shelf
support pieces

SHEET METAL PREDATOR GUARDS

Birdhouses or bird feeding stations attached to poles should be placed where squirrels, cats, or other unwelcome guests cannot leap from overhanging or nearby roofs or branches.

Also, guards should be placed on the pole beneath the feeder or house to prevent climbing from the ground.

You can make two kinds of guards. One type is a piece of tin wrapped around the pole and nailed to it. Animals will not be able to get a grip on the tin and cannot climb the pole. The other kind is a flaring piece of metal that looks like a lampshade and is a barrier the predator cannot pass.

A bird bath is used for both bathing and drinking, and is an interesting and entertaining addition to bird study in the summer. Birds will also come to a bird bath in winter if you use an electric heat tape to keep it from freezing.

A bird bath should be fairly large, shallow and easy to clean. It may be a store-bought bath mounted on a pillar, or half of an old truck tire placed on the ground. Be sure there is open space around the bath so that birds are safe from cats while they are bathing or drinking. A garbage can lid may be set on three or four posts of equal height, or a large upended drain tile. A flat rock in the lid will give it stability as well as provide a choice of water depth while bathing. In any case never allow the bird bath to dry out. Similar structures containing sand and dust may become very popular with birds.

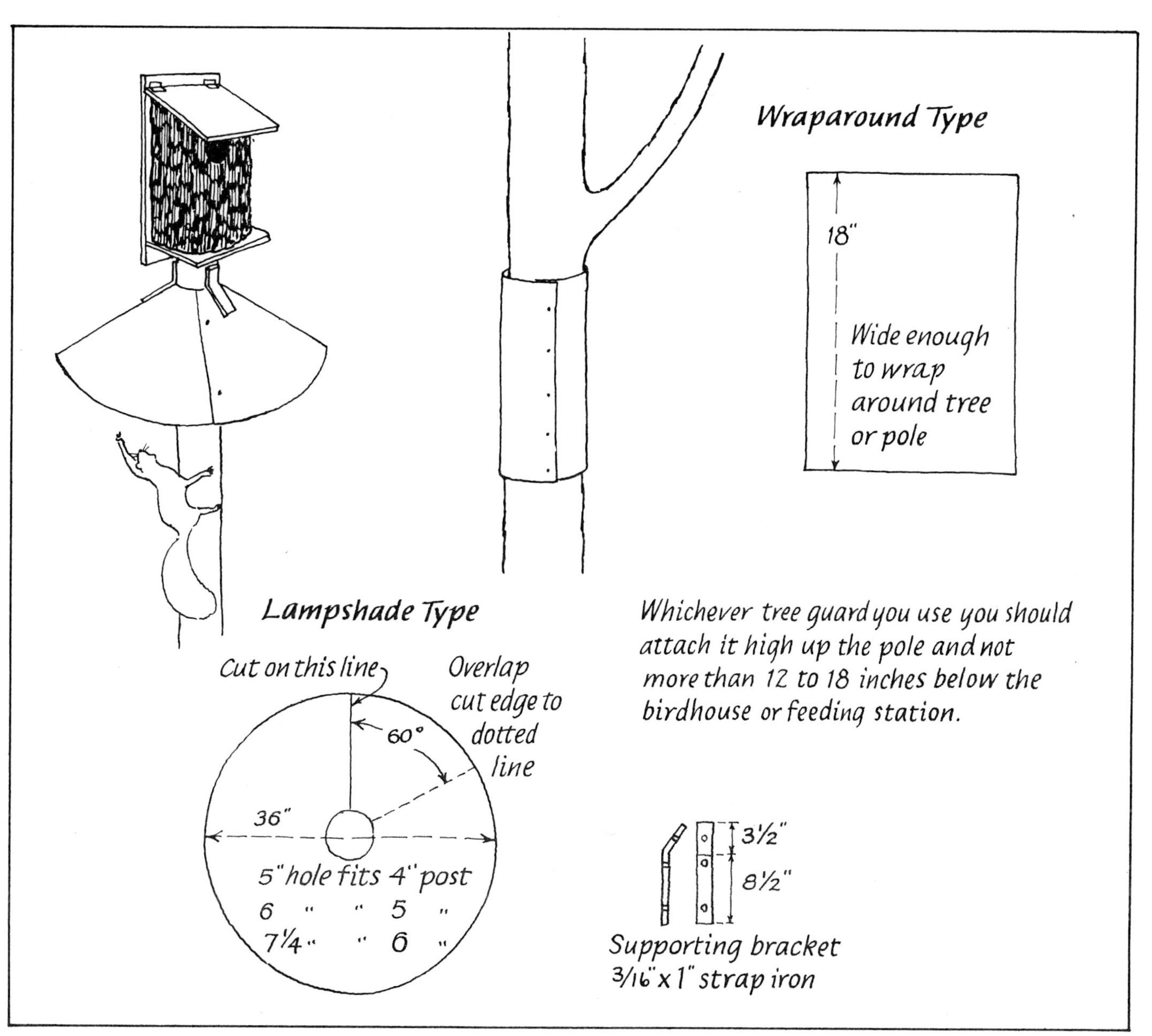

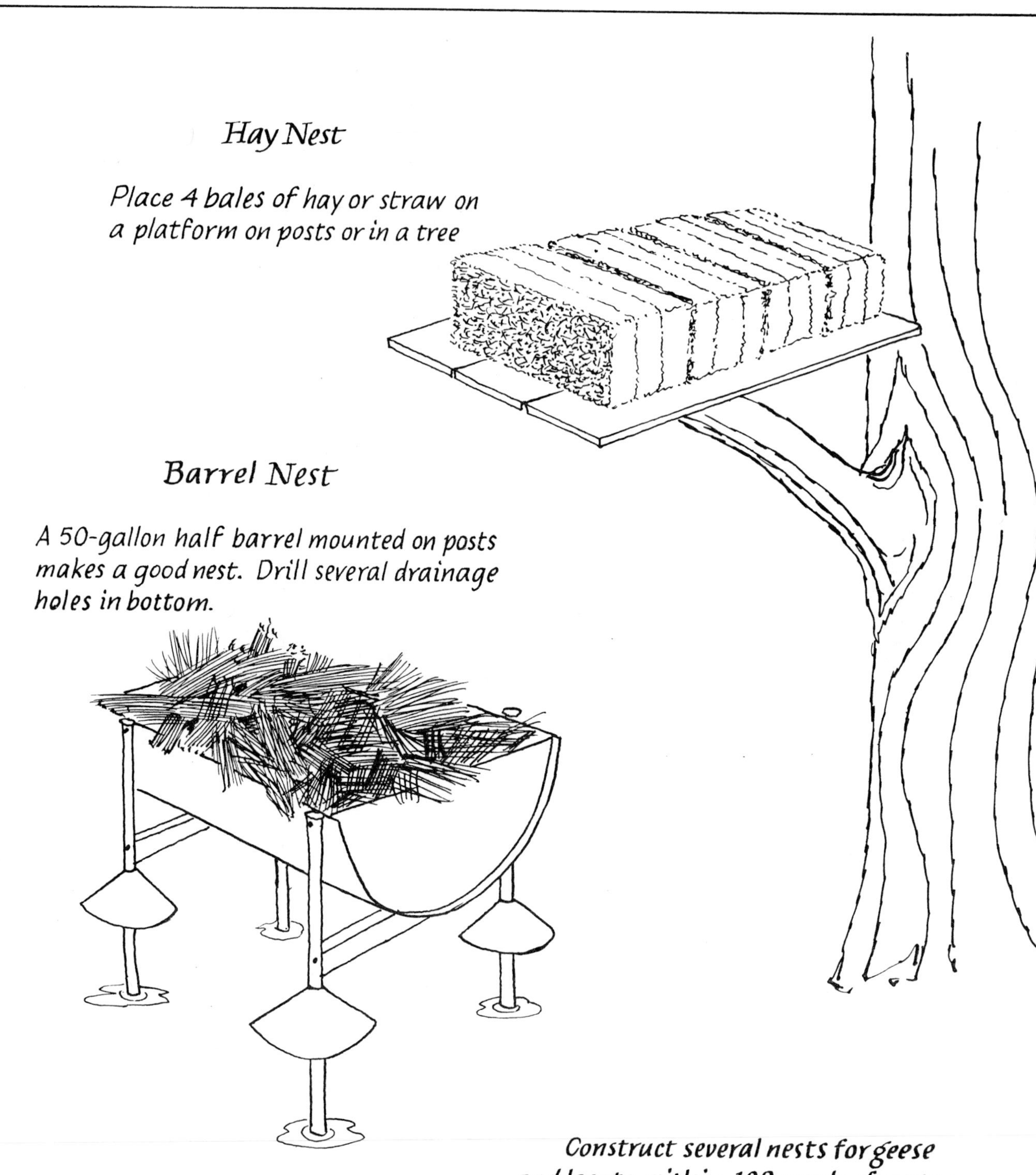

Construct several nests for geese and locate within 100 yards of water, or on posts in shallow water. Establish the nests no later than March 1. Several kinds of nests may be used to determine the most acceptable type.

Nests should be located a few feet above the ground, or if on the ground on an elevated site. Do not place nests closer than 100 yards apart.

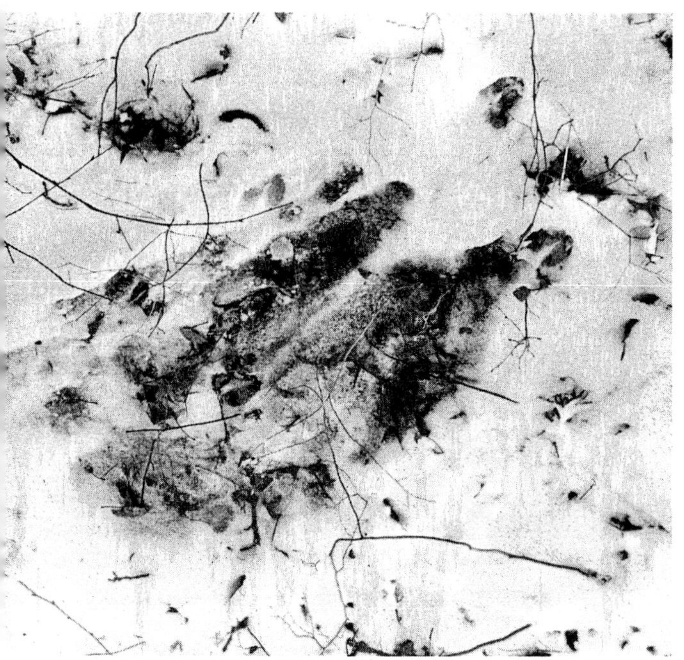

When deer bed down in snow they leave a distinctive mark. Photographs are the best means to record impressions in the snow.

When hard, take off the cardboard and separate the negative and positive casts with care. The positive cast is a duplicate of the original track.

Other tips:

After you gain experience, you will no longer need to measure. You can tell by the look and feel when the mixture is right — about the same as melted ice cream.

Materials other than plaster can be used to advantage. Paraffin as a negative for example, is easily removed from a plaster positive (by melting).

You may not need the cardboard strips if you can improvise earth dams for the plaster.

Carry materials in a knapsack with you in the field just as a photographer would carry a camera....just in case.

Make a "track pit," which is simply an area prepared especially for getting tracks. In a promising location (across a known wildlife trail, near a den, etc.) find a spot with fine sandy soil or other soil with suitable texture for good tracks. Dig it up — clean off all leaves, rocks, and other debris. Moisten if necessary and smooth with a board or broom. Make plaster impressions as soon as possible after tracks are made, since tracks may lose their sharpness when they dry. Some species can be attracted to a track pit with peanuts, apples, or other bait.

PHOTOGRAPHS OF ANIMALS

If you have ever tried to photograph wild animals, you already know that it is not easy. You will need a good deal of patience regardless of the technique you use.

Some animals, such as reptiles and amphibians, can be captured, photographed in a natural setting, then released. For others, such as some birds and small mammals, you can use food to coax them in close to you. For other animals and other techniques, you will need varying amounts of patience and equipment combined with stalking and "engineering" skills.

Blinds, described in the section on observing wildlife, are very useful. A good place for a blind is near a bird feeder.

If you have a tripod (or can devise some means of holding your camera still) and a way of releasing the shutter by remote control, you can put your camera where you expect the animal to be. Watch from a place of concealment some distance away and, when the animal is in the right place, take the picture. You may be able to devise a way to have an animal take its own picture.

For some cameras you can purchase remote control devices. Or you can use the diagrams shown here for ideas on how to make one for your camera and equipment. A flash will be useful since many animals are active at night.

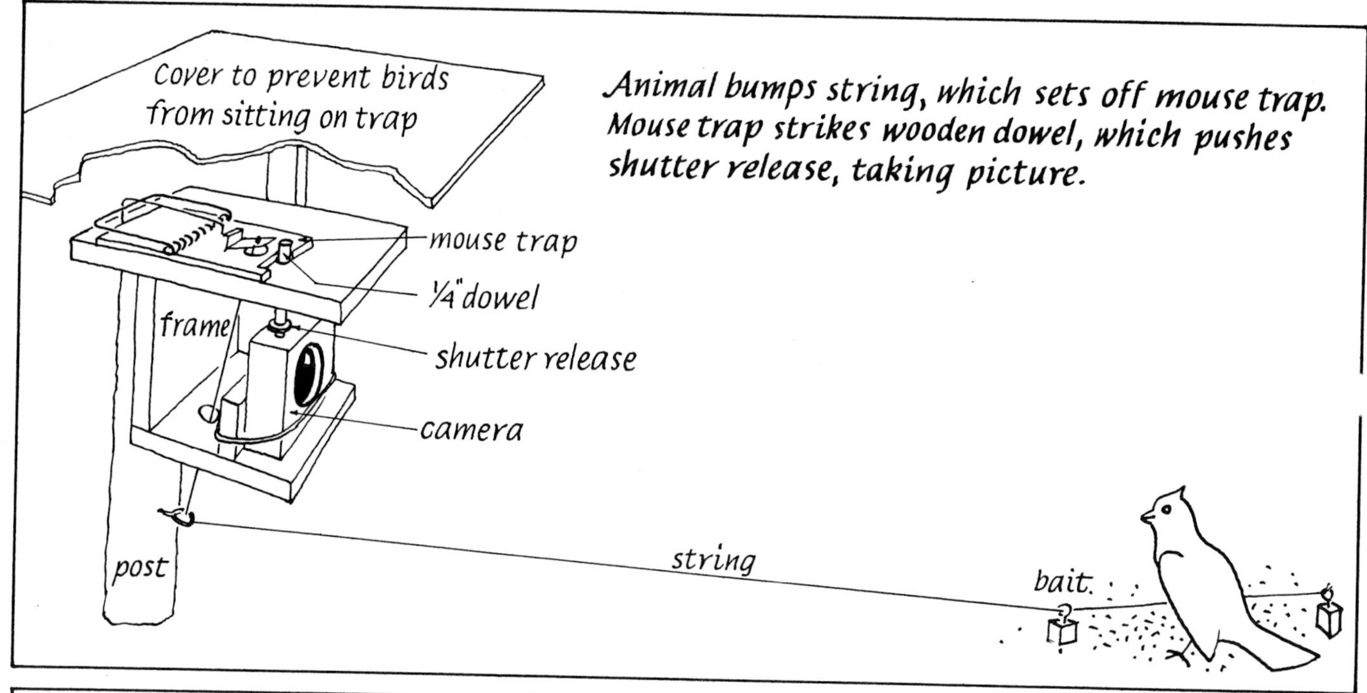

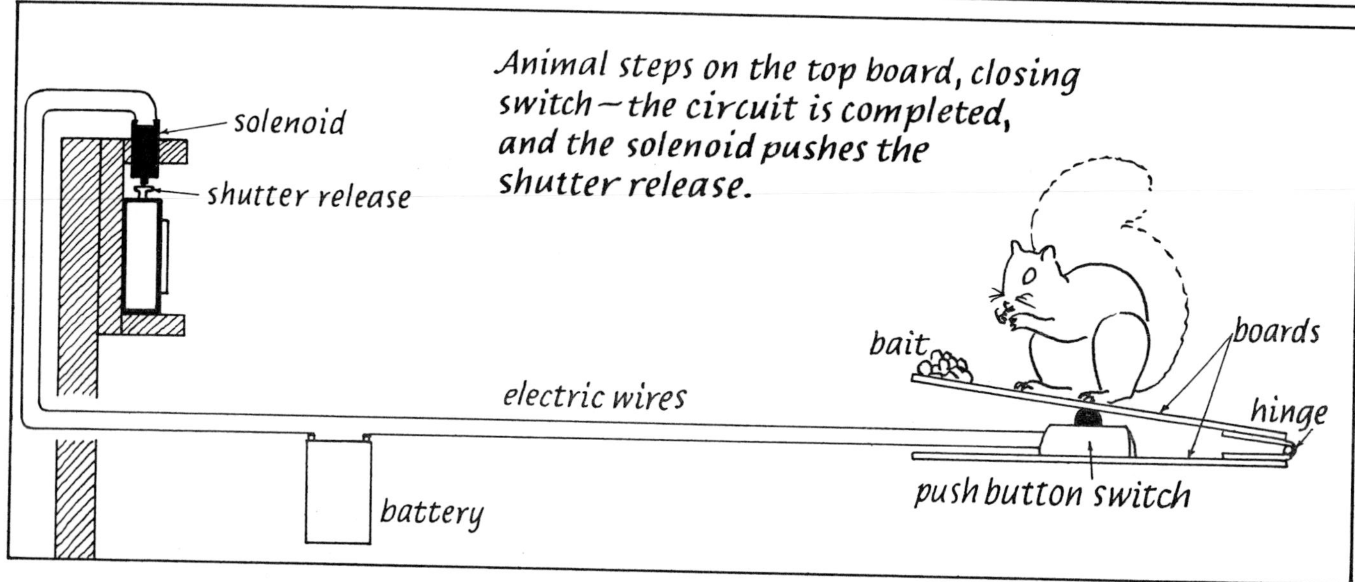

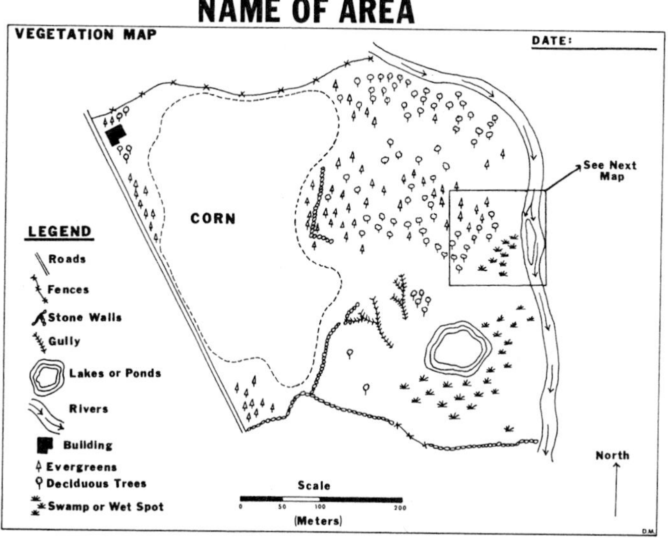

Large scale map

NAME OF AREA

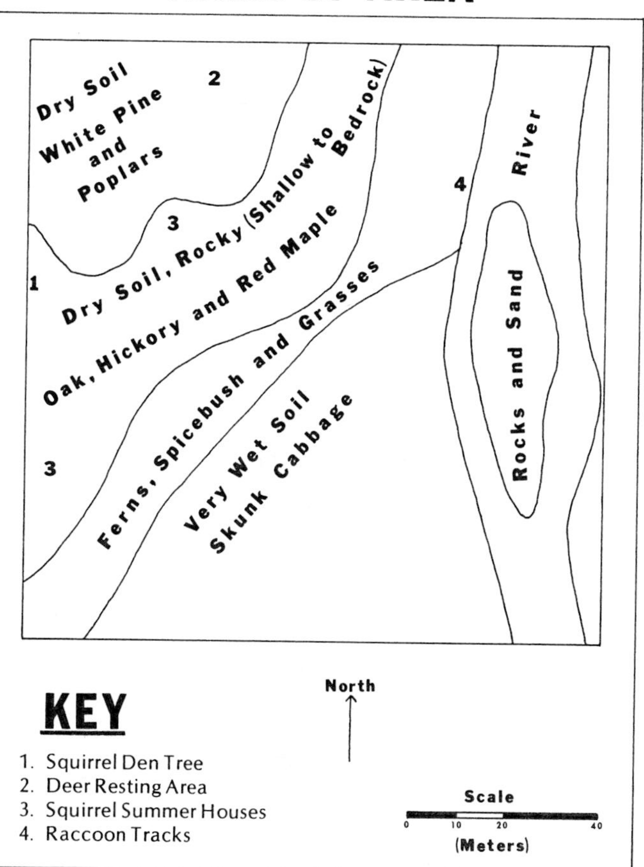

the route you walked. The map can be keyed to your field notebook.

You can map different aspects of your study area, such as depth of snow, amount of rainfall, wind speed, temperature variation, plant species distribution, soil types, habitat types, home ranges of various animals, nests, and so on. Many investigations will require that you look in science books, 4-H projects or other sources to learn how to set up your own measuring devices.

As part of this wildlife project you should look at each aspect of the area as a part of wildlife's environment. You should try to understand how each may have an effect on wildlife, and perhaps determine how wildlife distribution is affected by what you have discovered.

Large scale maps (i.e. 1:100) show more detail than small scale maps, and can be very useful. For example, the sample vegetation map shows a small area of woods and marsh.

A wildlifer like yourself sees much more, however, and can indicate additional information about the same area on a map of larger scale. For example, see the sample large scale map of the same area of woods and marsh. Using such a map will allow you to display much more detailed information about specific habitat resources and needs.

Wildlife and other observations can be recorded on large-scale maps very accurately, giving specific locations of nests, and animals of small home range such as shrews.

The uses of maps are limitless. They will help you learn about wildlife and help you tell others about your activities. Maps are a very useful part of an exhibit, or demonstration, or talk on your wildlife project.

total population. In the case of the woodchucks, you sampled a ten-acre field and found three burrows. Since the total hayfield acreage is 10 times as large as your sample, the total woodchuck population will be 10 times as large as your sample. You can set up an equation to solve mathematics problems like this:

$$\frac{10 \text{ acres}}{100 \text{ acres}} = \frac{3 \text{ burrows}}{X \text{ burrows}}$$

Cross multiply

$$10X = 3 \times 100$$
$$X = 30$$

A good check of your work is to take another sample in another field, and see if your results are the same, or reasonably close.

Similarly, you can estimate the squirrel population in a woods using a sample. Sit in one place for thirty minutes (the best time is sunrise) and count the squirrels you see. At the end of thirty minutes, estimate the average distance you can see through the woods. (It might be best to look from the place you have been sitting and select a point in the woods that is at your limit of observation [as far away as you could see a squirrel] then **measure** the distance to it). This distance is the radius of a circle, and you have been sampling the area within that circle.

For an example, let's say that you sat in a 40 acre woods for 30 minutes and observed 3 squirrels. You measure the distance to your limit of observation and it is 100 feet. Thus you have sampled a circle 100 ft. in radius.

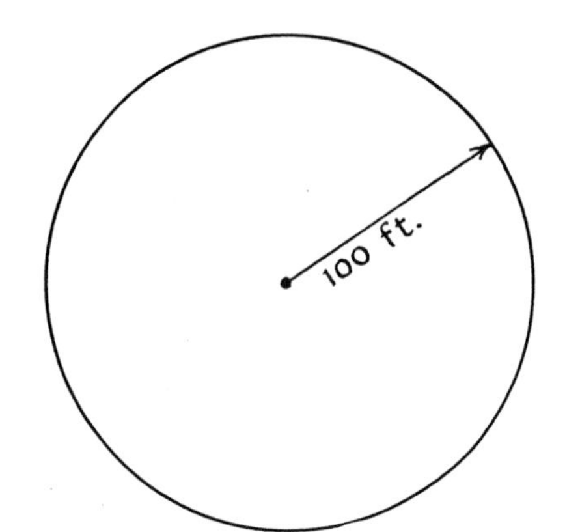

Area of a circle is Pi times the radius squared.

$A = Pi\ R^2$
$Pi = 3.14$
$R = 100$

$$A = 3.14 \times 100^2 = 3.14 \times 10000$$
$$= 31400 \text{ sq. ft.}$$

One acre equals 43560 square feet, so you observed

$\frac{31400}{43560}$ or about 0.72 of an acre.

Using mathematics again, you can find out how many squirrels there are in the entire 40 acre woods.

$$\frac{3 \text{ squirrels}}{0.72 \text{ acre}} = \frac{X \text{ squirrels}}{40 \text{ acres}}$$

Cross multiply

$$0.72X = 3 \times 40$$
$$X = \frac{3 \times 40}{0.72}$$
$$X = \text{approximately 167 squirrels}$$

Wildlife biologists usually speak of population "per acre". In this case, 167 ÷ 40 = 4.2 squirrels per acre.

Note that you can get this "squirrel per acre" figure without knowing the total acreage of the woods.

$$\frac{3 \text{ squirrels}}{0.72 \text{ acre}} = \frac{X \text{ squirrels}}{1 \text{ acre}}$$

$X = 3 \div 0.72 = 4.2$ squirrels per acre

When possible, you should repeat your census from different observation points, then average your distance you walked times the total width. (Total width equals distance you can see to the left plus the distance you can see to the right).

Thus when you have completed walking a "strip" and have recorded distance walked, width of strip, and number of animals observed, you can calculate the number of animals per acre. Multiply this by the number of acres in the parcel, and you have an estimate of the total population of the parcel. You can census more than one species at the same time using this method.

In underbrush the strip is narrower than in open woods.

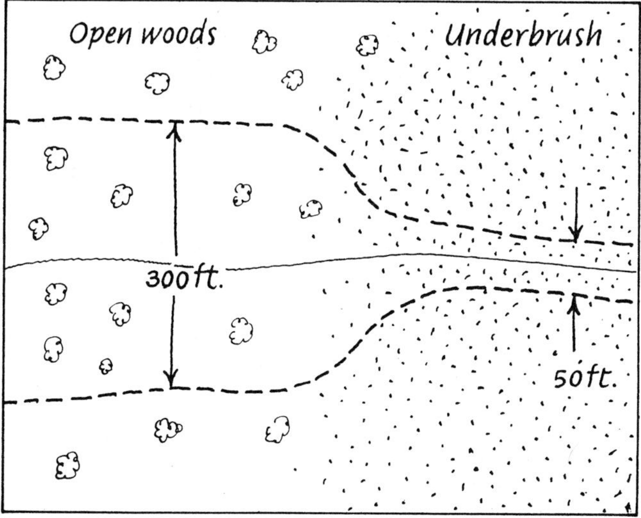

Sometimes, particularly in dense undergrowth, you must zig-zag in order to have a wide enough strip.

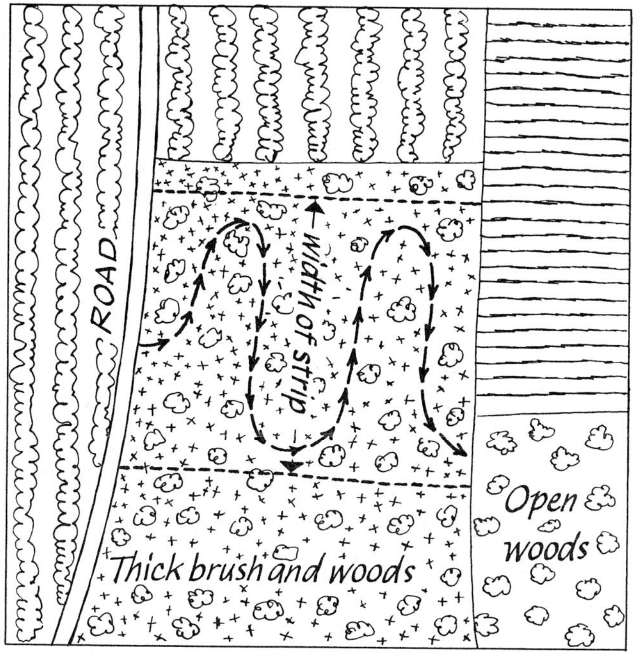

DRIVE CENSUS

For some kinds of habitat, observation is very difficult unless the wildlife is driven in to the open. Several people are necessary for a drive. The "beaters", or people to drive the wildlife, line up abreast close enough together to prevent wildlife from escaping unseen.

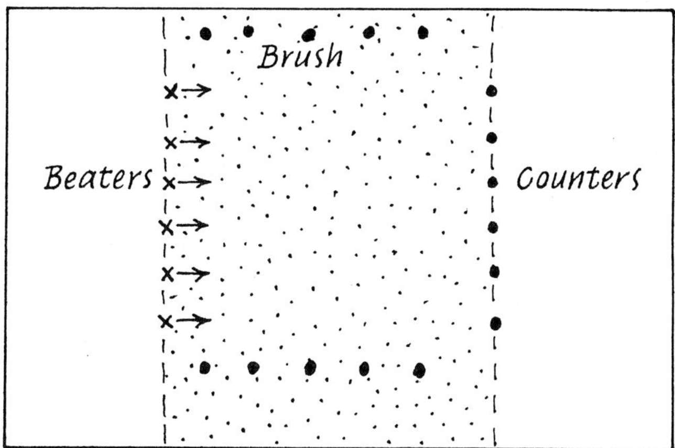

Counters line up at the opposite end and at the sides of the drive. The beaters then walk toward the counters, making noise to drive the wildlife ahead of them. Counters census all wildlife that goes past them, and beaters count all that go back past them.

Care must be taken that two people don't count the same animal. In open areas such as pastures or hayfields, beaters can drag ropes between them to flush out many rabbits, pheasants, or similar animals that would otherwise remain silent and unseen. A **well trained** dog can be very helpful, but a poorly trained dog will be a nuisance at best.

SPECIAL CENSUS TECHNIQUES

Many census techniques have been devised for particular species. For example, counting deer droppings can provide a good estimate of deer population. For training in these techniques contact an official of the state conservation department or read about them in books from a library.

MARKED ANIMALS

Professional wildlife managers and others who are licensed by proper officials sometimes use techniques which involve live trapping, marking, and release of animals. Do not attempt to trap birds or from a certain habitat. Mount and display with information on each plant's use to wildlife.

Write a letter to the editor of your local newspaper. Point out a wildlife situation that needs attention, or express your opinion on a controversy concerning wildlife the newspaper is covering.

Census the entire animal and/or plant population of a few square feet of vacant lot, roadside, or other area. Note which species are native and which were introduced from other parts of the world.

Make an anthology of wildlife poems by various authors. Write wildlife poetry of your own.

Observe (you will need binoculars) parent birds carrying food to young in a nest. Record number of trips per hour and kinds of food. Estimate total amount of various types of food the nestlings eat each day.

Identify a controversy involving wildlife in your area. Summarize the points of view of all sides of the issue.

Choose any species of wildlife in your area. Write a report, give a talk to your group, or prepare an exhibit on the species.

Rewrite the zoning laws of your town or city as if you were a beaver. Do the same thing for a hawk.

Observe a marsh, pond, meadow or other gathering place for wildlife from two hours before sunrise until two hours after sunrise. Record what you observe. Write a story or poem about your experience.

Make a scrapbook of newspaper and other articles concerning wildlife.

Prepare an exhibit on some aspect of your project for a fair, your school class, or a store window.

Make a balanced aquarium. Read about food webs in a pond, then collect plants and prey and predator species of animals. Set up the aquarium **carefully** following instructions you have found in a book on the subject. Try to strike a balance of prey and predator species.

Make a wildlife resource map of your school property, a park, a neighbor's property, or a similar place.

Watch television programs concerning wildlife. Make a list of concepts mentioned or implied.

Learn to prepare "study skins" of animals found dead along the roads. Check with your conservation officer, since you should know the laws concerning this.

In cooperation with your librarian, make a list of books in your library on the subject of wildlife. Include novels and poetry as well as biographies and other non-fiction. Using these books as well as other items, make a bulletin board or display to put up in your library during National Wildlife Week.

Observe a bird building a nest. Determine average distance traveled per trip. Calculate total distance traveled to build nest.

Write a report on a rare or endangered species.

Lead a field trip for a group of young children. Help them learn some basic facts and concepts about wildlife. Cause them to be interested in and care about wildlife.

Write a "Wildlifer's Diary" patterned after the January to December section of Leopold's *Sand County Almanac*.

Visit a state or federal wildlife management area or refuge. Interview officials and observe management practices. Write a report on the activities being conducted.

Raise earthworms. Write a report on their importance to all plants and animals.

Subscribe to a state or national magazine that deals with wildlife or read one regularly at your library.

"Adopt" a species of wildlife that occurs in your area. Observe it daily, or whenever possible, for a month or a year. Record your observations. Learn all you can about it from books, recordings, learned people, etc. as well as from your observations.

Locate a nest being built by a bird. Observe it closely during the nesting season and keep detailed records of activity. Include number of trips per hour when building, behavior when other birds, cats, etc. are nearby, number of eggs and when laid, hatching date, etc. Compare your observations to information published on that species in books.

Make crossword puzzles using wildlife terms. Make several using different themes, such as endangered species, food plants, predators, introduced species, etc.

Sketch, paint or draw an animal. Study the work of other wildlife artists.

Managing Small Woodlands for Wildlife

On a frosty, early spring morning a rapid "tat, tat, tat" can be heard coming from the woods, and a feeling of assurance fills us. Indeed, winter has ended and a new season of growth has begun. Most of us can identify the "critter" making the sound as a woodpecker, but do you know what kind of woodpecker? Why does it always make that type of sound from late winter on into summer? Where is it making the sound? Or more importantly, what if there are no woodpeckers "drumming" in woodlots? The presence of woodpeckers or chickadees, chipmunks or deer often makes the difference between an uninteresting collection of trees and an exciting woodlot. The tangible and intangible values of wildlife can enhance the importance of a woodlot both to the owner and to visitors.

Why does a wood thrush song lighten a day or make early rising worthwhile? Why do busy people pause to watch a doe with her fawns? What value can we place on these things? What are they "worth" to you as a private woodlot manager?

We cannot provide answers to all these questions. However, we will illustrate how one might manage a woodland to obtain these priceless, intangible (and sometimes tangible) values of wildlife, while maintaining compatible uses of the land for forestry, maple syrup and firewood production, agriculture, and recreation. The intimate knowledge of ecological relationships that you gain by working with wildlife can do no less than strengthen your sense of commitment to and appreciation of your woodlands.

Wildlife Management

Wildlife has both consumptive and nonconsumptive uses. Until recently, wildlife biologists had only gross estimates of the magnitude of nonconsumptive uses (for example, viewing wildlife, feeding birds, nature photography). Though research information is still far from complete, several trends are evident. In 1975, for example, nearly 50 million Americans engaged in wildlife observation, spending about 1.5 billion person-days at this activity. Of that number, 15 million people spent about 150 million person-days photographing wildlife. The economic importance of such activities is difficult to assess. However, some indication can be gained from examining specifically the hobby of bird watching.

One out of every 10 households in suburban America feeds garden birds, and over $500 million is spent annually by people interested in birds (for birdfeed, binoculars, cameras, etc.). In addition, a conservative estimate of the number of new people actively "birding" is about 2–3 million annually. In New York State alone there are 41 Federation of New York State Bird Clubs, with more than 10,000 members. This is not surprising, considering the large amount and diversity of potential wildlife habitats available to the public. The amount of money spent by people traveling to and from wildlife areas on food, fuel, and lodging has been estimated for various activities. Thus, attracting people to private woodlands well suited for birding activities can help local economies.

People enjoy seeing wildlife and, through their observations, form sets of values for individual species or groups of species (for example, deer, cottontail rabbits, and songbirds are usually favored, whereas rats and starlings are not). Through personal involvement and the educational efforts of conservation organizations and wildlife agencies, people's awareness of and attitudes toward wildlife are changing. Predators, for example, are being viewed not as villains, as depicted in folklore, or as heroes, as sometimes portrayed in the media, but rather as vital elements in the natural functioning of ecological systems. The need for wise, professional management of predators such as hawks, owls, foxes, and coyotes is becoming clear to the public.

Consumptive uses of wildlife, on the other hand, are relatively easy to assess economically. Since 1923, hunters in the United States have paid more than $2.5 billion in license fees, more than $762 million in taxes on sporting arms and ammunition, $71.2 million in taxes on handguns, and $11.5 million in taxes on archery equipment. In 1975, almost 21 million Americans hunted, spending about $5.8 billion on this recreation. All these numbers would increase considerably if fishing and the trapping of furbearers were included. Obviously, the consumptive use of wildlife is an important economic and recreational consideration in the United States.

The traditional emphasis in wildlife management has been upon game management because of the economic importance of game species and because hunters' license fees and taxes on their equipment fund almost all the management and research efforts by state wildlife agencies. However, the emphasis is now shifting toward a more holistic approach to wildlife management because of the efforts of enlightened wildlife biologists, sportspersons, and concerned citizens. Management for game species does not preclude management for nongame species. Natural selection of the most fit individuals through millions of years has favored the evolution of many animals best adapted to one or, at most, a few types of habitat (places where organisms live). Thus, management for a single species is not possible.

For example, many species of birds, including ruffed grouse, thrive in a certain type of forest. Therefore, management activities that enhance an area for ruffed grouse would also encourage other species adapted to that same habitat type. If management for game is properly carried out on a piece of land, then all wildlife values are enhanced by creating many different habitat types. These managed areas provide a mosaic, or patchwork, of areas more suitable to a greater variety of species than would be found in a single habitat type.

For example, one can perceive New York State as a mosaic of different vegetation types (such as wetlands, grasslands, croplands, hardwood forests, conifer forests, and alpine). These types are seldom found either as pure stands of a single species or as large unbroken blocks of a single type (except perhaps in the Adirondack Mountains). The result of this mosaic is the meeting of field and woods or different forest types in many areas. The famous naturalist Aldo Leopold called these transition zones *edges* and suggested that the kinds and density of game species in an area were a function of the amount of edge. He observed that an edge was richer in plant species and structure (trees, shrubs, and grasses) than either the adjacent fields or woods. We now recognize that more diverse and structurally complex habitats usually contain more bird species and other forms of wildlife than do simple ones (for example, a grassland usually is more simple structurally than a woodland and contains fewer bird species).

About 90 percent of the potential woodland wildlife habitat in the northeastern United States is privately owned (71.6 million acres [28.6 million ha]). Consequently, the quality of woodland habitat for wildlife depends on the discretion and management objectives of these many owners. For this reason, we wish to present some approaches for managing small woodlands for wildlife and for enhancing wildlife habitats in woodlands where the production of timber, pulpwood, firewood, or maple syrup is the primary goal.

Ecological Principles

Understanding a few basic ecological principles is necessary before one can successfully address the complexities of wildlife management. Unfortunately many forest and wildlife management decisions in the past have neglected such principles and have often resulted in economic, social, and biological disasters. An easy way to introduce such ecological principles is to consider briefly the various levels of biological complexity—simple to the complex.

Cell

The cell is a basic biological unit that is able to maintain itself biochemically and structurally. Though individual cells have a definite set of life requirements, single cells are normally too minute to be a direct concern to a land manager. Though single-cell animals and plants live throughout the forest, they go undetected without the aid of a microscope. However, cells are also the building blocks for larger organisms.

Individual

Cells with common functions are combined to form tissues and organs, and these then form the components of individual plants and animals. Larger individuals, whether a tree, shrub, grass, or animal, are often of direct interest to landowners. Plant and animal species, through aeons, have adapted to the rigors of the environment by the process of natural selection. This process dictates that the best adapted individuals shall reproduce successfully and , thereby, pass their likeness on into the future with their offspring. Thus, an individual organism will have a characteristic set of requirements optimal for its growth and development. Two of these requirements are defined by *habitat* and *niche*. Simply stated, an animal or plant can live in an area that provides food, cover (shelter), water, and space. This area then is called its habitat. Niche, on the other hand, is difficult to define accurately because it encompasses many ecological aspects of an organism's existence. However, the niche has been simply defined as the ecological role (or profession) of the organism in its environment. The key to successful wildlife management is closely tied to the manipulation of habitat and consideration of niche. This will be discussed further throughout this bulletin.

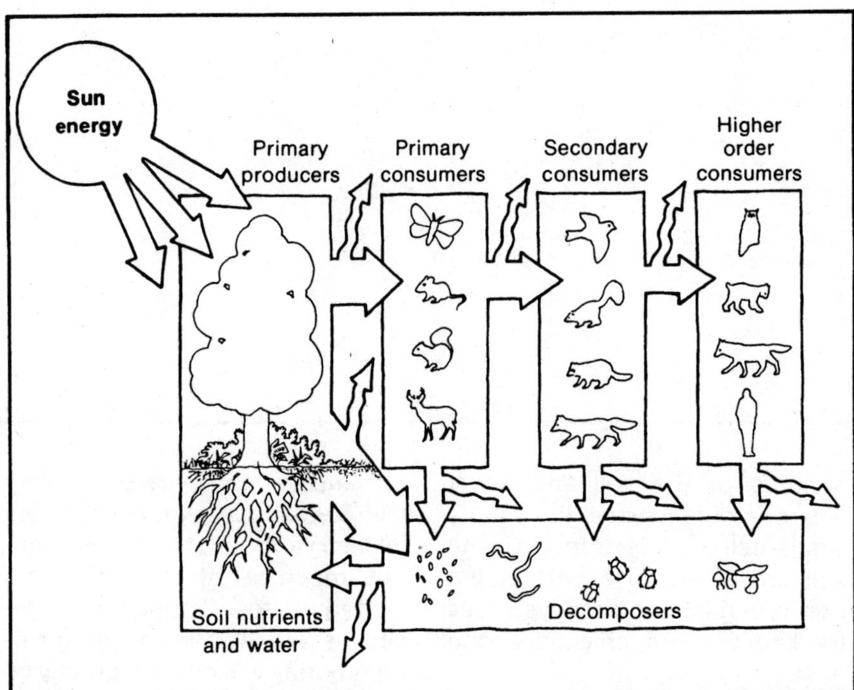

Figure 1. *Schematic of a forest ecosystem showing energy flow (*straight arrows) *and energy losses* (wavy arrows).

Population

A population is a group of individuals of the same species that freely interbreed. One of the problems in attempting to manage a population is defining the boundaries of the population. Many management schemes designed to benefit a species are unsuccessful because they are able to manage not the entire population but only segments of it. This point will be considered later when cooperation between neighboring landowners is discussed.

Community

Whereas a group of individuals of the same species forms a population, an assemblage of species in a given area can be a community. A community is composed of different species that interact in many ways. The habitats of some species overlap, and any change in the various habitat factors will probably alter the distribution and abundance of some of the species. Both plants and animals can be involved. Hence, a typical northeastern hardwood forest can be considered a community of plants and animals that are fairly characteristic. An adjacent field and its associated flora and fauna would compose another community.

When different organisms have similar life requirements and these are in limited supply, competition for these requirements will occur. Competition can exist between species and within a particular species. Competition between animals can be active, such as seen in territorial aggression, or subtle, such as with competitors exhibiting differential food-capturing efficiencies. Competition between plants is typically indirect, involving subtle differences in abilities to acquire needed resources. Root growth characteristics and differences in utilizing low light levels are two important features. For example, deep-rooted plants may have a competitive advantage over shallow-rooted species when water is scarce. The species composition of the community can be affected when management or any natural process gives a species a competitive advantage over another species. Then, the superior species may eventually be able to exclude its competitor from the area.

Ecosystem

A community can be viewed as being simple or complex. For example, the bird community of a red pine stand is simpler than that of a tropical forest of the same size. However, ecologists recognize that no single individual organism exists alone, but rather interacts with many others. A definable group of interacting plants and animals along with their physical environment (for example, soil and water) is termed an ecosystem (see fig. 1). An ecosystem includes not only large organisms but all physical, chemical, and biological components of the soil and aerial environments. Hence, the simple single-cell organisms found in the soil are as much a part of the northern hardwood ecosystem as the beech, birch, chickadee, and deer.

Ecosystems are not static, but are in a dynamic equilibrium with short- and long-term changes in the environment. Both composition and numbers of plants and animals change through time. Our view of a woodlot as a permanent, unchanging collection of trees and wildlife results from observing this ecosystem for a relatively short time, namely, our lifespan. If we could compress 100 years into a few minutes, we would have a very different view of the woodlot ecosystem.

A continental ice mass covered most of the Northeast during the ice age 10,000 years ago; dramatic changes in plants and animals occurred as the ice receded. A series of plants and animals progressively invaded the bare areas left by the glaciers, each community making the environment more hospitable for another. Ecologists call this *primary succession;* and its outcome takes a long time, for soil-forming processes usually need to be initiated before higher plants can become established.

Secondary succession is easier to observe, it being the natural progression of communities following a relatively minor disturbance, such as fire or farming. Old field succession can be seen in its various stages throughout much of the northeastern United States. Though the process is similar, the resulting tree community will depend greatly on the geographic location. Normally an early stage in succession is called a *seral community* (or seral stage), whereas the final community is termed the *climax.* However, even so-called climax communities are not static, given a long time frame marked by periodic disturbances.

Agriculture in the northeastern United States reached its peak in the mid- to late 1800s. For example, over 80 percent of the forest land outside the Adirondack Mountain region of New York was cleared for farming by this time, only a remnant of the former extensive forest that covered most of the state being left. New York led the nation in timber production in 1850, cutting a volume of timber never equalled in the state again. However, much of the cleared land was marginal for agriculture; and as mechanization increased, these lands could not compete with more productive farmlands and were subsequently abandoned. So great was this farm loss that between 1880 and 1930 the area being farmed in New York was reduced by nearly 5 million acres. The depression years continued the exodus of farmers, and by the 1960s less than one-quarter of the farmers were turning out more than 33 percent more products on less than half as much land as in 1900. These trends are continuing.

The abandonment of cleared land initiated the process of ecological succession (see fig. 2). Once a field was released from agricultural use, the bare ground was colonized by hardy weeds. Many weeds are best adapted to invading and growing on disturbed soil sites under harsh environmental conditions. As these weeds stabilized the soil and slightly modified its character, conditions became more suitable for other plants, such as grasses and forbs, which, in turn, invaded the area. In time, shrubs and trees replaced the herbaceous plants, and a forest developed, eventually dominating the site. The plant species colonizing the site can be variable, as can the length of time that the process of succession takes to reach the forest stage. Much of the farmland abandoned in the 1930s is now young forests. In many northeastern states these forests are typically overcrowded stands of beech, birch, and maple.

Changes in animal communities occur along with plant community changes. For example, meadowlarks and meadow voles, common in grassy fields, are replaced by song sparrows,

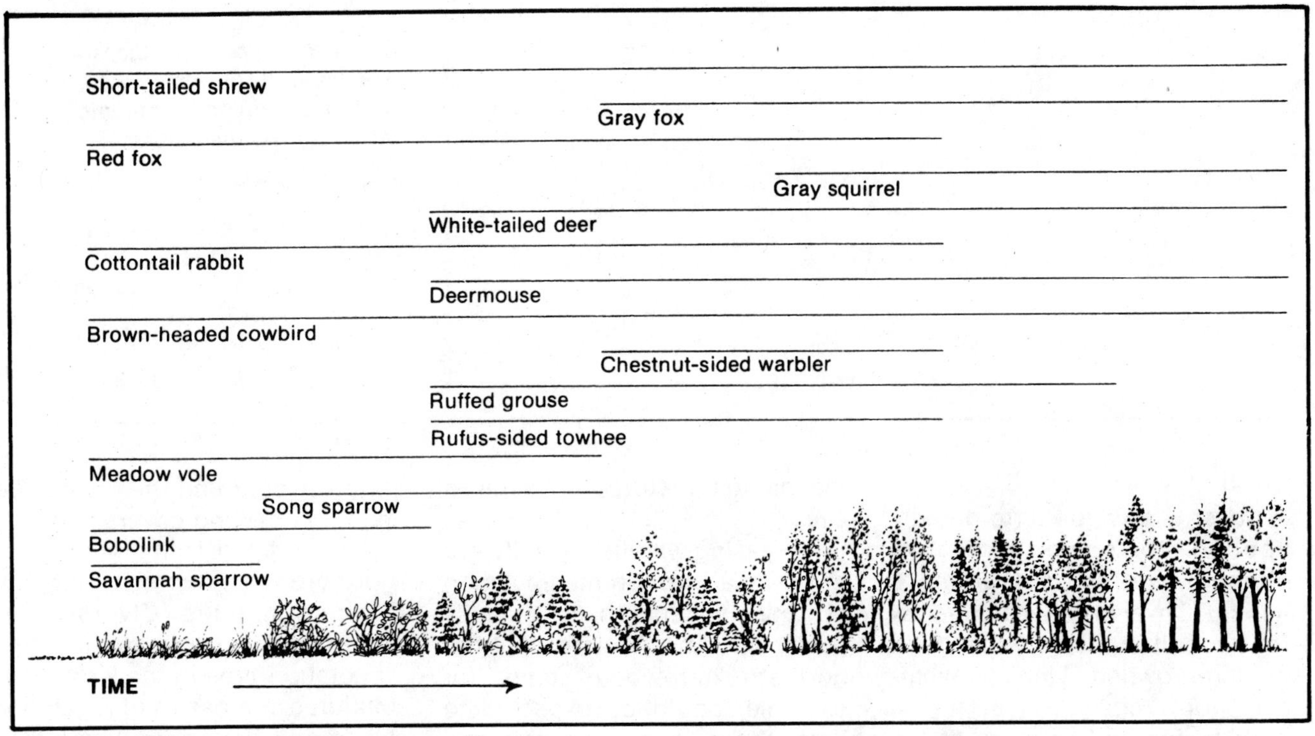

Short-tailed shrew
Gray fox
Red fox
Gray squirrel
White-tailed deer
Cottontail rabbit
Deermouse
Brown-headed cowbird
Chestnut-sided warbler
Ruffed grouse
Rufus-sided towhee
Meadow vole
Song sparrow
Bobolink
Savannah sparrow
TIME

Figure 2. *Old field succession showing typical progressive changes of vegetation and wildlife with time.*

towhees, and rabbits in the shrub-grass stage. Thus, we can accurately predict which wildlife species are likely to inhabit a given habitat. Furthermore, because wildlife species require different habitats, we can manipulate habitats to favor those species desired.

Forest succession can be retarded or accelerated, depending on one's management goals. If, for example, one wishes to maintain some grassy openings in the forest, periodic mowing or burning will discourage the invasion of woody plants. (Obviously, caution must be observed in burning any vegetation.) On the other hand, forest succession can be accelerated by planting trees or by selectively cutting certain vegetation. In fact, massive reforestation programs during the 1930s resulted in about 600,000 acres (240,000 ha) of conifer plantations in New York. Hence, many landowners now find conifer plantations intermittently mixed within their natural hardwood stands.

Wildlife populations can be managed effectively only when we have some idea of the natural history and ecology of the animal species involved. Often we have recognized only one or two critical elements of a species' habitat requirements because it is extremely difficult to precisely define every habitat requirement. For example, a critical requirement for an animal might be a nest or perch site, a particular stage in the vegetation succession, or a particular type of vegetation. The amount and quality of special requirements are subject to our modification.

Elements of Thrifty Wildlife Populations

Wildlife managers generally agree that the thrift of wildlife populations is intimately linked to four primary factors: food, cover, water, and space. These factors define an animal's habitat. The first three often are susceptible to manipulation, but the last one may be more difficult to alter. In the following discussion we will present various methods for maintaining good food, cover, and water resources for wildlife. The importance of snags (dead trees) in a woodlot in providing both food and cover will also be illustrated. Then we will show how wildlife values can be integrated with forest land-use operations. Finally, we will present suggestions for planning and manipulating wildlife habitat in woodlots typical of the northeastern United States.

The amount and quality of these elements determine the carrying capacity of the land for a species. The term *carrying capacity* is often used to refer to the maximum number of animals a unit of land can support during the most unfavorable time of the year. We emphasize that this is not a constant number, that the carrying capacity of a piece of land fluctuates in response to environmental changes on it.

Figure 3. *Typical northeastern woodland:* (top) *unmanaged, and* (bottom) *managed for multiple uses including wildlife habitat.*

Key

Nature trail

Conifers

Observation blind

Released orchard

Brushpiles

Cover

Cover is a vague term broadly applied to some protective element within an animal's habitat. Cover may be a hedgerow for a rabbit or a spruce tree for a golden-crowned kinglet. Whatever form cover takes, it will provide for one or more of the necessary functions in the lives of animals: breeding, nesting, hiding, loafing, sleeping, feeding, and traveling.

Research has helped identify the cover requirements of game species, but little is known of these requirements for nongame animals. Many wildlife species are found in habitats having diverse plant species or plant growth forms (that is, plant shapes, sizes, leaf types). Consequently, replacing a mixed hardwood stand with a monoculture (a single-species vegetative community), such as a pine plantation or a cornfield, results in a predictable loss of many wildlife species. Hardwood forest residents would be replaced by conifer specialists (animals that use conifers almost exclusively) as the plantation grew to maturity. On the other hand, if a patch of conifers were planted in a hardwood stand, they would provide habitat for conifer specialists and cover for other species, like white-tailed deer, ruffed grouse, and wood thrushes. Animal diversity is often a function of plant diversity and of the patchiness or arrangement of the habitat features on a given site.

Increasing wildlife diversity in a given area through manipulation of the vegetation is readily possible. An 80-acre (32-ha) northern hardwood stand, for example, could be expected to hold about 15 species of mammals and 60–80 species of birds (fig. 3A). This diversity in a given habitat type is known as *within habitat diversity.* If that same woodlot (fig. 3B) was modified by timber harvesting, plantings, or habitat improvement work so that various 0.5–2.0-acre (0.2–0.8-ha) vegetative patches were established (such as fire lanes, a pond, an opening, and a conifer patch), predictable changes would take place in the animal species present. The mosaic of habitat types would increase the animal diversity of the area. Although specific areas, such as the conifer stand, would probably have a decrease in both habitat and animal diversity, the entire woodlot would show an increase. Increasing the *between habitat diversity* provides different conditions for wildlife in the altered sites. Blackburnian warblers and golden-crowned kinglets should colonize the conifer patch. Wood ducks and red-winged blackbirds might nest around the pond; and frogs, salamanders, and fish would also live there. Song sparrows and towhees would find suitable cover in the cut area, and juncos would find the grassy fire lane fine nesting cover.

Middle-aged to mature, mixed northern hardwoods have a higher species diversity of breeding animals than any other vegetation type in the Northeast. Mixtures or mosaics of vegetation types and the edges where they meet have greater diversity than any single vegetation type. Maintaining edges and open spaces is often an important management practice.

Brushy fence rows and hedgerows are examples of edges that provide cover for wildlife. With the advent of mechanized farming, many brushy fence rows and hedgerows have been removed to increase the agricultural yield. Consequently, many species of animals that use these have declined in numbers because they have lost the necessary cover element in their habitat.

Hedgerows also provide safe travel lanes between woodlands. A woodlot isolated from other woodlands by open fields is a habitat "island," which may have fewer species of wildlife than nearby woodlands. The variety of species found in an isolated woodlot depends upon many factors. Woodlot size, plant diversity, distance to other woodlands, and animal mobility and population density all influence the species diversity of the woodlot. A major factor is the accessibility of the isolated

A

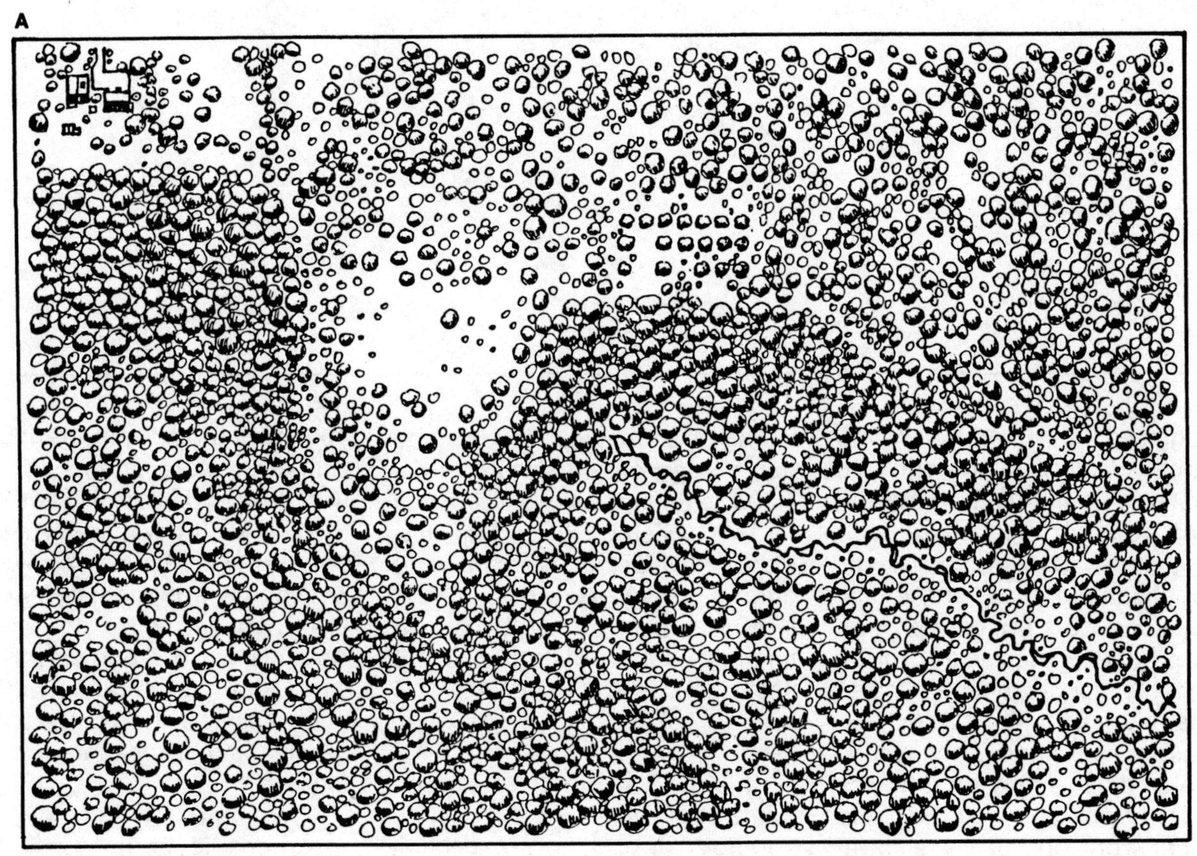

B

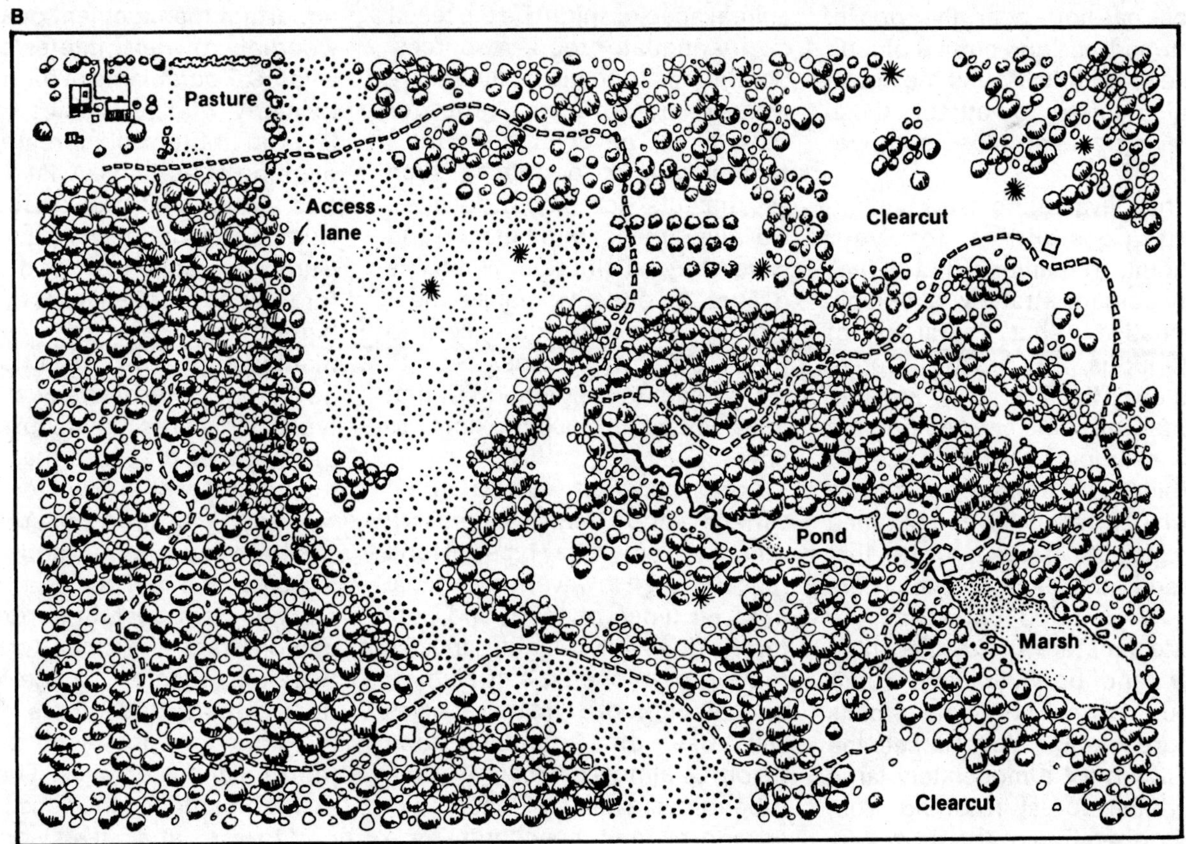

woodlot to the nearest colonizing source. Colonization can be facilitated by creating brushy fence rows or hedgerows with living trees between the "island" habitat and the "mainland" forest. These corridors not only provide travel lanes, but also provide habitat for species adapted to that edge type of habitat (such as catbirds, cardinals, pheasants, rabbits, deer). Many rural homes isolated from their woodlot could benefit from one of these travel lanes passing near the house. Planting trees and shrubs of food value to wildlife around the house would serve to attract those species traveling along a hedgerow.

When evaluating the management possibilities for your woodlot, remember that a no-management strategy is a viable alternative. That is, areas of contiguous, unbroken forest canopy offer the only suitable habitat for some species of birds (for example, the worm-eating warbler). Maintaining a mature patch of forest, such as illustrated in figure 3, helps provide that needed unbroken forest. There may be a good opportunity to locate a mature stand adjacent to your land boundary and contiguous with your neighbor's mature stand. We can see the possibility of a moderately large unbroken forest resulting from the cooperation of several nearby landowners. Notice also that our hiking trail design follows the outer edge of the mature forest stand to minimize the disturbance to area-sensitive birds. Management activities, such as firewood cutting, should take place in the late summer or early fall to minimize the disturbance to nesting birds and mammals.

Food

All animals must eat other animals or plants to survive. A woodlot devoid of expected animal species might be the result of inadequate food resources. Sometimes food plants also serve as cover (for example, shrubs for rabbits), or cover plants form a forage base for food items (such as insects on tree foliage). However, the location of food and cover may be different. When this occurs, an effective management strategy is to provide access to food by travel lanes or to manipulate the vegetation so that food will be in close proximity to cover.

Some animals eat a great variety of food items (generalist); others eat only a few types of food (specialist). However, no animal uses all types of food, and only rarely does any wildlife species rely on only one type of plant or animal for food. Still other species will use an abundant food resource almost exclusively when it becomes available. Mast (such as acorns and beechnuts) is a good example of a periodically abundant food. Squirrels and jays will even store acorns for later use; deer and bears will develop a thick layer of winter fat (stored energy) while feeding on acorns. Seasonally abundant berry crops are also attractive to wildlife. Animals eat the berries for their succulent pulp and unwittingly help disperse the plant seeds to other suitable locations via their feces.

The manipulation of food resources is perhaps the most important management goal for a woodlot owner interested in wildlife. Food plants of high value to many wildlife species can be favored in firewood, forestry, and planting operations. A list of trees and shrubs that provide food for wildlife is included in Appendix 1. Careful selection of food plants for their cover qualities is another benefit derived from habitat manipulation. Also, selection can be made for a diversity of food types, for plants that mature early or late, and for those that retain their fruits well into winter.

Creating a good juxtaposition between food, cover, and watering sites is a realistic and fruitful management goal. In figure 3 we demonstrate the importance of this juxtaposition to the robin, deer, rabbit, and others. These manipulations indirectly provide food for these animals. The deer and rabbit hide in the dense cover or forest and feed on the herbaceous growth in the fire lane

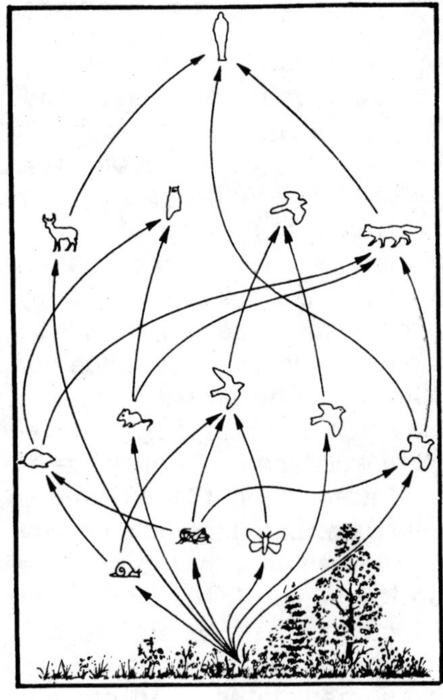

Figure 4. *(Above) Over-mature hardwood forest with snags and wolf trees useful to various wildlife species.*

Figure 5. *(Left) A simplified food web showing energy flow between various animal species.*

or grassy opening along with the robin. And when the cold and snow of winter drives the robin south and buries the grass and acorns, both the deer and rabbit will browse on the shrubs and tree seedlings found in the forest openings that were created by logging or firewood cutting.

A tree growing in the absence of competition from other trees will often produce a large, widespread crown with many branches. These characteristics, coupled with a short stature, have occasioned the label "wolf tree" (see fig. 4). Such trees usually produce poor quality timber and are typically eliminated from a woodlot by a forester. They may, however, produce more fruit or mast than a merchantable timber tree of the same species. Recognizing which wolf tree species are good food producers and maintaining them in a woodlot or hedgerow will greatly benefit wildlife.

Insects are a vital food source for most birds and several species of woodland mammals. Since insecticides tend to produce temporary reductions in insect numbers and some of them may kill wildlife directly, these chemicals should be used only with care and restraint.

This last point demonstrates the interaction between plants and animals. Plants use the sun, water, and nutrients to grow, and the insects eat the plants or other minute animals. The insectivorous birds then eat many of the insects. Insecticides break some of the links of this complex food web and may have serious effects on the forest community.

Figure 5 illustrates part of the food web discussed. What organisms would be affected by indiscriminant application of a general-purpose insecticide? How might insecticides affect your plans for recreation on your land?

Snags—cover and food

Snags are dead trees that are still standing (see fig. 4). They provide both food and cover and, thus, are important in the distribution and abundance of many wildlife species (see Appendix 2). Snags are used primarily as nesting, feeding, or perching sites. Until a few years ago, foresters systematically removed snags because of their potential for harboring disease and insect pests and for attracting lightning. The attitude toward snags is changing. Many bird species that nest in snags eat insects and help to prevent serious insect outbreaks. Other snag nesters, such as squirrels, provide meat and sport hunting. Still others, like raccoons, provide revenue from trapping; and others, like flying squirrels and deer mice, are unique, aesthetically pleasing, and functional elements in a forest ecosystem. In addition, where snags are lower than the surrounding canopy, the lightning threat is actually of minor consequence.

Once a tree dies, the slow process of decay begins. As the heartwood softens, woodpeckers will excavate nesting and roost cavities in a snag. After they abandon these sites, other wildlife species (secondary hole nesters) may use them (see Appendix 2). Some live trees also are used by primary hole nesters (species that excavate the initial hole), but often these trees are diseased, decadent, or dying.

Not all snags are of equal

quality or suitability in providing nesting habitat for birds (see Appendix 3). Basswood and beech are good cavity-producing trees, but most oaks (except black oak) are not. Small trees may be suitable for some bird species but not for larger wildlife. Short-lived species such as aspen will often provide suitable snags before the forest matures. Trees infected with fungal heartrot will often provide suitable cavity material sooner than will the natural death and decay process in sound trees. Trees notorious for heartrot, like beech, should be considered as potential wildlife nest trees.

Snags are classified as either hard or soft snags. Soft snags are punky and weak; and though they provide excellent foraging areas, they are neither as long lasting nor as good for nesting habitat as are the long lasting, sturdy hard snags.

Much still needs to be learned about which trees are the best cavity producers and which species produce natural cavities suitable for larger animals. Nevertheless, to maintain the maximum possible populations of aesthetically pleasing and economically important birds and mammals, snags should not be removed indiscriminately in forestry or firewood-cutting operations. If some of the trees have to be removed, the tallest and largest trees should be maintained, and no fewer than three hard snags or live trees with heartrot and two soft snags per acre (about six and four per ha) should be kept. Some smaller snags and potential snags (large, decadent trees) should be maintained as well. Taller trees also are used for perch sites by a number of bird species, including eagles, hawks, owls, and vultures. An individual evaluation of which snags are being used can be made by observing cavities drilled within the snag or droppings accumulated beneath the snag. Even snags left in clearcutting operations increase the diversity of birds within the cut area. Obviously, snags that present a safety hazard should be removed, for example, a large soft snag near a building or public area or those overtopping electrical lines.

Water

Water is an essential resource for all living things, but not all wildlife need standing water. For those that do require it, a creek, spring, or pond will serve the purpose. Management of water resources can take several forms. An important management objective is the protection of the woodlot's watershed (all the area drained by a creek, stream, or river). This can be ensured by following proper logging practices, maintaining the vegetation along the stream bank or spring, and preventing overgrazing or other activities that cause serious soil disturbance or erosion (such as off-road vehicle use). If free water is not readily available all year, developing a seasonal spring may create a needed water supply during the times when water has usually been unavailable.

Small impoundments will attract waterfowl and other animals to an area. Ponds can be created by dredging out a small area or damming an existing small watercourse or spring. Ponds serve not only as wildfowl nesting and feeding sites but also as rest stops for migratory waterbirds. If the pond is sufficiently large or deep enough, fish can be stocked to provide recreational fishing. Fish will also attract fish-eating wildlife (for example, mergansers, kingfishers, ospreys, minks). Muskrat control may be needed in such impoundments.

Fish numbers can be increased in streams by constructing artificial deflectors and pool diggers that provide suitable habitat for fish. Secondarily, these stream improvements may enhance the use of the stream by waterbirds for feeding or rearing their young. Bank stabilization by stream-side vegetation will also increase the stream's value for wildlife. The results to be expected from stream improvement will depend upon the size of the stream and the streambed substrate. Large streams or very small streams with impermeable bottoms would prove most difficult to manage. Before any stream modifications are initiated in some states, appropriate permits must be obtained from the regional or main office of the state's conservation department or other natural resource agency.

Additional habitat manipulation

Some aspects of improving wildlife habitat were discussed in the previous sections. Still other projects that would benefit wildlife, particularly birds, can be accomplished easily. Studies show that many species of secondary-hole nesting birds are limited by the lack of suitable nest holes. If your land has been cleared of snags or if few are available for birds, you can supply birds with snags or you can erect nest boxes throughout your woodland.

In mature stands that lack standing snags, selected trees can be girdled and killed (see Appendix 3). As these trees deteriorate, they will form useful wildlife snags. Consult a professional forester or wildlife specialist before attempting such an operation. Tree culling can fit well into a sound forest management program, but killing trees indiscriminately could greatly degrade the future economic value of your woodlot. This

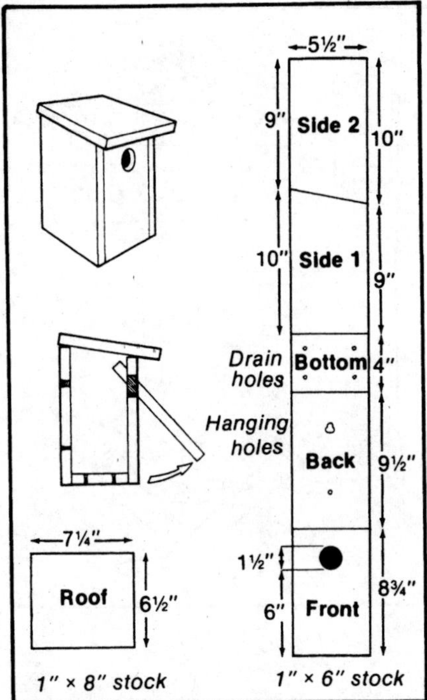

Figure 6. *Eastern bluebird box construction.*

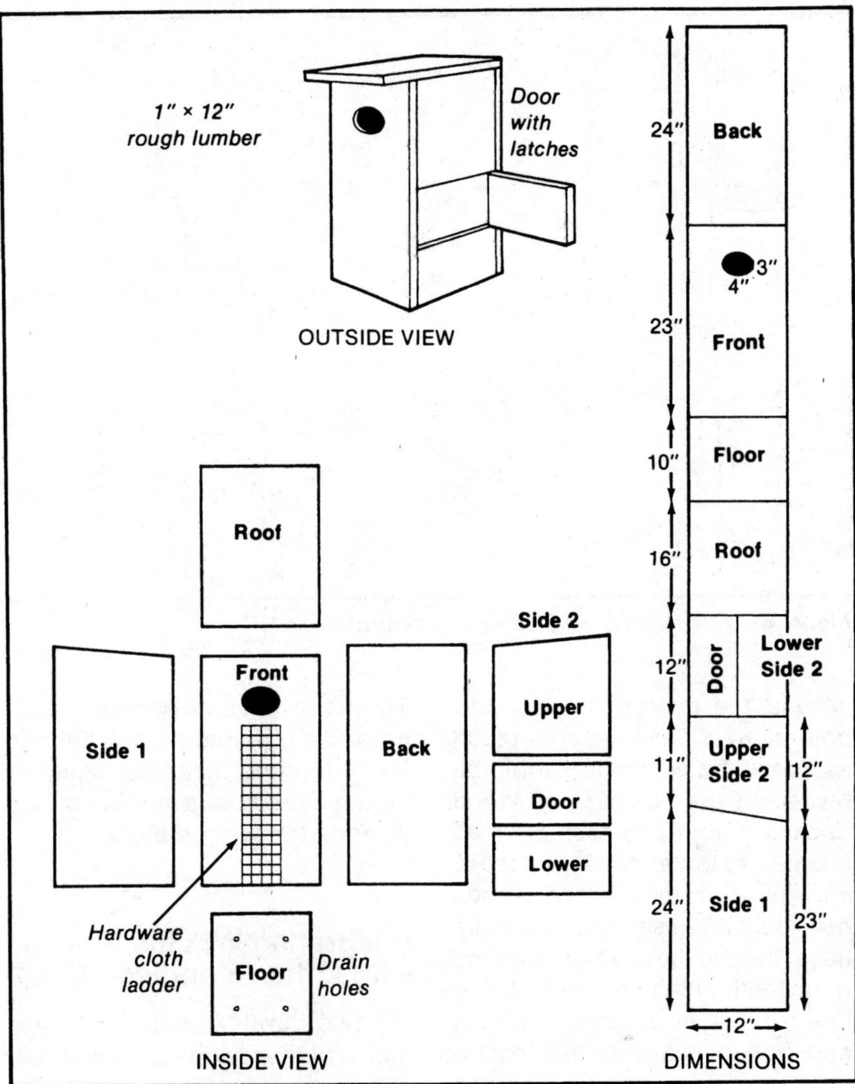

Figure 7. *Wood duck nest box construction.*

general subject will be discussed later in this bulletin.

Another way to create nesting cover is to build and distribute nest boxes. There are many types of and designs for birdhouses, and each is suited to a particular bird species. The construction of two types of nest boxes is illustrated in figures 6 and 7. These boxes are ideal for either the eastern bluebird or the wood duck.

Both bluebird and wood duck populations in the Northeast have suffered from a loss of habitat through snag removal and other forestry measures. However, extensive nest box programs for wood ducks, acting together with specific timber-harvesting regulations, have resulted in a dramatic increase in wood duck numbers. The management of wood ducks ranks with the wild turkey, white-tailed deer, and pronghorn restoration programs as one of the highlights of successful modern wildlife management. Unfortunately, bluebird populations have not fared so well, but a more active role by interested landowners in erecting bluebird boxes could cause a favorable change in the future.

Wood ducks will initially enter wooden boxes more readily than metal ones. However, once the birds become accustomed to using wooden boxes, they should be replaced (during the late fall) with metal boxes since these are more secure from predators. Boxes should be placed on a pole within the standing water of a pond or against a tree a short distance inside the forest edge of a mature woodlot. The boxes can be placed from 4-20 feet (1.2-6.1 m) above the ground or water surface. Nest boxes in woodlots for wood ducks should be located within ½ mile (0.8 km) of a pond, large stream, or river where the hen can eventually take her hatched brood. The number of boxes placed in an area will depend on the number and size of suitable water bodies nearby. Begin conservatively, for too many boxes in an area may attract enough birds to cause serious competition between them (an example of the need of wildlife for space). Each nest box should be protected by a predator shield, which is usually a metal apron

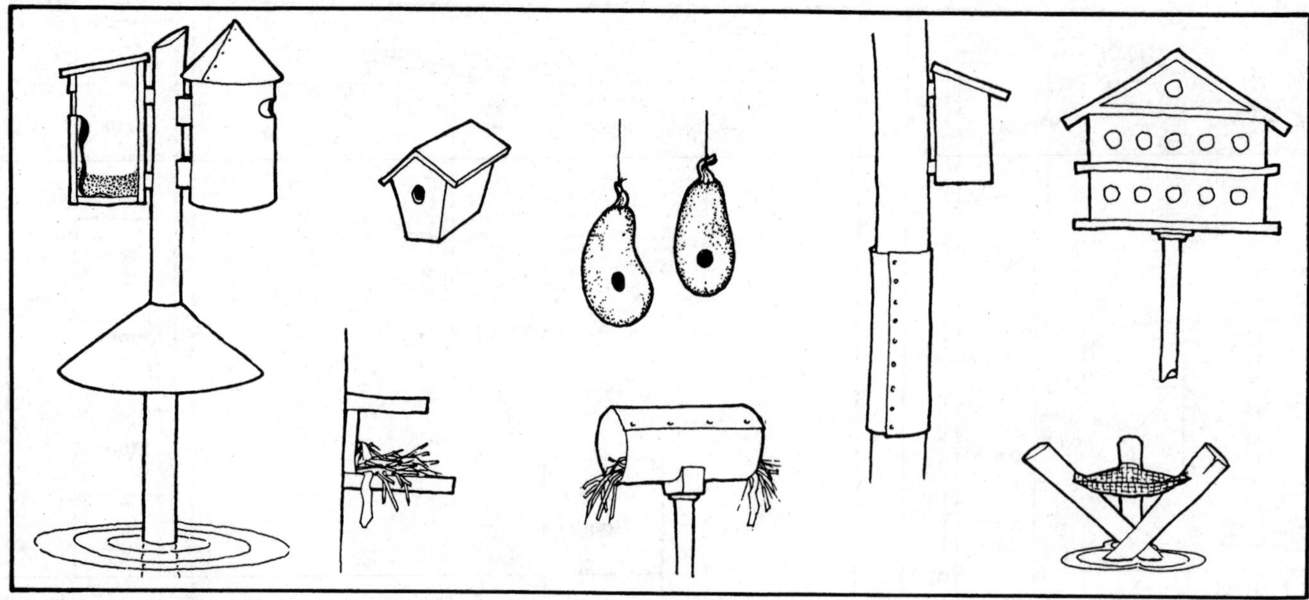

Figure 8. *Examples of various bird nest structures.*

around the base of the support pole or tree. Nest material (such as straw and sawdust) should be placed in the boxes since wood ducks do not carry nest material.

Bluebird boxes can be placed in an open field or in open woods near fields. These boxes typically have hinged lids, which can be removed for cleaning or removing undesirable bird eggs. Starlings and house sparrows will sometimes use bird boxes. Starlings are serious competitors with native species for nesting cavities. If starlings or house sparrows are using a box, the nest and eggs should be removed. Starlings, house sparrows, rock doves, and monk parakeets are all exotic (that is, nonnative) birds and are not protected by law. All other birds and their eggs are legally protected and may not be destroyed or removed from their nest.

Many other species of birds, such as screech owls, wrens, chickadees, and crested flycatchers, will accept nest boxes. The type of nest box, its hole diameter, and location (both habitat and height of box) will determine what species of birds are likely to use the nest box. Table 1 gives some nest box sizes, entrance diameters, and heights for attracting specific species. Figure 8 provides a number of box designs for various birds.

Integrating Wildlife Values with Other Woodland Uses

Trees and forests provide numerous economic, ecological, and social benefits to people. In the Northeast, where individual, privately owned acreages are small and productivities are low, many landowners strive to enjoy a variety of uses from their property. This process, termed *multiple use,* is not new to forestry, and in principle it dictates that a forest can provide a compatible set of "products." These forest products include timber, pulpwood, firewood, maple syrup, Christmas trees, and various recreational opportunities. All these products can be viewed as a commercial crop bringing a direct economic return to the landowner. On the other hand, they may be noncommercial and bring only intangible returns. Of course, the money saved by heating your home with firewood, by those dinners centered around venison or maple products, and by the construction poles used around the house or farm do represent an indirect economic advantage of wise woodlot management.

The irony of the situation is that full-scale, commercial forest management is seldom economically justified on small acreages in the Northeast. This is not for the want of a strong market, for hardwood sawlog prices have never been better. Instead, the problem arises from the high cost of various management activities (including property taxes) that must go into producing a timber crop. A recent economic study has indicated that the break-even point may be near 50 or 60 acres (20–24 ha). Obviously, people own woodlands for a variety of reasons, and the production of commercial timber may not be a primary concern.

In this section we will briefly illustrate how wildlife habitat values might be integrated into other woodland uses. We will see that various trade-offs will be made to meet an owner's specific management objectives. Remember, these remarks are only

Table 1. Nest Box Specifications

Bird species	Cavity floor	Depth	Entrance above floor	Hole diameter	Height above ground
	(inches†)	(inches)	(inches)	(inches)	(feet†)
Chickadee	4×4	8–10	6–8	1⅛	6–15
Titmouse	4×4	8–10	6–8	1¼	6–15
Nuthatch	4×4	8–10	6–8	1¼	12–20
House wren	4×4	8–10	6–8	1–1¼	3–10
Bluebird	5×5	8–10	6–8	1½	5–10
Tree swallow	5×5	8–10	6–8	1½	5–15
Purple martin	6×6	6	1	2½	15–20
Great crested flycatcher	6×6	8–10	6–8	2	5–20
Screech owl	8×8	12–15	9–12	3	10–30
Kestrel	8×8	12–15	9–12	3	10–30
Wood duck	12×12	24	18	3×4	10

† 1 inch=2.54 cm 1 foot=0.3048 m

an introduction to this complex subject. For additional information, consult the references at the end of this bulletin or contact your local Cooperative Extension office or state forester.

Timber management

The most traditional product from a woodlot is wood fiber. The basic principle of forest management is to manipulate a given plot of ground to produce a commercial timber crop economically. Simply stated, forest management involves establishing, cultivating, and harvesting this crop. Though often ignored in practice, each activity can be adjusted slightly to integrate wildlife habitat enhancement into the total land management program.

For those desiring hardwoods, ecological succession resulting in hardwood stands will readily occur on most abandoned fields in the Northeast outside the conifer areas. Furthermore, stump and root sprouts and understory seedlings will spring up following a timber harvest. In fact, foresters normally do not recommend planting most hardwood species since survival rates are notoriously poor. On the other hand, conifer stands in many areas are established primarily by planting young seedlings. In both cases the low stature of young trees can provide both cover and food for a variety of wildlife species (see Appendix 1).

Stand establishment is not a major concern to most woodland owners. Many rural landowners are faced with too many trees rather than not enough. In New York State a typical hardwood stand or conifer plantation is overstocked; that is, there are too many trees per unit area. A given area of land will only grow a certain amount of wood fiber, determined by the environmental, or site, factors associated with the area. It can be dispersed over numerous small stems or concentrated in larger trees. Since bigger trees normally mean higher-value sawlogs, the idea is to reduce the density of stems to a point where the entire site is fully used by the optimum number of trees. This necessitates weeding, or thinning, the average woodlot. Because of the general conditions of most woodlots, thinning is the most common timber stand improvement recommended by foresters in the Northeast.

When thinning a woodlot for commercial timber production, a forester might remove all crooked, forked, diseased, and dead trees; wolf trees would also be culled (fig. 9). Future crop trees would be identified based on species, size, and form; and other trees crowding these individuals would be marked for removal. Marked trees can all be cut at one time, or they can be removed as the crop trees grow and become progressively more crowded. Such intermediate cuttings can produce pulpwood or, if the trees are large enough, even sawlogs. Recently, these thinnings have often ended up as firewood.

Based on our understanding of animal habitat needs, we should all see that a wildlife manager would strongly disagree with the preceding thinning operation. Many of the initially culled trees might be suitable wildlife trees. From a wildlife point of view, all snags and wolf trees should not be cut. Wolf trees are particularly valuable if left along hedgerows and travel corridors. We recommend for early removal trees poor in form that do not produce mast or berries. Next, trees of little food value that are crowding valuable crop trees should be cut. Figure 9 shows how we might thin a woodlot to meet some wildlife needs, but still upgrade the timber-producing capabilities of the woodlot. However, trade-offs between timber, firewood, and wildlife habitat will need to be considered, and decisions will depend upon the personal preferences of the landowner (see Appendixes 1 and 3).

A thinning operation will leave a considerable amount of debris even after the stems are removed for firewood or pulpwood. This debris, consisting primarily of tree crowns and large branches, can be cut into manageable sizes and stacked. When interspersed throughout a woodlot, these brush piles will serve as cover for many small animals (fig. 10). In addition, living brush piles can be made by cutting through a tree stem only until the tree falls and allowing it to remain partially attached to its stump.

The greatest economic return from traditional forest management activities comes when the crop trees are harvested and sold for sawtimber. Normally, sawtimber trees must be at least 16 inches (41 cm) in diameter at breast height (4.5 ft or 1.3 m). Appendix 3 indicates the relative value of numerous forest tree species common to the Northeast. Woodlot owners primarily interested in a commercial timber harvest can plan this activity to enhance their overall wildlife habitat. Several methods of logging are used throughout the United States, but two are of special interest in this area. The first method is selection logging in which some trees of all age classes (uneven-age management) are removed during the operation (fig. 11); the second is clearcutting in which all the trees (even-age management) of a given area are cut (fig. 12).

Figure 9. *Hardwood forest showing alternative management strategies.*

If you sell stumpage to a private company, you have the right to insist upon the proper harvest of trees to protect watershed and wildlife values. Further, when selling trees, you can designate which trees may and may not be cut. In this way you can avoid "high grading" of your timber stand by the contractor. High grading involves removing only the most valuable timber in a selection cut. Selection cutting, in the classic sense, is often not done because of these practices. In any event, snags and wolf trees of high value to wildlife should be maintained.

Clearcutting means the removal of all the trees on a plot. If a clearcut is performed carefully with respect for the soil and landscape, the overall animal diversity of an area should increase because younger forest and brush stages (seral stages in succession) will develop on the clearcut site. Several recommendations should be considered by woodland owners planning to use a clearcut method. The size of the clearcuts should be relatively small (0.5–10 acres [0.2–4.0 ha], depending on area available for harvest and economic feasibility). Clearcuts should be dispersed over the area and not concentrated. In addition to being aesthetically pleasing, irregularly shaped clearcuts produce the maximum amount of edge (fig. 12). Again, snags are a major consideration since they provide nesting cover in a young forest before the natural cycle of the forest would provide them.

Maple syrup production

Maple sugaring in the early spring is a popular commercial and recreational activity carried out by many woodland owners throughout the northeastern United States. Although maple sap can be obtained from all native maples, sugar maple, also known as hard or rock maple, is considered the best. Managing a sugar bush has quite a different objective from managing for timber production since wolf trees are to be favored. The ideal sugar tree has a wide, deep, and open crown for high sugar

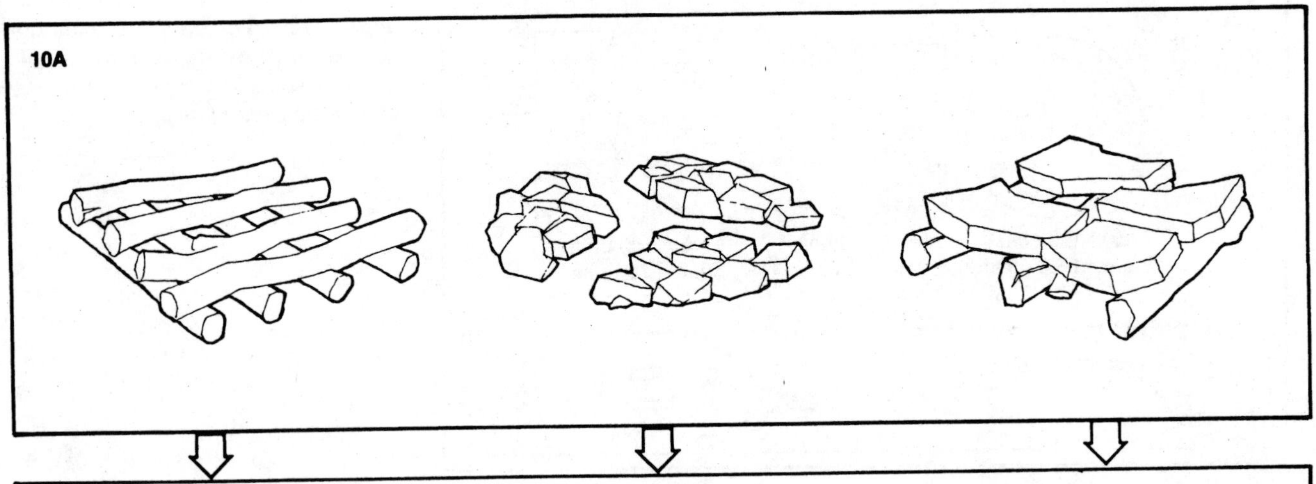

10A

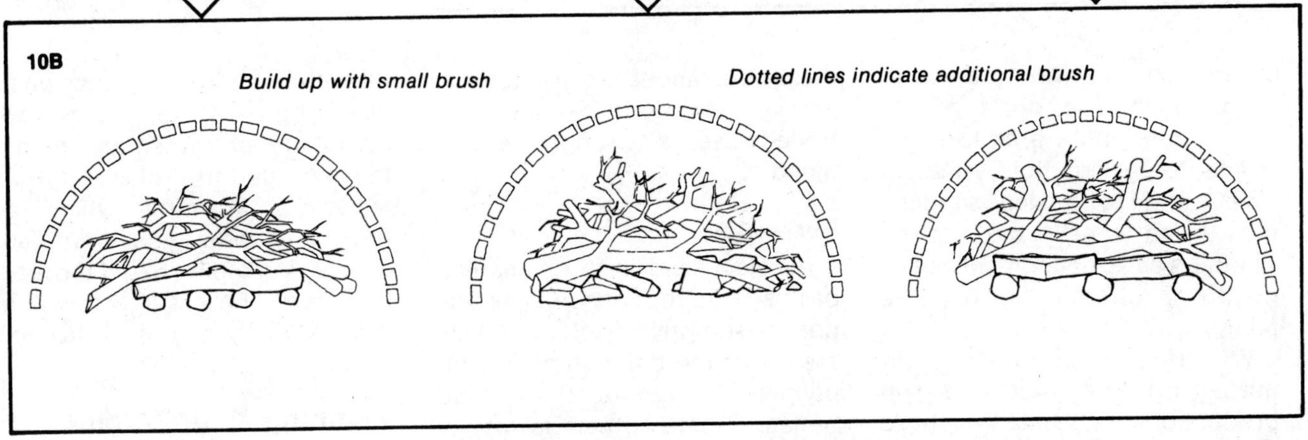

10B

Build up with small brush

Dotted lines indicate additional brush

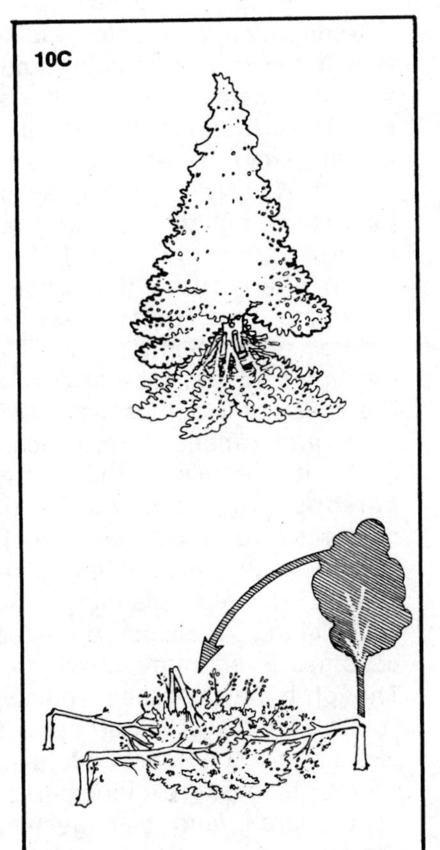

Figure 10. *Construction of dead and living brush piles showing* (A) *base construction methods,* (B) *dead brush pile construction, and* (C) *living brush piles with conifers or hardwoods.*

Figure 11. (Below) *Hardwood forest after a selection cut.*

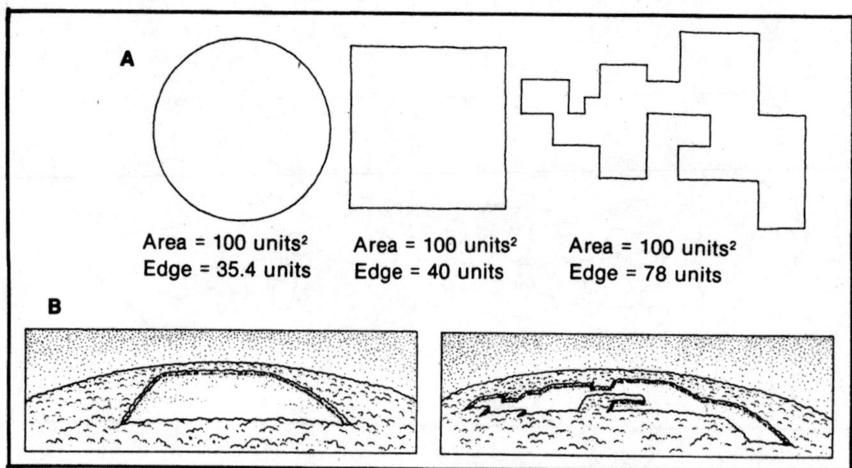

Figure 12. *The effects of clearcut shape on* (top) *the relationship of area to edge and* (bottom) *the aesthetic perspective.*

production. In thinning a young sugar bush, the goals are to convert the entire area to sugar maple, to develop the best sugar trees, and to hasten seedling growth to renew old stands. Thinning can be accomplished by girdling, chemicals, or tree felling.

Wildlife considerations in managing for maple syrup production are similar to those discussed earlier. The development of wolf trees and snags would enhance wildlife habitat. On the other hand, developing a sugar maple monoculture could greatly reduce woodlot diversity. But a sugar bush, when viewed as one component of a larger land management scheme, might be advantageous.

Christmas tree production

Christmas tree farms are merely conifer plantations that are intensely managed (planted, fertilized, protected, shaped, and cut) to produce a well-shaped, dark green tree in 6 to 10 years. A stand of Christmas trees might serve well to increase the total habitat diversity of your property, while still producing a valuable, short-term tree crop. However, many plantation owners indiscriminately use a variety of pesticides to control insects, diseases, and unwanted weeds and brush. Remember, many of these substances are also toxic to animals; so their careful, controlled use is strongly recommended.

Recreation

As discussed at the beginning of this bulletin, consumptive and nonconsumptive uses of wildlife are major recreational outlets for people throughout the United States. Some other forms of recreation are also compatible with wildlife habitat enhancement. Hiking and skiing trails, as well as access roads, constructed through your woodlot, may be used by larger wildlife. Camping areas and berry fields will provide increased edge as well as a diverse environment. However, some recreational activities may not be compatible with wildlife. Snowmobiling and the use of "off-road" vehicles are two possible examples of conflicting use.

Summary

Remember, a diverse environment is more pleasing to most persons, and it aids wildlife. Strive to develop a total land management plan that will provide for a variety of habitat types. If you are fortunate enough to own a large amount of property, different forest "products" can be derived from different parts of your property—a sugar bush here, a hardwood timber stand there, a clearcut or old field somewhere else. High wildlife diversity will surely be promoted by such a mosaic pattern of land use. However, knowing what you have and what you want, and developing a plan to get there are the keys. These subjects will be discussed in the following section.

Planning Your Wildlife Management Strategy

Managing a woodlot for wildlife is a long-term, continuing activity. A clearcut patch will not remain so indefinitely, nor will a useful snag remain standing forever. To realize the greatest long-term benefit for wildlife, careful planning should be undertaken from the onset. Adequate time spent planning before undertaking a wildlife management project will ensure the most efficient use of one's time and financial resources. Since it is unlikely that many persons will have sufficient resources to implement simultaneously all the wildlife modifications desired, planning and establishing realistic priorities becomes even more important. Though it may not seem so now, you may find that the process of planning for the future of wildlife on your land is an exciting part of your overall land management project.

Figure 13. *An inventory base map.*

Key

Hayfield

Snags

Shrub hedge

Brushy field

Wetland

Aspen

Conifer plantation

Mature hardwood

Wolf tree or den tree

Pole stage hardwood

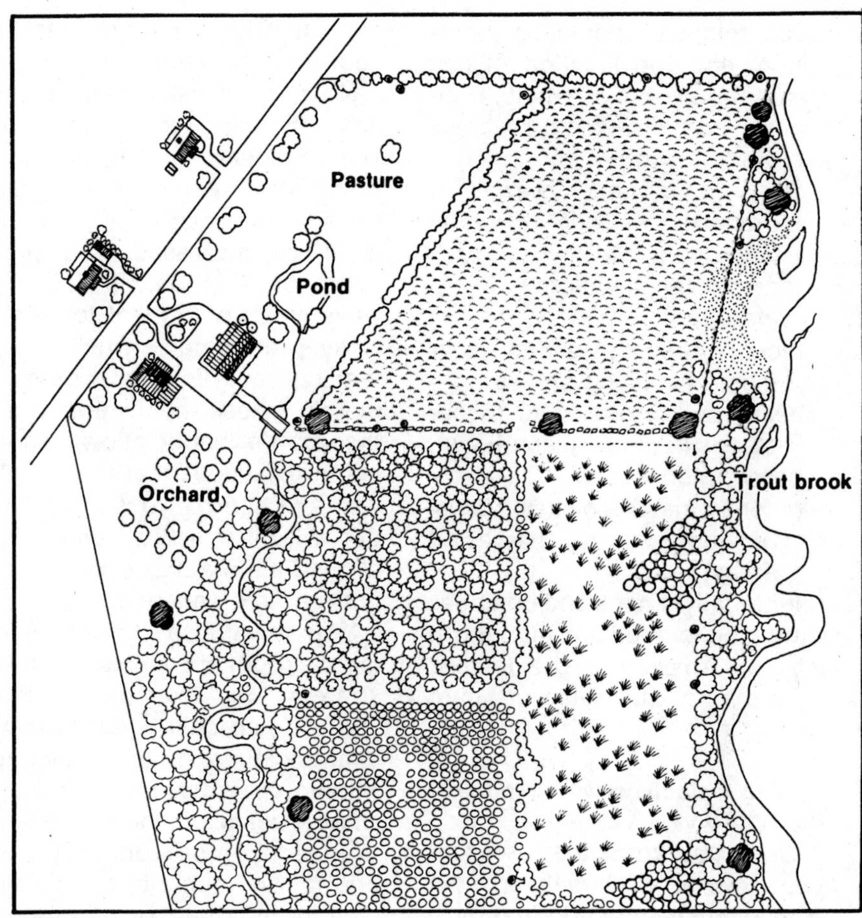

An important initial consideration is whether you intend to conduct a management program solely on your own property or if you would like to work with adjacent landowners. Combining the land, financial, and time resources of several landowners with adjoining property can increase the total size of the wildlife habitat improvement area, increase the diversity of resources available (for example, one landowner may have an existing water source while another has a conifer plantation), and further enhance overall interest in wildlife habitat improvement work. There is one obvious pitfall: the greater the number of people involved, the greater the chance of someone not following through with his or her commitment to the wildlife management plan. The potential advantages and disadvantages of multiple-landowner involvement must be weighed carefully.

Mapping and inventorying

Before you can intelligently manipulate the biological and physical resources of your land for wildlife, you must know what resources exist in an area, their precise location, and their relative utility to various management techniques. To begin this inventory you first need to know exactly where your land is located. This may sound odd, but many landowners do not know the precise boundaries of their property. Locate and mark the boundaries of your land on the ground. Next, you will need an inventory base map (fig. 13). In most instances it will probably be best to make this map yourself rather than to rely on existing maps, such as topographic maps and county soils maps, since you will want the largest scale possible. Topographic maps and soils maps are valuable aids and should be consulted; but because of their relatively small scale, they are not ideal resource maps. County or town planning boards may have maps of a more appropriate scale, and these agencies should be queried. If you have only recently purchased your land, you should check with the county Agricultural Stabilization and Conservation Service and Soil Conservation Service offices to see if they have ever worked with a previous owner in developing a map of the property.

Once a base map outlining your land is completed, key details, such as the location of roads, buildings, streams, ponds, marshes, swamps, woodlots, and fields, can be added. Delineation of soil types, slope, and drainage is also useful for planning water impoundments and planting sites. Work of this type soon becomes a job of resource inventorying. Though the items mentioned can be obtained from secondary sources like topographic maps, aerial photographs, and soil surveys, information in more detail will be needed and will require some footwork and careful observations.

The species and age makeup of your woodland (both canopy and understory vegetation) and brush thickets should be determined, and the location of key areas should be designated. Of primary concern would be areas like the following:

old, abandoned, overgrown orchards (or even individual wild apple trees),
thornapple (hawthorne) thickets,
hickory, beech, oak, or other mast-producing groves,
heavy coniferous cover (cedar stands, pine plantations),
berry patches, and
recently disturbed sites (burns, blowdowns, or harvested areas).

Additionally, snags and den trees should be located and marked on the map. An example of a detailed base map is illustrated in figure 13.

Setting objectives and establishing priorities

Once you know the resources you have to work with on your land, management priorities must be established. Such planning considerations may seem like common sense, but they can be overlooked easily in the enthusiasm for actually "doing something." Careful planning ensures that management efforts will have the desired results.

Plans serve another purpose; they help to evaluate your progress in accomplishing your management objectives. They provide a basis for redirecting your efforts at some time in the future in case circumstances change. They can also add continuity to wildlife management efforts should land ownership happen to change.

The first question that must be answered is, Will your management objectives be primarily for forest products and secondarily for wildlife "products," or will wildlife management be your primary concern? If you do not know which forest management opportunities are possible on your land, find out.

Next, you must decide how much time and money you would like to spend initially and over subsequent years. For instance, if the amount of edge on your land is to be increased, you could approach this objective in two ways: you could plant food- and cover-producing shrubs along the border of your woods or merely cease cultivation along the border and allow woody plants to invade the area naturally. The first alternative is expensive, but will give results quickly; the second alternative costs nothing, but requires patience.

You must also remember the logical order of your management strategy. For example, perhaps you are particularly interested in enchancing your land for aquatic wildlife. If there is currently only a small stream on the property, it would make more sense to put top priority on impounding a section of it rather than building wood duck boxes; they can come later.

Keep the following points in mind when developing your strategy for managing wildlife:

- The plan must be biologically possible. It must rely on wildlife enhancement from existing soils, plants, and water resources or from the introduction of suitable native plants, creation of water impoundments, and construction of structures appropriate for the wildlife species.
- The plan must be economically possible. It must have critical activities spaced out over a sensible time span and be designed within your ability to follow through on the plan. Annual objectives are helpful.
- The plan must strive to increase the wildlife productivity of your woodland on a sustained basis. The long-term carrying capacity of a variety of wildlife species must be enhanced. The more nearly self-sustaining the system, the more likely will be its prolonged attractiveness to wildlife. A management plan demanding extensive, costly manipulation of vegetation is likely to be abandoned before its completion.
- The plan should be directed primarily at maintaining or increasing plants and animals native to the area. Once this is accomplished, thought could be given to reestablishing locally rare native species. Introduction of exotics is seldom a productive course to follow and is not generally recommended.
- Finally, and most importantly, does the plan personally satisfy you by meeting your management objectives and desires? If not, something is wrong.

Getting in Touch with Wildlife

Sound planning and management aimed at enhancing the wildlife values of a woodlot will result in a greater diversity of animals on your property. However, how is this greater diversity going to be enjoyed? Increased success at hunting or trapping will be an obvious return for the consumptive wildlife user. But what about nonconsumptive appreciation? Unfortunately, many people are not "in touch" with wildlife; that is, they know little about the life and times of the many creatures around them. Having an intimate knowledge of wildlife, their distribution, abundance, and behavior not only expands our appreciation for wildlife resources, but also gives us clues as to the "health" of the forest.

One way to achieve these insights is to record wildlife activities and occurrences in a log book. In the naturalist's world these books are field notes. They may be as extensive and detailed

H Gutiérrez 1979 Journal 245

Sapsucker Woods and nearby areas, Ithaca, Tompkins Co, New York

22 March 0630: The second day of spring! Clear, crisp morning as Wanda Richburger and I have our first morning run of the year. We noted many birds singing as we passed through Sapsucker Woods: Brown Creepers; downy, hairy, and pileated woodpeckers all drumming on the snags in swamp; chickadees; white breasted nuthatches; tufted titmice, and Robins all could be heard in the woods. Once we left the woods into scrub lands of arrowwood and marshy areas we spotted redwinged blackbirds and common grackles announcing territory. On further through grassy fields, we saw only a lone meadow lark. I guess our summer nesting birds haven't arrived. After 2½ miles (see route taken below), we turned back anxious to hear more of the woodland species at Sapsucker Woods Bird Sanctuary. We

grass
Warren Rd
Hwy 13
arrowwood thickets
Sapsucker Woods Rd.
woods

are lucky to have the sanctuary near us. It is always so evident to me how important the snags are to the hole nesting birds - and also to us! Tired after the run but really pleased at this fine spring day.

Figure 14. *Sample format for field notes showing a typical journal entry.*

as one wishes. Figures 14 and 15 are sample formats for field notes developed by an early California naturalist, Joseph Grinnell. Such formats have been adopted by many people throughout the world. Each page should contain all the information shown, with each page numbered sequentially. This standardization is important should you drop your notes or, more importantly, should someone else try to read your account of the changing forest and wildlife. Notes of this kind often are valuable resources, which frequently are stored in the archives of libraries for their historical and scientific value. They, or copies, can also be passed on to each consecutive owner as a record of the land. A logical and organized set of notes is one way of assuring that the notes will be maintained rather than discarded.

For convenience, we have found that a notebook that holds 5-by-7-inch (12.7-by-17.8-cm) notebook paper is easiest to handle in the field and to store. Do not make the mistake of taking notes in different notebooks with different paper sizes. This only leads to later confusion and frustration.

Two useful categories of field notes are the journal and the species account. The journal (fig. 14) is an appropriate place to record daily events when observing wildlife. Your activities (such as cutting brush, logging, or skiing), weather, description of areas visited, and special notes of interesting things encountered are all included as entries in the journal. You may also wish to record your feelings. Field notes differ from a diary in that they have the directed purpose of serving as a repository for contact with wildlife, changing land use, changing vegetation, your management efforts and their results. So often we have wondered about the history of wildlife in a state, region, or the nation; accurate field notes could help provide this information. Field notes were written by explorers and naturalists like Audubon, Muir, and Nuttall, but little is known of the

Figure 15. *Sample format for field notes showing a typical species account.*

R.J. Gutiérrez
1979

Brown Creeper
Certhia familiaris

②

260 Sapsucker Woods Rd, Ithaca, Tomkins Co. New York

10 March 0830: Saw my first brown creeper in my yard - near the bird feeder. It always amazes me how they are so inconspicuous during the summer, fall, and winter. I think that I shall start an account of these little birds today in the hopes of learning a little more about them

Cornell University Campus, Ithaca, Tomkins Co. New York

20 March 0745: Heard a creeper singing his trill notes in the woods behind Fernow Hall - never had noticed the critters there before. 1030: walking to the library heard a creeper calling from the same woods (same bird?).

Sapsucker Woods Rd, Ithaca, Tomkins Co., New York

21 March 1635: A brown creeper at the feeder tree. Although I've seen them here several times recently they don't seem to use the suet bag, yet this "clever" bird has learned(?) to pick up the suet pieces the woodpeckers drop. Interestingly, however, the bird doesn't leave the tree but reaches out from the tree and picks up suet on the ground. Its feet always holding on to the tree.

suet

suet flakes

early landowners' contact with natural things. Perhaps they did not view wildlife as you do, and their not recording this information reflects this difference. How often have you wondered about the history of your own land? Even trying to recall days past to another person is a tedious effort for which little accuracy can be assured after but a few years.

A species account (fig. 15) is developed when one is interested in a particular species and wishes to record specific information about it. A different account is undertaken for each species studied. This method improves upon the rate of retrieving information about an individual species. Hunters can record the locations and yearly fluctuations of game; or perhaps the success of your wood duck, bluebird, or other bird houses can be recorded over time. Through these notes you become intimately involved with a species because you care enough to take time to observe it.

Margaret Morse Nice, a homemaker, became interested in the song sparrows that frequented her backyard in Ohio. She began taking field notes on the birds' behavior and natural history. Before long she became engrossed with the study of song sparrows and eventually published papers on the biology of the song sparrow, which are considered classics by modern professional ornithologists. She continued her study of birds, writing many more scientific papers on them, and became an inspiration to amateur ornithologists everywhere. Ms. Nice's story illustrates how the secrets and mysteries of wildlife can be observed, unraveled, and appreciated by a careful, patient observer with a field notebook. Young people find great reward in studying animals and recording what they have seen in their notebooks.

Over time you can see how your wildlife populations have changed through your efforts or as a result of forest succession or nearby changes in land use. Carefully recorded field notes will give information to help you manage your land in the future. If you are not inclined to write extensive notes, lists of wildlife seen through the year and your specific efforts are worthwhile notes to record.

What Can Be Done: A Case History

To indicate beneficial management changes in the landscape for wildlife or to speculate on the outcome of managing a woodland area is often not difficult. The type of improvements suggested here are relatively easy to carry out. However, a concrete example of a retired farm where an owner has made improvements specific for wildlife would be valuable. One such example is provided by the Gustav A. Swanson family.

The Swansons purchased the 88-acre (35-ha) North Star Farm in Upstate New York in 1948. There had been only 10 previous owners of the farm (of whom 5 covered 132 years). The area was primarily field crops and grassland maintained by cultivation and mowing. As pointed out earlier, old field succession proceeds rapidly to mature forest stages if land is left undisturbed in the Northeast. On the North Star Farm succession was reversed on some areas by building ponds and marshes; natural succession continued on 20 acres (8 ha); succession was hastened on 40 acres (16 ha) by tree and shrub planting; and 15 acres (6 ha) of grassland were maintained by annual mowing (see fig. 16).

Recreation, rather than scientific study or economic gain, was the prime consideration for management on the farm; so the planning was casual, but aided by the Soil Conservation Service. Classic wildlife management steps included census, evaluating productivity, diagnosis, and control. The specific management practices employed were as follows:

Plantings

Trees—about 40,000 conifers of 8 species; a few osage orange, mountain ash

Shrubs—roses, Russian olive, autumn olive, elderberry, winterberry, barberry, redosier dogwood, filberts, highbush cranberry

Vines—bittersweet and releasing wild grape

Food patches—corn, buckwheat, millet, sunflower, birdsfoot trefoil (lime and fertilizer used)

Aquatic plants—wild rice, *Butomus*, cattail, duck potato, sago pondweed, *Phragmites*, rice cutgrass, water smartweed

Stocking mallards, barn owls, great horned owls, quail, pheasants

Creating water areas—8 ponds and marshes

Grasslands maintained by mowing

Nest boxes for tree swallows, bluebirds, purple martins, wrens, wood ducks, woodpeckers

Control of feral house cats

Trail system built with observation cabin in the woods

Winter bird feeding near the house

Fish stocking for fish-eating birds

Using duck decoys

Providing perches

The results of the work have been remarkable in that 177 species of birds have been recorded in 18 years, including 100 species seen annually. Fifteen species of waterfowl, 4 herons and bitterns, 2 grebes, 7 shorebirds, kingfishers, and other marsh birds were attracted to the ponds and marshes. The grebes, kingfishers, herons, mergansers, and ospreys made good use of the fish-stocking effort. The grasslands attracted upland sandpipers, bobolinks, meadowlarks; and the savanna, grasshopper, Henslow's and Vesper sparrows. Tree swallows, starlings, and house wrens used the nest boxes. The perches were used by all the swallows, ducks, and kingfishers. Many species of birds (such as woodcock, ruffed grouse, and many warbler species) responded to the natural succession of plants and the plantings. In addition, other wildlife that responded to management included deer, red fox, raccoons, woodchucks, gray squirrels, three species of tree frogs, three other frog species, toads, newts, salamanders, water and garter snakes, turtles, and fishes (brown, brook, and rainbow trout, bass, perch, minnows, channel catfish, and others). The farm became a wildlife paradise.

This project was undertaken with the help of professional conservation agencies. The type of assistance that the Swansons received is briefly summarized below. Unfortunately, some of these assistance programs are no longer available; so inquire early in your planning process.

- County Soil Conservation District and U.S. Soil Conservation Service: cooperator plan and maps, soils mapping, design and supervision of construction of two fish ponds, tree and shrub planting stock and transportation and arrangement for planting, design and supervision of construction of two diversion ditches
- N.Y.S. Department of Environmental Conservation, Forest Resources Subdivision, and the Forest Practice Act: cooperator tree planting plan, trees furnished free in earlier years and at $5 per 1000 in later years from the state nursery
- N.Y.S. Department of Environmental Conservation, Division of Fish and Wildlife: designed and constructed two wildlife marshes and five small potholes and assumed proportion of construction cost, furnished most of shrub

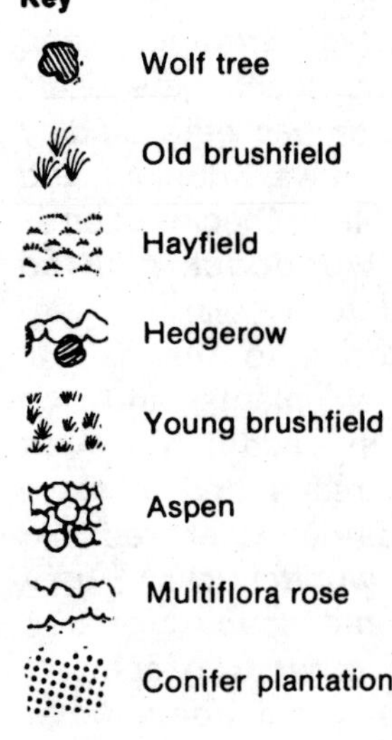

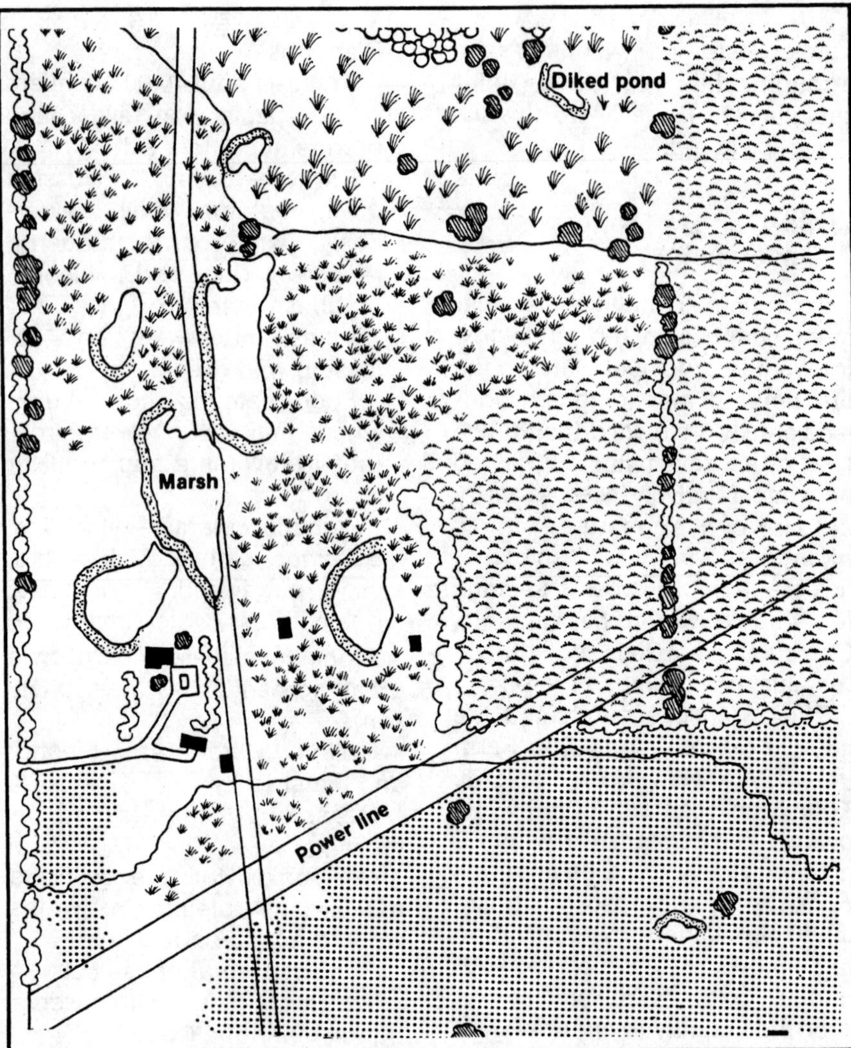

Figure 16. *Base map for the North Star Farm in Upstate New York.*

planting stock free of charge and provided planting service for many of shrubs at less than cost under habitat development project

• USDA, ACP Program: shared cost of tree planting, some shrub planting, liming and fertilizing and planting birdsfoot trefoil field, and constructing one of the ponds

• USDA, Soil Bank Program: rental of 8-acre (3-ha) field retired from corn and grain production

• Cooperative Agricultural Extension Service, both county agents and specialists from Cornell University: running soil tests; advising on fish stocking, tree planting, water supply, nuisance wildlife control, gardening, naturalizing of flowers, etc.

The North Star Farm is a study in creating the elements of a good wildlife area. Creating diversity in vegetation types and providing food, cover, water, and space were the simple rules followed (fig. 16). Maintaining field notes allowed the Swansons to diagnose the results of their efforts and kept them in touch with wildlife. Remember, this success story can be repeated by those of you who wish to do so.

Conclusion

The future of wildlife habitat in the Northeast is in the hands of the private landowner. Therefore, the responsibility for the direct care and husbandry of woodland wildlife belongs to the small woodland owner. Studies show that landowners care about their land for reasons beyond its economic value, but that they often lack the background information to maximize wildlife values on their lands. A few examples of how a woodland owner can enhance and maintain good wildlife habitat have been provided in this bulletin.

Once again, the clear spring air is carrying the sound of woodpeckers. But it is 5 years hence, and the woodpeckers' drumming now takes on a different meaning. A little downy woodpecker drums on a snag you left in a small forest clearcut, a hairy woodpecker stakes out his territory from a snag you left in your firewood–cutting operation last fall, and the granddaddy of all, the pileated woodpecker, "punishes" the huge dead elm up the forested creek, an area that you have decided to leave as mature woods.

FISH MANAGEMENT IN NEW YORK PONDS

Contents

3 Kind of fish to stock
5 Pond location and construction features
7 Stocking regulations and sources of fish
8 Biology and management of trout ponds
12 Biology and management of bass-shiner ponds
14 Biology and management of bass-bluegill ponds
16 Biology and management of other species
17 Pond maintenance
20 Regional offices of the New York State Department of Environmental Conservation

FISH MANAGEMENT IN NEW YORK PONDS

There are more than 40,000 ponds in New York State and new ones are being constructed at the rate of about 1,000 a year. Of the various pond uses, fishing is one of the most popular because it provides recreation for the whole family, and the fish caught are tasty and nutritious.

The purpose of this publication is to discuss:

- Factors to consider in deciding which fish species to stock.
- Design and construction features particularly important in fish ponds.
- Where and how to obtain fish for a pond.
- Growth, survival, reproduction, and yield that can be expected from a fish pond in New York.
- Management practices for obtaining satisfactory fishing from your pond.

Information presented here is based largely on results of 12 years' work on more than 150 ponds in Central New York State. The recommendations given should apply to ponds across New York that have surface areas up to 2 acres and maximum depths of 7 to 15 feet.

Kind of Fish to Stock

Ponds can be used for trout if the water does not become too warm during summer months; otherwise, they should be stocked with fish that thrive in warmer water. The only warm-water species recommended at present are a combination of largemouth bass and golden shiners or a combination of bass and bluegill sunfish. This section discusses some of the factors that might influence the pond owner's choice between trout and warm-water species.

Water temperature

For trout, it is important that *bottom* water in the pond remains *cool;* for bass, shiners, and bluegills, it is important that *surface* water becomes *warm.*

Survival of trout in New York ponds is influenced more by maximum summer water temperature than by any other factor. Although pond trout can withstand water temperatures as high as 80° F. for periods of one or two days, prolonged periods of water temperature above 74° F. will cause trout to die. Whether a pond will be suitable for trout depends chiefly on how long the coolest water, near the pond bottom, remains above 74° F. for any one period.

Bottom water temperature, which may differ from that of the surface by as much as 12° F., can be measured accurately with a maximum-minimum thermometer or with a glass thermometer suspended in a tin can (fig. 1). To suspend the thermometer, make one pencil-sized hole in the top of a quart can of motor oil, empty and wash it out. Punch three very small holes in the top rim of the can and attach a wire bridle for suspending it, as shown. Use an unframed thermometer with the degrees on the thermometer stem itself.[1] Insert the thermometer through the hole in the can and secure it with a rubber band to suspend the bulb in the lower part of the can without its touching the sides. Obtain a stout bamboo pole 15 feet long and attach a 10-foot length of heavy twine connecting the bridle to the end of the pole, as illustrated.

Fill the can with water to make it sink. With the pole, hold the can out over the deepest part of the pond (usually about 16 ft out from the middle of the dike) and lower it to the bottom. Leave the can on the bottom for at least three hours to allow the water in it to reach the temperature of its surroundings. Then carefully raise the can to the surface, disturbing the water in it as little as possible. Bring the can to shore and read the thermometer immediately, keeping the bulb well immersed in the can of water.

Taking a series of bottom water temperatures during the last two

---

[1] Thermometers of this kind are stocked or can be ordered at hardware and photographic supply stores.

Figure 1. Temperature of the pond's deepest water can be accurately measured with thermometer suspended in an empty oil can. See directions in text.

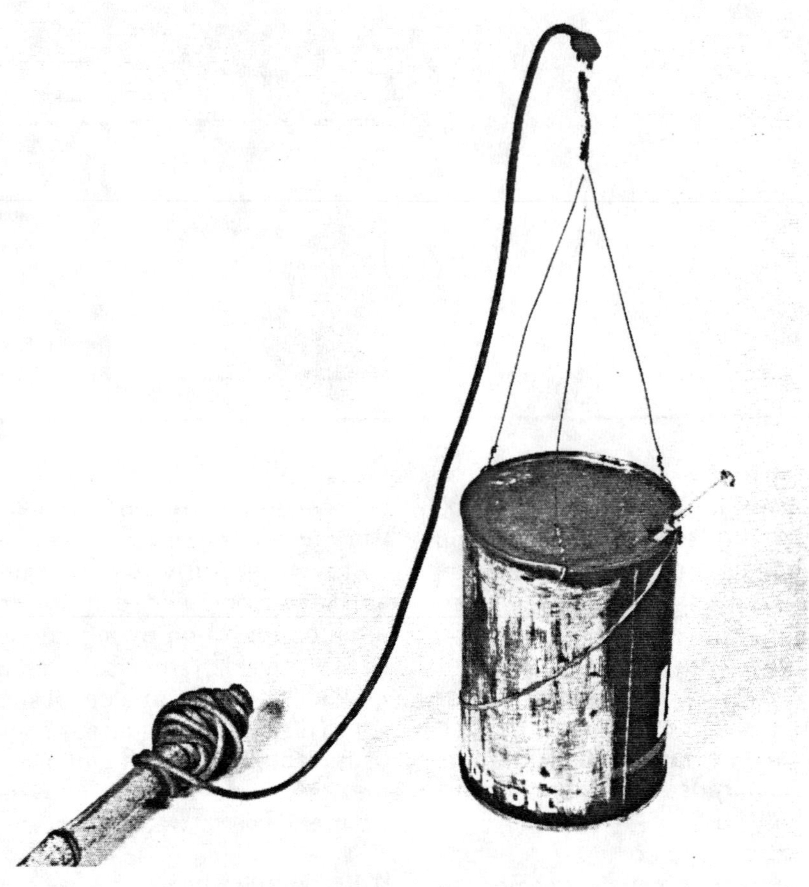

or three weeks of July will give you an idea of what to expect from your pond.

Satisfactory growth and reproduction of warm-water species occur when the surface water of the pond becomes warm enough. For bass and shiners the temperature should be above 72° F. and for bluegills 80° F. for several weeks each summer. New York ponds probably never get too warm for these species. To determine a pond's suitability for warm-water species, the owner should measure surface temperatures periodically during the summer. This can be done by placing a thermometer in undisturbed water, 12 inches below the surface, but not touching the bottom. Read the thermometer, still immersed, after about five minutes.

New York ponds can be divided into three groups according to their summer water temperatures. *Cold-water ponds* are those whose surface temperatures seldom, if ever, rise above 72° F.; trout should be stocked in all of these. *Cool-water ponds* are those whose bottom temperatures rise above 74° F. for only short periods and whose surface temperatures exceed 72° F. for periods of several weeks but only infrequently reach 80° F. or above; trout or the bass-shiner combination will do well in these. *Warm-water ponds* are those whose surface temperatures remain above 80° F. for considerable periods in summer; these should be stocked with the bass-shiner or bass-bluegill combination.

Source of water

If a pond has a permanent supply of spring water—that is, if there is some water running out of the pond at all times—and the pond has a maximum depth of at least eight feet, then it is practically certain to support trout in almost any year. Many ponds fed entirely by runoff water from the surrounding watershed are excellent trout producers, although trout survival in these ponds may be poor in unusually hot summers. In ponds fed entirely by runoff water, chances of summer trout mortality are less in those located at higher elevations, in those having a maximum depth of at least 10 feet, and in those ponds that receive some shade.

In a pond where bluegills are desired, springs will be a liability if they cool the water enough to retard or prevent their spawning.

Pond size

It is practical to use ponds as small as one-tenth acre (surface area) for trout, because these fish can be stocked at high rates. The bass-shiner combination will thrive in ponds of one-fourth acre and even one-sixth acre if the pond has an average depth of four feet or more. Usually the bass-bluegill combination should be stocked only in ponds larger than one-half acre. This combination may succeed in a pond as small as one-third acre *if* the pond has all the recommended construction features *and* can be carefully managed.

Effect of water plants

Water plants become a problem in most ponds if they are not controlled periodically by chemical or mechanical means. The owner's choice of fish may be influenced by the amount of time and money he or she can spend on control. Information on the control of large plants and algae in farm ponds is available in Cornell Information Bulletin 107, *Aquatic Plant Management and Control.*

In trout and in bass-shiner ponds, moderate amounts of plants (covering up to one-fourth of the pond's surface area) seem to increase fish production. However, most biologists recommend that a bass-bluegill pond be kept free of plants, and thus the bass-bluegill pond owner must usually practice more intensive control. If the pond is overflowing, a permit must be obtained for the use of any weed control chemical.

Kind of fishing provided

Trout, bass-shiner, and bass-bluegill ponds differ somewhat in the kind of fishing they provide. Because pond trout are usually hard to catch during the summer months, trout ponds offer most fishing during the fall, winter, and spring. Bass and bluegills provide most fishing during the spring and summer months.

Under New York conditions the difference in total pounds of fish produced with the three types of stocking described here is not large.[2] Trout ponds can support average annual harvests of about 20 to 40 pounds per acre (depending on the number stocked), and bass-shiner ponds can provide bass harvests averaging about 25 pounds per acre per year. Bass-bluegill populations can support average harvests of about 15 pounds of bass and 35 pounds of bluegills per year.

Although trout and bass ponds are more commonly underfished than overfished, it is still possible to "fish out" trout and bass. Fishing quality usually deteriorates fairly rapidly in a pond that is subject to uncontrolled fishing.

Main drawbacks with each stocking method

Trout seldom reproduce in farm ponds, seldom survive beyond three or four years, and usually must be restocked every two years to maintain satisfactory fishing.

In bass-shiner ponds, shiners usually become extinct during the first five years after stocking. Smaller bass then tend to become too numerous and stunted. If this occurs, some of the smaller bass (between 8 and 10 inches) must be harvested.

In bass-bluegill ponds, bluegills usually produce more young than the bass will eat. Bluegill growth rates then decrease. If too many of the smaller bluegills are present, fishing deteriorates; moreover the bass population may suffer from bluegill competition for food and space. Crowded bluegill populations need to be thinned by trapping or seining; it may even be necessary to drain or poison the pond and begin again.

Which species should you stock?

If yours is a *cold-water pond,* stock trout.

If you have a *cool-water pond,* stock either trout or the bass-shiner combination. Remember that trout have to be restocked every two or three years. If you have a new pond and do not know whether to start off with trout or bass-shiners, it might be best to begin with trout; because pond trout are short-lived and almost never reproduce, it is easy to switch from trout to bass-shiners whenever you wish. On the other hand, once warm-water species are established in the pond, it is impossible to change over to trout without first killing off the entire warm-water population by draining or by using chemicals, either of which may present difficulties.

If you have a *warm-water pond,* stock either bass and shiners or bass and bluegills. The bass-shiner combination usually produces more bass fishing (but *only* bass fishing) and requires less management. Bass-bluegill ponds provide fishing for two species, but are usually more time-consuming to manage. In ponds smaller than one-half acre, bluegill numbers may be very difficult to control.

Pond Location and Construction Features

The importance of proper location, design, and construction of any pond cannot be overemphasized. Technical assistance on these matters can be obtained from the Soil Conservation Service, and other aid may be available through the Agricultural Stabilization and Conservation Program. Every prospective pond owner should consult the county agricultural agent for specific information on the pond services available in the county and on the design and construction of ponds. The following discussion is limited to those aspects of the location and construction of ponds of particular importance in fish management.

Location

For satisfactory fish production, the pond should be located where sufficient depth and the best possible water supply can be obtained.

A location near the house is

[2] Detailed stocking recommendations are given in later sections.

essential if the pond is needed for fire protection. This location also lessens the chance that unauthorized persons will fish or stock the pond; either action can have adverse effects. Fish ponds should not be located where they will receive barnyard drainage.

A pond to be used for fish production should not be located where it will receive silty runoff from land regularly cultivated. Such runoff interferes with production of fish food organisms and reduces fish production. As silt deposits build up, the pond gradually becomes too shallow.

Size, depth, and slope

If properly constructed and intensively managed, ponds as small as one-tenth acre are suitable for trout, ponds down to one-sixth acre are satisfactory for bass and shiners, and ponds of one-half (occasionally one-third) acre or larger can be used for bass and bluegills. Of course, the larger the pond, the more fish it will support and the more fishing it will provide.

Trout require cool or cold water, even in midsummer. The deeper the pond, the cooler its bottom water will remain. For trout, New York ponds with a year-round supply of spring water should have a maximum depth of at least 8 feet. Seven feet is occasionally enough when springs feeding the pond are exceptionally large. Runoff ponds should be 10 feet deep for trout, although somewhat shallower ponds will give good results in some years.

Bass and shiners thrive in cool or warm water, bluegills in warm water. Thus ponds fed by large springs will seldom be suitable for these species. When most of the pond's water comes from runoff, the water level and, consequently, the water depth tend to fluctuate. The water level is usually lowest in late summer. For satisfactory production of bass or bluegills or both, fluctuations in water level should not be severe, and the pond's maximum depth should never be less than about 7 feet. This means that maximum depth in late spring should be at least 8 feet.

It follows that if a pond is to be used for irrigation, maximum depth after water withdrawals should be at least 7 or 8 feet.

All sides of the pond should have 2:1 slopes out to a point where the water is always at least 3 feet deep. This minimizes the area of shallow water where plants thrive and lessens plant problems considerably. In trout ponds shallow water is also undesirable because it warms up quickly during sunny weather and warms the whole pond when mixed with the deeper water by wind action.

Water supply

For New York ponds fed entirely by runoff water, a five-acre watershed is generally adequate to maintain a one-acre pond. If there is some permanent supply of spring water, the watershed area can be reduced proportionately. If the watershed is larger than necessary, the excess water flushing through the pond interferes with the fish's food chain by carrying out nutrients and plankton. Large outflows may also permit the fish to leave the pond and may endanger the dike. Unneeded runoff water can be kept out of the pond by constructing a diversion ditch.

Whenever possible, water bypassed from an adjacent stream should not be used to supply a farm pond used for fish production. Practically all streams contain undesirable fish of various kinds, and some of these eventually find their way into most by-pass ponds. Streams frequently carry heavy silt loads, especially after heavy rains. In many cases the stream water becomes too warm for trout.

If it is essential to use by-pass water for a fish pond, contamination by unwanted fish can be prevented or minimized if the water enters the pond through a pipe whose outlet is at least 2½ feet above the maximum pond level (fig. 2). The water falls into a box about 2 feet square, or larger if

Figure 2. If a by-pass water supply must be used, this box with screened bottom may keep out weed fish.

large amounts of water enter the pond. The sides can be wood or sheet metal and are about 16 inches high. The top of this box is open, but the bottom consists of plastic window screening (about 15 meshes to the in.), thoroughly reinforced from below by wooden or metal slats. The box is mounted securely on four legs; water from the inflow pipe falls directly onto the screening. The screen should be at least 6 inches above maximum water level. The construction must be sturdy, and all parts should be protected against rust and rot. Fish entering through the pipe are deposited on the screen where they die from lack of water or from being beaten against the screen by the falling water. Experience will determine how often it must be cleaned to keep debris out of the box. This will vary with the season.

Use tile or pipe to lead spring water from the place where it first appears above ground into a trout pond. This method can keep the inflowing spring water as much as 15°F. cooler than if it were allowed to trickle into the pond above ground. The tile need not be buried much below ground level.

Water control structures

A combination trickle tube and drain pipe is particularly desirable in any pond to be managed for fish production. Although this structure is expensive, fish are less likely to escape through it than over a spillway. If only a spillway is used, it should be as wide and level as possible to spread the outflowing water in a thin sheet. A small wooden dam two to four inches high across the spillway tends to prevent escapes. If a screen is used for this purpose, it should not be more than four inches high because it soon becomes clogged and merely acts as a dam.

A drain pipe is an important asset in any fish pond. If the pond develops leaks, it can be drained and repaired. If undesirable fish enter the pond, it is often easiest to remove them by draining. If bluegills become seriously overcrowded, or if partial winterkill occurs in bass-bluegill ponds, it may be best to drain the pond and begin again.

Fencing

Livestock should not have access to a farm pond. Their trampling and wading not only endanger the dike, but keep the water turbid and reduce the production of fish food organisms.

Stocking Regulations and Sources of Fish

Before fish can be stocked or restocked in any pond or other water, permission to do so must be obtained from the State Department of Environmental Conservation through the regional fish manager.[3] The procedure is simple, and there is no charge for the permit.

Fish for stocking privately owned ponds must be obtained from commercial hatcheries. The program under which the United States Fish and Wildlife Service supplied fish through local Soil Conservation Service offices has been discontinued. Your local Soil Conservation Service office or the regional fish manager for your area should be able to provide a list of commercial hatcheries in New York and neighboring states. A list of these hatcheries is also available from the New York State Department of Environmental Conservation, Bureau of Fisheries, 50 Wolf Road, Albany, New York 12201. Hatcheries operated by the New York State Department of Environmental Conservation do not supply fish for privately owned ponds.

In some counties the Soil and Water Conservation Committee has coordinated a group purchase of fish from reliable suppliers. Check with your local Soil and Water Conservation office to see if such a program is available in your area. The major advantage

[3]A directory of regional offices of New York State is given on page 20 of this bulletin.

of a group purchase is a reduction in shipping costs and, possibly, a large quantity discount in price.

Biology and Management of Trout Ponds

Kinds of trout

Brook trout (fig. 3) or rainbow trout (fig. 4) are equally suitable for New York ponds. Many people consider the brook trout to be better eating. Although neither species is difficult to catch in the cooler months of the year, it is easier to "fish out" a brook trout population. On the other hand, rainbows are generally considered to be more spectacular fighters. A mixture of these two kinds of trout can be stocked in a pond to provide greater variety of fishing. If both kinds of trout are stocked, they should be roughly the same size so that one group will not prey heavily on the other.

Brown trout (fig. 5) *are generally unsatisfactory in New York ponds* because they are more difficult to catch than either brook or rainbow trout. Thus browns provide poor to mediocre fishing and a low yield on the investment. Also, the old brown trout remaining in a pond prey heavily on the fingerlings introduced for restocking.

Trout are unable to compete successfully with most other fish in a pond because these other fish multiply rapidly and monopolize the food. Contaminating species will ruin the pond for trout production until the entire fish population is killed off and a new trout population established. There are a few kinds of small, nonprolific minnows that might not interfere with trout production. However, it is very difficult to obtain these "harmless" minnows without getting some harmful ones as well. For these reasons, no minnows or other fish of any kind should be stocked. Pond trout thrive on an insect-rich, fish-free diet.

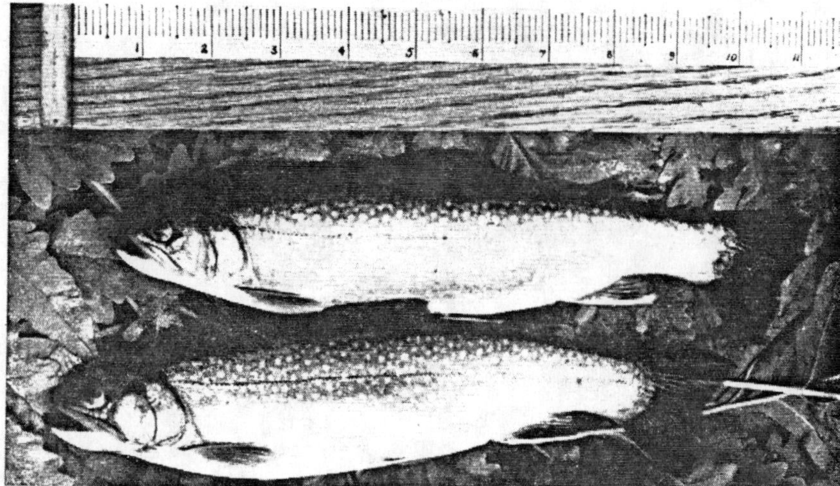

Figure 3. Brook trout.

Figure 4. Rainbow trout.

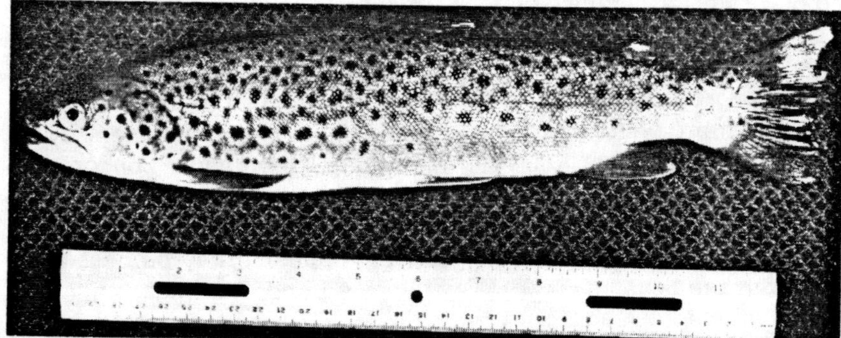

Figure 5. Brown trout.

Stocking recommendations

Either spring fingerlings (2 to 3 in. long, 2 or 3 months old) or fall fingerlings (5 to 6 inches long, 7 or 8 months old) can be used in stocking farm ponds with trout. Both types reach catchable size about the same time, that is, in the spring following stocking. However, results with spring fingerlings are much more variable and unpredictable than with fall fingerlings, except in ponds containing no fish and fed by strong, permanent springs.

When trout are obtained from commercial hatcheries in the East, spring fingerlings usually sell for about $28 to $60 per hundred and fall fingerlings for about $34 to $95 per hundred FOB. At these prices, fall fingerlings usually provide considerably more catchable size trout per dollar invested than will spring fingerlings. It is very uneconomical to purchase trout larger than about six inches for pond stocking.

Thus, *it is usually best to use fall fingerlings for trout stocking n New York ponds.*

Trout should never be stocked during the warm season. Spring ingerlings, if stocked, should be planted no later than May 1; fall ingerlings should be planted after September 30.

In most New York ponds, 600 all fingerlings (or 2,000 spring ingerlings) per acre of pond surace should be stocked to produce he maximum yield of fish consisent with satisfactory growth. Some ponds that are ideal for rout can be stocked at rates of 00 fall fingerlings per acre. Ocasionally trout in ponds located n exceptionally low-lime soils t high elevations will show satisactory growth only when stocked t 400 fall fingerlings per acre.

When the pond owner obtains tock, he or she should take speial precautions that the trout ill enter the pond in good condion. The hatchery person may dvise the owner concerning umber and size of containers to ring along. Thoroughly clean lastic garbage cans with covers an be used to transport trout 00 fall fingerlings per 30-gal an), although larger tanks, with overs, are often more satisfacry.

Trout should be transported nly in the cool or cold weather f spring or fall. If there is danger that the tank's water temperature will rise above 55°F. during transit, then ice should be packed around the tank. *If ice is to be placed in the water used for carrying fish, it is absolutely essential to use ice made from nonchlorinated water since very minute quantities of chlorine will kill fish.* If the fish are to be transported considerable distances, then the water should receive oxygen. Oxygen-producing tablets (2 per milk can) can be used and are available in sport and bait shops.

When stocking trout, place the can or bucket in the pond and tip it gently on its side so that the fish can swim out. Do not plant them near the overflow structure. If the temperature of the water in the pond differs from the temperature of water in the transport tank by more than 5°F the fish should be "tempered" gradually to the pond temperature over a period of 1 to 2 hours. Tempering can be done by adding pond water slowly to the transport tank. Remember to obtain a state permit before transporting or stocking fish.

Growth

Brook and rainbow trout grow at about the same rate in New York ponds. Average lengths and weights in spring and fall for three years after stocking are given in table 1. In a pond stocked with either 2,000 spring fingerlings or 600 fall fingerlings per surface acre, the trout generally average about eight inches long by the following spring. Growth rate generally decreases as the fish grow older and is usually somewhat faster in summer than in winter.

Growth rates vary considerably from one pond to the next. Trout probably grow a little more slowly in the first few months after a pond has filled, before it has built up a large supply of aquatic insect life, the trout's principal food. Also trout tend to grow more slowly in soft (acid) water than in hard (alkaline) water.

Survival

Survival of pond trout tends to fluctuate with annual variations in average summer temperature. In the first year after stocking, survival also varies with the size of fingerlings stocked. During the summer following stocking as *spring* fingerlings, the survival is highly variable, averaging only about 30 percent. In the two succeeding summers, average survival is about 50 percent. Overwinter survival of trout in each year of pond life is commonly 60 and 80 percent.

The dotted line in figure 6 shows the average number of brook or rainbow trout remaining in an *unfished* pond during the three years following stocking at a rate of 600 fall fingerlings (or 2,000 spring fingerlings) per acre. If lower stocking rates are used, the number of survivors at any time will be proportionately less.

From the graph it is clear that

Table 1. Average lengths and weights of pond trout in the first three years following stocking

	First year		*Second year*		*Third year*	
	Spring	*Fall*	*Spring*	*Fall*	*Spring*	*Fall*
Length, inches	8.1	10.1	11.1	12.8	13.5	14.2
Weight, ounces	4	8	10	14	17	22

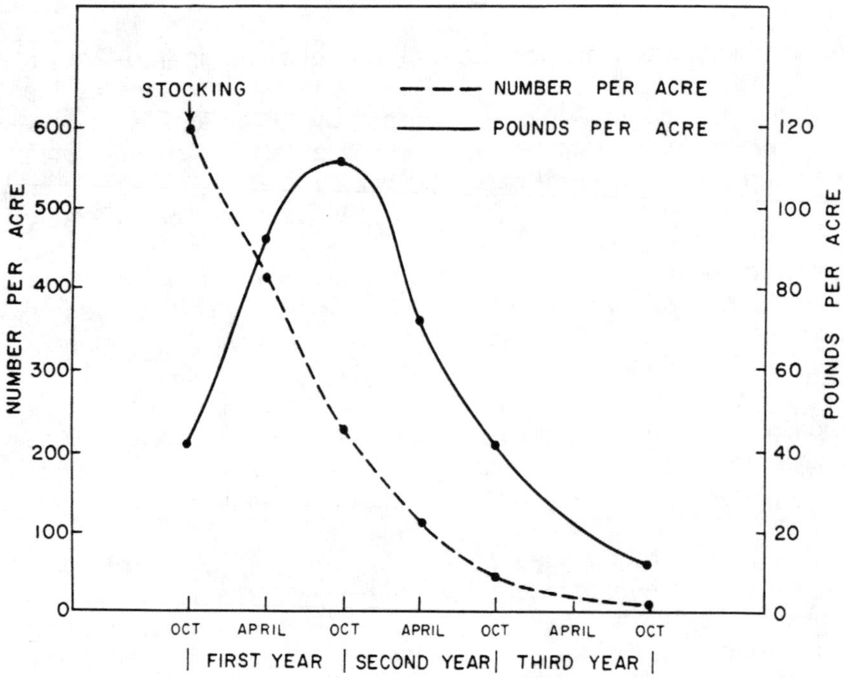

Figure 6. Numbers and pounds of trout remaining in an unfished pond after stocking with 600 fall fingerlings per acre.

Table 2. Relation between number of trout per acre harvested in the first year and number per acre that could be harvested in the second year after stocking. Average figures for ponds stocked at rates of 300 and 600 fall fingerlings per acre

Number of trout per acre		
Harvested in first year	*Available for harvest in second year — When stocking rate was:* 300/acre	600/acre
0	35	70
50	25	60
100	15	50
150	5	40
200	—	30
250	—	20
300	—	10

few trout remain after three years in a pond, and four-year-olds are a rarity, as is also the case in most other trout waters of the state. Fish mortality from natural causes is normally a gradual process and takes place more or less continuously, even through the dead fish are very seldom seen.

Reproduction

Because most ponds lack a suitable spawning site, pond trout rarely reproduce, although they may go through the act of spawning. A suitable spawning site for trout consists of a gravel area through which a good flow of water percolates during the incubation period, supplying the eggs in the gravel with fresh, oxygen-rich water and keeping them from being smothered by silt deposits. In a very few ponds having exceptionally large and concentrated springs, limited trout reproduction has occurred naturally at times or has been achieved by placing beds of gravel in suitable locations. To date no method has been discovered for achieving adequate natural reproduction in the average spring-fed pond without resorting to modifications and additional construction which require considerable outlays of time and money.

Trout production

The total poundage of trout present in a pond at any time following stocking is the net result of two opposing trends: growth, which increases poundage; and deaths, which reduce it. When the growth rate exceeds the death rate, there is a net increase in total poundage, and vice versa. The continuous line in figure 6 shows the total pounds of trout present in an *average unfished* New York pond during the three years following stocking with 600 fall (or 2,000 spring) fingerlings. Under these conditions, total poundage reaches a maximum, averaging about 110 pounds per acre by fall of the first year following stocking, when about 230 trout (dotted line, same graph) remain. One year later only 41 pounds (45 trout) are left.

Fishing trout ponds

Figure 6 shows that usually over 90 percent of the stocked trout in an *unfished* pond will have died from natural causes two years after stocking. For maximum yield, a pond owner should therefore harvest as many trout as possible during the first two years.

The longer an owner waits before starting to harvest the trout, the lower the harvest will be. Consider the example of a Mr. Dow and a Mr. Jones, who start out with identical one-acre ponds, each stocked with 600 fall fingerlings. Natural deaths occur at the same rate in both ponds. In the first year after stocking, Mr. Dow harvests 165 trout, but Mr. Jones does no fishing in order to let his fish get larger. The second year both men fish equally hard and catch equal percentages of their remaining trout populations. The numbers of fish caught and remaining in each pond would be:

	Mr. Dow		Mr. Jones	
	Caught	Left	Caught	Left
First year after stocking	165	115	0	230
Second year after stocking	35	5	70	10
Total Catch	200 (75 lb)		70 (50 lb)	

Although Mr. Jones caught twice as many two-year-old fish as Mr. Dow, Dow's total catch for the two years was nearly three times as great in numbers and about 50 percent more by weight. Furthermore, the difference between numbers of fish left in the two ponds at the end of the second year was insignificant.

Large two-year-old trout remaining in the pond at restocking usually eat some of the newly introduced fingerlings. To minimize this predation, trout should be fished heavily during the second year following stocking.

The proportions of trout to be harvested in the first and second years after stocking are largely matters of individual preference. Table 2 gives the number of trout most likely to be available for harvest in the second year when some particular number was harvested in the first year. This information is given for *one-acre* ponds stocked either at 300 or 600 fall fingerlings per acre. If yours is a one-quarter-acre pond, you would divide all the numbers in the body of the table by 4 and make proportionate adjustments for ponds of other sizes. Remember that these figures are based on *average* trout survival. In any particular pond, the number of fish available for harvest in the second year is likely to differ from that in the table.

Pond trout are generally much easier to catch in spring and fall than in summer, and it is unwise to count on harvesting large numbers of them between late June and early September. The most successful method of fishing may vary with the season and with the individual fisher's skills. Fly fishing, worm fishing, and spinning are all effective.

New York ponds also afford opportunities for winter ice fishing, with either worms or weighted artificial lures. The latter may give best results when moved up and down in short jerks, a foot or two above the bottom. Out-of-season fishing for any species can be done only by the holder of a fish pond license, members of the immediate family, and employees (see page 17).

Minnows should never be used for bait when fishing trout from ponds. If they escape and later reproduce in the pond, they will usually ruin it for trout production.

Restocking trout

From what has already been said about trout survival in ponds, it is clear that a pond should be restocked every two years to maintain adequate fishing.

Fall fingerlings are recommended for restocking. They are much less likely to be eaten by the large "holdover" trout of the previous planting than are the smaller spring fingerlings.

The pond can be restocked either with 600 fingerlings per acre every two years or with 300 per acre each year. The latter management plan maintains a more even mixture of one- and two-year-old trout.

Feeding

At the stocking rates recommended, trout grow rapidly on just the natural food produced in the pond. Although supplemental feeding may increase the growth rate an inch or two per year, it is rather expensive.

Some pond owners may wish to feed their trout, either as a hobby or to maintain much larger trout populations than the 600 per acre recommended. This would be a way to increase the fishing potential, especially in a small pond. Pelleted trout food is available through farm supply stores. Trout usually form the habit of surfacing for pellets that are tossed on the same area of the pond each day. Add only as much food as will be eaten immediately. Otherwise, the decomposing food may foul the water and suffocate the trout (see fish kills, page 17). Feeding should probably be done only in ponds having some year-round spring water supply and should not be continued beyond September 1.

Fertilizing trout ponds

A single application of inorganic fertilizer at the rate of about 300 pounds of 10–10–10 per acre can be applied to a newly dug pond as it is starting to fill. This is not a necessity but tends to hasten the establishment of a natural food supply. More fertilization than this endangers the trout.

In some New York ponds the addition of about 1,000 pounds of commercial fertilizer per acre per year may suppress aquatic plant growth. However, fertilization at this rate is usually directly harmful to trout or indirectly harmful since it increases the risk of winterkill (see page 18).

Annual applications of about 300 pounds of fertilizer per year tend to increase trout growth. However, this also stimulates plant growth so much that the pond may become practically useless.

Biology and Management of Bass-Shiner Ponds

The bass-shiner combination is recommended for *cool-water* and *warm-water* ponds whose owners desire sport fishing for bass. This combination will likely prove satisfactory in ponds of one-sixth acre or larger where plants are present but not abundant.

Kinds of bass and shiners

In this bulletin "bass and shiners" refers to a combination of largemouth bass (fig. 7) and golden shiners (fig. 8). Largemouth bass are recommended on the basis of their proven ability to grow and reproduce in typical New York cool-water and warm-water ponds. Smallmouth bass might be equally successful and desirable in New York ponds, but this is not yet known.

The golden shiner is one of a number of minnows occurring naturally in New York. It prefers quiet waters with plants on which to deposit eggs and is quite prolific. Bait dealers successfully raise the golden shiner in bait ponds as described in Cornell Extension Bulletin 986, *Raising Bait Fish and Crayfish in New York Ponds.* Many anglers consider it to be the best bait fish of our native minnows.

Figure 7. Largemouth bass.

Figure 8. Golden shiner.

Stocking recommendations

Suitable ponds should be stocked with 100 bass fingerlings (1 to 2 in. long) and about 400 golden shiner adults (2½ to 4 in. long) per surface acre. Golden shiner adults are commonly available from bait dealers for $10 to $20 per hundred. Bass prices are given on page 14. In most New York ponds under one acre in surface area, bass predation usually eliminates the golden shiners within four years. Bass populations usually will continue indefinitely without any other fish species present. They will reproduce in normal years and show moderate growth to maximum lengths of 15 or 16 inches.

Growth

Growth rates vary considerably from pond to pond. Table 3 contains data on average size attained by bass in some experimental New York bass-shiner ponds. Shiners did not grow to a very large size in these ponds; the largest one found was 8.2 inches long. A 16-inch largemouth bass can swallow an 8-inch golden shiner.

Survival

As with growth, survival rates vary considerably from one pond to another and from year to year. In *unfished* experimental bass-shiner ponds, the number of original bass declined from 100 per acre at stocking to an average of about 60 per acre five years later (broken line, fig. 9).

In bass-shiner ponds, shiner populations usually reach a peak about two years after stocking and then diminish in numbers, probably because of bass predation. In some of the experimental ponds where this combination has been tested, shiners have become extinct four years after stocking; in others they have survived for six or seven years. However, bass have continued to thrive in all the tested ponds, even those where shiners have been absent for three years. How long this will continue, or whether shiners need be stocked at all, is now being studied.

Reproduction

Usually bass first reproduce as two-year-olds in New York ponds, but occasionally may not reproduce until they are three or four years old. Once bass have repro-

Table 3. Average lengths and weights of bass, in experimental bass-shiner ponds at midsummer during years following stocking

	Year after stocking				
	First	Second	Third	Fourth	Fifth
Length, inches	8.3	11.1	13.1	14.2	15.4
Weight, ounces	5	12	18	22	25

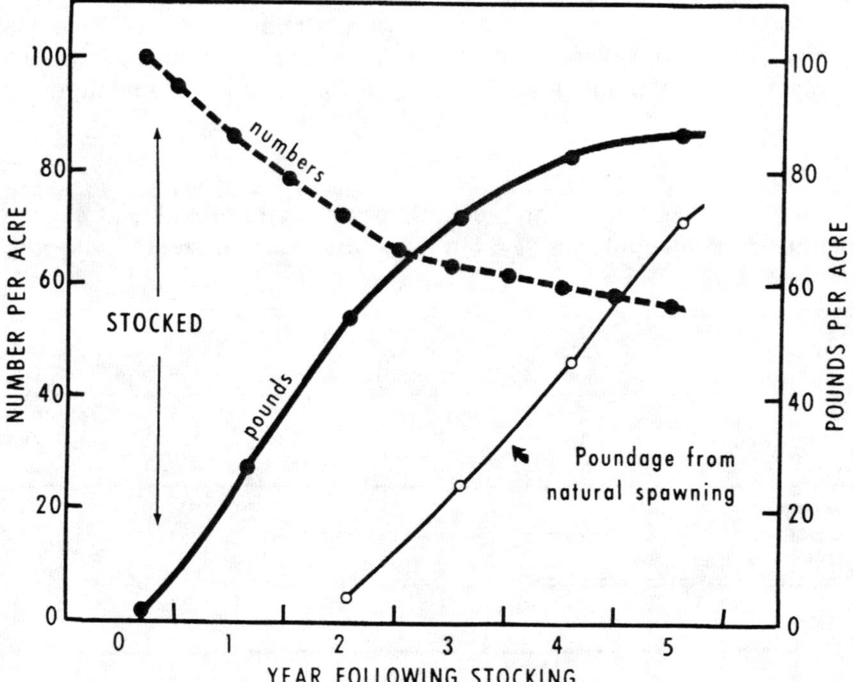

Figure 9. Average total numbers and pounds of largemouth bass in experimental bass-shiner ponds. **Heavy lines:** *stocked bass remaining in an unfished pond.* **Thin line:** *poundage of naturally produced bass in ponds where stocked bass were fished moderately hard.*

duced, they usually spawn successfully in each succeeding year, shiners being present or not.

Shiners reproduce the year following stocking and each year thereafter so long as adults are present.

Bass production

Total poundage of original bass in unfished experimental ponds increased to an average of 85 pounds per acre five years after stocking (heavy solid line, fig. 9). The thin line of figure 9 shows how the average poundage of young bass, spawned in the pond, increased when the originally stocked bass were subjected to moderate fishing pressure.

Fishing bass-shiner ponds

Bass should not be fished until they have reproduced successfully; that is usually not until two years after stocking. Thereafter, they can be fished intensively, *but only a limited number should be removed at any one time.* It is quite possible to remove most of the large original bass in a quarter-acre pond in an evening's fishing; if this is done, fishing will be poor for at least a year or two.

Experiments have shown that, on the average, bass spawned in New York bass-shiner ponds reach a 10-inch size when three years old. Since no bass are spawned in the pond until two years after stocking, it follows that the original stock of bass must provide all the bass fishing for at least the first four years after stocking. Knowing the average mortality rate of bass in bass-shiner ponds, it can be determined that the average bass-shiner pond should support harvests of about 22 bass per acre per year from the second through the fourth summer after stocking. Thereafter the bass spawned in the pond should be fished at about this same rate.

About four years after stocking, some bass-shiner ponds become crowded with bass 8 to 10 inches long. Where this occurs, a good proportion of such smaller bass should be caught and removed to give those remaining a chance to grow. If the larger bass, say those longer than 15 inches, are returned to the pond, then these larger bass will also help to thin out the population of smaller ones. A 15-inch largemouth can swallow an 8-inch largemouth.

Harvesting the smaller bass and returning the larger ones may also serve to maximize both the sport and the total catch from a bass-shiner pond.

Fertilizing bass-shiner ponds

Bass-shiner ponds do not require intensive fertilization. To hasten the development of a natural food supply, a newly constructed pond might be fertilized at the rate of about 400 pounds of 10-10-10 fertilizer per acre for the first year or two. A method of applying fertilizer is given on page 16.

Biology and Management of Bass-Bluegill Ponds

The bass-bluegill combination is recommended for *warm-water ponds* larger than one-half acre and deep enough throughout to make plant control practical, whose owners can harvest at least 165 bluegills per acre per year (see page 15).

Kinds of bass and sunfish

Largemouth bass has been the species most generally used with sunfish in ponds. The suitability of the smallmouth bass for this purpose in New York is not known. Of the sunfishes native to New York, the bluegill is the most suitable for pond stocking. Other native sunfish either grow more slowly, have a smaller maximum size, or overpopulate ponds more rapidly than bluegills. No sunfish other than bluegills should be stocked, except possibly the redear (see page 17).

Bass-bluegill stocking recommendations

Government agencies have recommended 100 bass fingerlings (1 to 2 in. long) and 1,000 bluegill fingerlings (about 1 in. long) per acre, both to be stocked during the same summer. At present there is no strong evidence that these stocking rates should be changed or that the time of stocking should be altered. At commercial hatcheries in New York State, two- to three-inch bass fingerlings cost about $70 per hundred, and one- to two-inch bluegills cost about $25 per hundred FOB.

Growth

Table 4 contains data on average size attained by bass and bluegills in experimental bass-bluegill ponds in New York. Bass growth is usually a little slower in these than it is in bass-shiner ponds.

Survival

The broken lines in figures 10 and 11 show the average numbers of bass and bluegills, respectively, remaining in *unfished* experimental bass-bluegill ponds during the years following stocking. For both bass and bluegills, survival differs markedly from one pond to the next, even among ponds that seem very similar physically and biologically.

Reproduction

As in bass-shiner ponds, bass generally first reproduce as two-year-olds in bass-bluegill ponds. They reproduce fairly regularly thereafter. Bluegills usually first reproduce as yearlings and regularly thereafter. In New York ponds, bass spawn once, in late spring or early summer. Bluegills may spawn more than once during the summer, depending on

Table 4. Average lengths and weights of bass and bluegills in experimental bass-bluegill ponds at midsummer during years following stocking

	Year after stocking				
	First	*Second*	*Third*	*Fourth*	*Fifth*
Bass					
Length, inches	8.3	10.1	12.0	13.6	14.8
Weight, ounces	5	10	15	20	24
Bluegills					
Length, inches	5.0	6.4	7.4	7.8	8.2
Weight, ounces	2	4	6	7	8

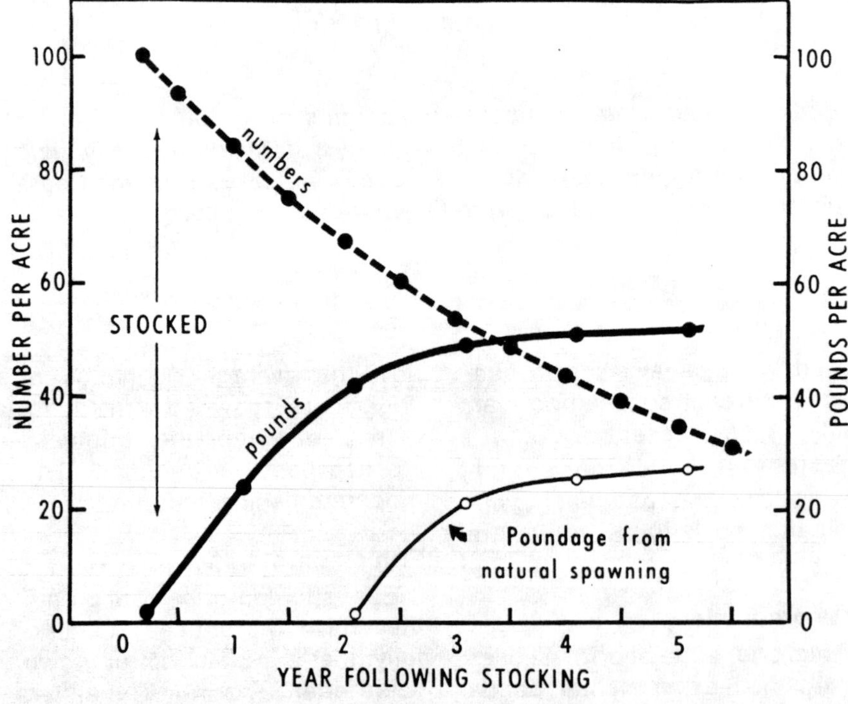

Figure 10. Average total numbers and pounds of largemouth bass in experimental bass-bluegill ponds. **Heavy lines:** *stocked bass remaining in an unfished pond.* **Thin line:** *poundage of naturally produced bass in ponds where stocked bass were fished moderately hard.*

water temperatures. Bluegill reproduction is frequently so successful that bass cannot keep them under control; this leads to overpopulation and stunting of bluegills.

Bass and bluegill production

The heavy continuous lines in figures 10 and 11 show standing crops, in pounds per acre, of original bass and bluegills, respectively, in average unfished experimental bass-bluegill ponds. The thin lines show how populations of bass and bluegills, spawned in the average pond, increased when original stocks were subjected to moderate fishing pressure.

Fishing bass-bluegill ponds

Essentially the same considerations apply to bass fishing in bass-bluegill ponds as were stated for bass-shiner ponds (page 13). The *bass* harvests from bass-bluegill ponds will likely average less than bass harvests from bass-shiner ponds. The two reasons for this are that apparently bass survival is usually lower in bass-bluegill ponds, and that it takes four years for bass spawned in the average bass-bluegill pond to reach 10 inches but only three years to do this in most bass-shiner ponds. Thus the average bass-bluegill pond can support annual harvests of only about 11 bass per acre from the second through the fifth year after stocking. Perhaps bass fishing might improve somewhat after five years, but reliable information on this point is lacking.

Because bluegills usually first spawn as yearlings, and their young reach a size of about 6.5 inches when three years old, the original bluegill stock must provide all bluegill fishing for the first three years following stocking. In the average, well-managed bass-bluegill pond, about 165 bluegills per acre can and should be removed annually during the first three years following stocking. If the pond owner prefers to wait until original bluegills are two years old and therefore larger, then she or he should harvest about 215 bluegills per acre during each of the second and third years following stocking. If the pond does not become crowded with small bluegills, fishing should continue at about this level. In terms of weight, average bass-bluegill populations can support annual harvests of about 15 pounds of bass and 35 pounds of bluegills.

Two important points follow from these findings. The first is that *New York bass-bluegill ponds will not support unlimited catches.* The second point is that after the second year *about 15 times as many bluegills as bass can and should be harvested.* On a weight basis this is about 2 to 3 pounds of bluegills for every pound of bass removed.

If bluegills become crowded, as they frequently do, large numbers of them should be removed either by angling, with seines, or with traps. Figure 12 shows a chicken-wire trap that is easy to build and operate. Several such traps should be used, with the number depending on pond size and the speed with which a bluegill reduction is desired. The traps should be fished for at least

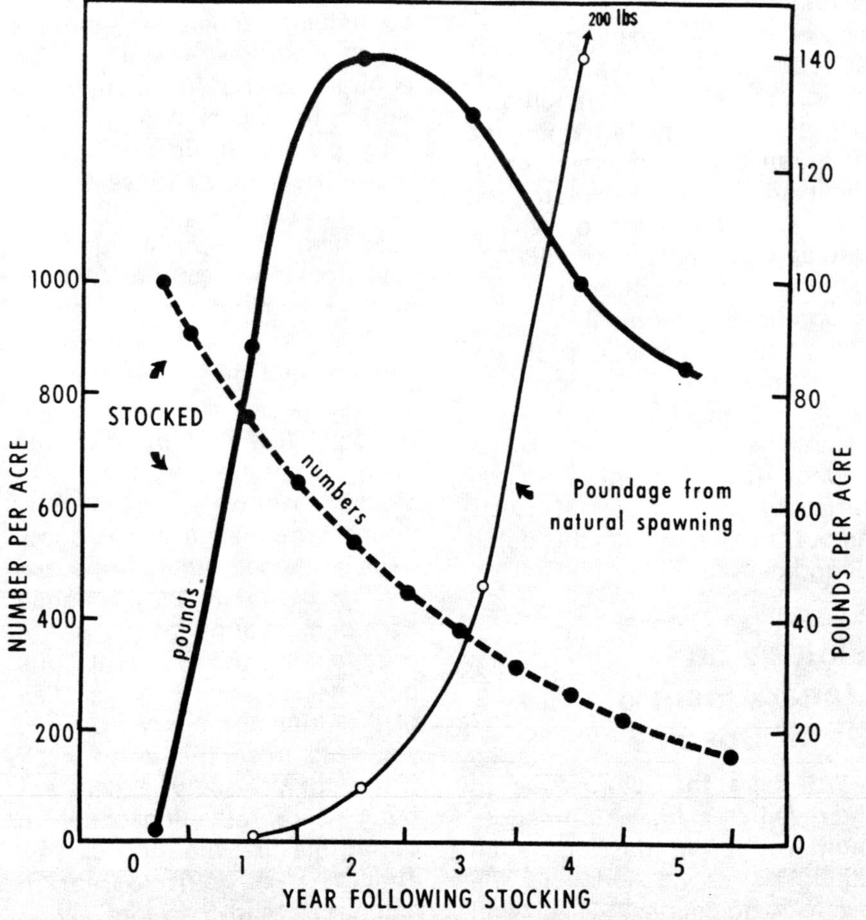

Figure 11. Average total numbers and pounds of bluegills in experimental bass-bluegill ponds. **Heavy lines:** *stocked bluegills remaining in an unfished pond.* **Thin line:** *poundage of naturally produced bluegills in ponds where stocked bluegills were fished moderately hard.*

Figure 12. Trap for harvesting bluegills. Made from chicken wire of one-inch mesh. Door is for removing fish.

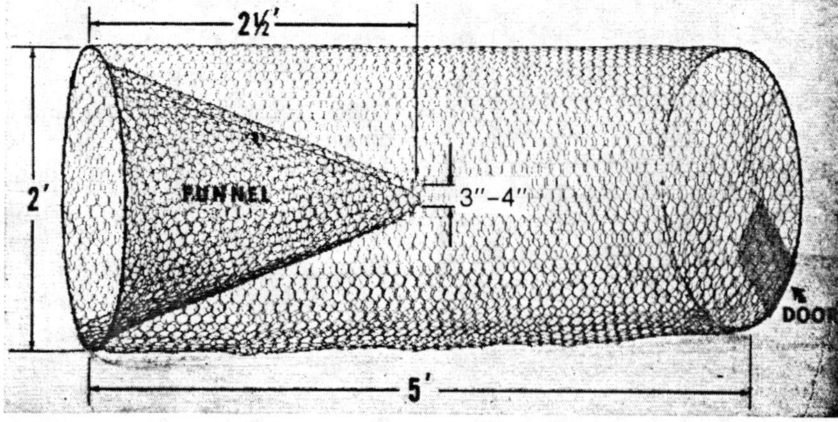

two weeks during June, July, or August and emptied daily. Baiting them with cottage cheese suspended in a cloth mesh bag may increase the catch. Bass usually do not enter the traps.

Infrequently, bass become crowded in bass-bluegill ponds. Intensive angling for 8- to 10-inch bass probably will reduce their numbers sufficiently.

Fertilizing bass-bluegill ponds

Heavy fertilization is generally recommended for bass-bluegill ponds in southern states. One purpose of such fertilization is to produce dense plankton blooms which serve to shade out plants and prevent their growth. Another purpose is to increase production of bluegills and possibly bass.

In New York ponds, fertilization does not always result in plankton blooms, and the fertilizer then merely serves to increase plant growth. Also, the large amounts of organic matter formed may use up all the oxygen in the pond while decomposing in winter and thus suffocate the fish. For these reasons heavy fertilization is not recommended for most New York ponds; it may be relatively safe only in the larger, deeper ponds.

Pond owners who decide to try producing a plankton bloom should apply an inorganic commercial fertilizer such as 10-10-10 from late spring to mid-August. (The formula recommended in the South, 8-8-2 or 20-20-5, is not readily available in New York.) The fertilizer need not be broadcast; simply cut a large rectangular 'window' in one side of the bag and carefully lower it, window up, into 18 inches of water in the windward corner of the pond. If a bloom does not develop in several weeks, another bag should be added at another location in the pond. Thereafter, an additional bag should be added when the plankton bloom shows signs of diminishing. To develop and maintain a satisfactory bloom in a one-acre pond may require 1,000 pounds or more fertilizer per acre of pond surface annually.

If plants become a problem, these should all be removed by either chemical or mechanical means before more fertilizer is added. Also, it is pointless to add fertilizer to a pond if large amounts of water flush through it periodically.

Biology and Management of Other Species

What are the alternatives to the given stocking and management recommendations? Can other species be added to the given combinations? These and similar questions are often asked; some suggestions follow.

Largemouth or smallmouth bass alone

It was found that experimental largemouth-bass-golden-shiner ponds tend to become bass-only ponds because the shiners often become extinct. But bass continue to thrive after shiners are no longer present. Bass-only ponds, containing either largemouths or smallmouths, might provide enough fishing for many New York pond owners. Whether bass-only ponds would provide as much fishing as bass-shiner ponds during the first two to four years is not known. A suggested trial stocking is 150 bass fingerlings per acre.

Channel catfish

This species has been tested in some New York ponds. Survival immediately following stocking was very low in most ponds. Where survival was good, catfish attained quite large sizes (up to 12 lb) as they reached ages of eight and nine years. Reproduction was spotty; in one pond it first occurred when fish of the original stock were three years old, in another when stock was eight years old, and in another no reproduction occurred during the first nine years. This species is difficult to rear in hatcheries; and therefore, stock is usually hard to obtain.

Brown bullhead

Bullheads (sometimes called

"catfish") are quite popular in New York. Many pond owners are interested enough in this species to add it (usually illegally) to whatever species were stocked in the pond. Usually the results are unsatisfactory.

Bullheads often reproduce in ponds. They frequently overpopulate the pond and stunt at a small size. Bullheads stir up the mud of the pond searching for insects living there. If the bullheads are crowded, they may keep the pond almost permanently roiled. The muddiness interferes with growth and reproduction of other species in the pond and also reduces the value of the pond for swimming and as a source of domestic or stock water.

Yellow perch

Yellow perch have been tried in a few New York ponds. They are very good to eat, and populations that are not crowded can furnish good pan-fishing. Information available indicates that perch tend to reproduce abundantly and soon overpopulate the pond with stunted fish. Apparently they are not cannibalistic enough to control their own numbers when stocked either alone or with species that are not fish eaters.

It has been suggested that perch might act as a buffer in a bass–perch–bluegill combination in ponds by serving as an alternate forage species for bass and also as an additional predator on bluegills. This is probably partly true, but it is likely an oversimplification of what the effects really are when these three species are stocked together. As yet there is no firm basis for conclusions about this species combination in New York ponds.

Redear sunfish

Redear sunfish (also called "shellcrackers") are popular pond fish in the Midwest and South, in combination with largemouth bass or bass and bluegills. They have not been tested in New York. In other areas they grow somewhat faster than bluegills, are less prolific, but sometimes are more difficult to catch than bluegills. Perhaps this species might be used as an alternative to bluegills in suitable ponds of southwestern New York.

Pond Maintenance

Fish-pond license

As stated in Section 11-1911 of the Fish and Wildlife Law, the holder of a license or "any member of his immediate family, and any person actually employed by him in the cultivation of his farm or the management of the licensed pond may without license . . . take fish of any size, in any number, at any time, in any manner permitted by the Department."

Application for a fish-pond license should be made to the regional office (see p. 20). There is no charge for the license. Privately owned ponds used in connection with camps, motels, or hotels are not eligible for this license. Fish that have been caught from a pond may be transported off the pond owner's property only when certain regulations are observed. For these and other regulations, see Section 11-1911 of the Fish and Wildlife Law.

The pond license described above permits owners to plan fishing and management to suit themselves. Thus trout may be fished in fall, winter, and spring when they are most readily caught. Similarly, bass may be fished in spring before plants become a problem. If warm-water species become crowded, small fish may be removed. There are, therefore, important advantages in possessing such a license.

Clearing muddy water

If the pond is still muddy with suspended clay three months after it has filled, the clay can usually be precipitated by adding *ground agricultural limestone* (calcium carbonate). This material is commonly available in farm supply stores. An application of 1,000 pounds per acre will usually suffice to clear the water and keep it clear for two or more years. There is no danger of an "overdose" since limestone is harmless to fish and in fact tends to increase the pond's productiveness. Other chemicals, such as gypsum and alum, will also settle out suspended clay, but these substances tend to acidify the water. Fish production is lower in acid waters.

Do not use lime or quicklime (calcium oxide) which may kill the fish.

Preventing fish kills

Partial or complete fish kills are not uncommon in New York's ponds. After a kill has occurred, it is often difficult or impossible to determine its cause with certainty. Information in this section may assist a pond owner in making an educated guess about the cause of a fish kill, and also indicates how the risk of kills can be lessened.

1. Oxygen depletion

For respiration, fish depend on oxygen that is dissolved in the water; if there is insufficient oxygen in the water, the fish suffocate. Fish suffering from suffocation can be seen struggling and gasping at the surface. All or most of the fish are affected at the same time. The fish die with the mouths open and gills flared out.

Summer kills caused by suffocation usually occur between 4 a.m. and 8 a.m. During the night, green plants, fish, insects, bacteria, and other animals remove oxygen from the water, and so the oxygen concentration in the water reaches its lowest point in early morning.

The process of decay also requires oxygen. During the winter months when the pond is ice covered, the animals, higher plants, and most bacteria and fungi are dependent on the oxygen in the trapped water, plus any oxygen that may enter with inflowing water or may be given off by well-lighted green plants living under the ice. Large amounts of decomposing animal or plant matter in the pond may then use up the oxygen and thus cause fish to suffocate.

Kills from oxygen depletion, either in summer or in winter, occur most frequently in New York ponds that are small and shallow and have dense plant growths or in ponds treated with large amounts of fertilizer or manure. The chances of kills from suffocation can therefore be lessened by building deeper ponds; by avoiding heavy fertilization, including barnyard drainage; and by controlling weed growths, particularly in late summer. Chemical weed killers should not be used later than mid-September.

2. High water temperature

Of the fish species recommended for New York ponds, only trout suffer kills caused by high temperature. When water temperatures throughout the pond remain warmer than about 74° F. for more than a few days, trout begin to die. This type of kill is usually progressive rather than sudden as with suffocation. At any particular time during the hot spell, some dead fish may be noted on the bottom or floating on the surface. Dying fish behave in an abnormal manner; they appear sluggish or very inactive, or may swim slowly in circles or in spirals.

Because high-temperature kills usually are gradual and because carcasses that float usually drift ashore and are soon disposed of by racoons, skunks, and other animals, it is possible for a large or complete temperature kill to take place without the owner's knowledge.

If a temperature kill occurs in a trout pond during a summer with approximately average temperature, the owner should consider restocking with bass and shiners or bass and bluegills.

3. Toxic substances

Occasionally fish are killed by the introduction of poisonous materials into the pond. Such substances include various insecticides (such as rotenone, toxaphene, DDT, dieldrin, endrin, and organophosphates), sprays containing large amounts of copper compounds, and many chemicals containing chlorine. The dying fish show various symptoms, depending on the kind and amount of toxic material introduced.

To avoid such kills, the above insecticides should not be used on the pond watershed, and equipment used for applying these and other sprays should never be filled, emptied, or rinsed in the pond or tributaries to it.

Eliminating undesirable fish

When a pond has become contaminated with fish species other than those stocked, it may be necessary to eliminate them and start over again. Often this is most easily accomplished by removing all the water from the pond by draining, siphoning, or pumping. It is important that the pond bottom become *dry*.

If the pond cannot be dried, the fish can be killed with rotenone, an inexpensive chemical which interrupts oxygen transfer in the gills. In the very low concentrations used for killing fish, rotenone is entirely harmless to animals *except* for swine, which might be poisoned by drinking treated water. It is *illegal* to use rotenone in any body of water without first obtaining a permit to do so from your regional fish manager of the Department of Environmental Conservation. Special permission must be obtained each time it is necessary to poison a pond. Detailed information on treating ponds with rotenone is available from your county agricultural agent and from your regional fish manager of the Department of Environmental Conservation.

Controlling muskrats

Muskrats damage ponds by burrowing into the banks. The burrow starts about six inches below the water line, slopes upward, and is usually four to five feet long. Such burrows may cause leaks and dangerous amounts of erosion. When the burrows collapse these problems are magnified.

If possible, the prospective builder should locate the pond in an area well removed from other water bodies, including streams, which are potential sources of muskrat infestation.

Whether muskrats are present or not, the pond banks should be kept mowed so that if damage occurs, it can be seen and corrected promptly. Mowing also reduces the amount of protective cover for muskrats. Cattails and other emergent vegetation should be removed from the pond since these plants provide both food and cover.

Muskrats should be removed at once when there is evidence that they are damaging a farm pond. They are most likely to move in during the spring or fall when the official trapping season is usually closed. The simplest approach is to obtain a 'rider' on your fish pond license authorizing you to trap muskrats from your pond at any time for nuisance control purposes. A pond owner who does not have a pond license can obtain a *temporary* trapping permit from the regional game manager.

Steel traps[4] are relatively inex-

[4] This is the type consisting of 2 steel jaws that snap shut.

pensive, and are effective if set properly. Of these, the "stop-loss" or "killer" models are more efficient although more expensive. Number 1½ or number 2 traps should be used.

Individuals inexperienced in trapping techniques can use cage-type live traps, which have spring action doors, to remove muskrats. The traps are baited with carrot slices. Although the cost per trap is several times more than for steel traps, only a few live traps are necessary to effectively trap a pond; and since they catch the muskrats alive, pond owners can release the animals at some distant point if they wish.

If a pond is constantly invaded and damaged by muskrats from nearby water areas or if the dike is especially narrow, the pond owner may wish to rip-rap the shoreline with small rocks or heavy gravel. These materials should be extended at least one foot above normal water level and at least three feet below it, in a layer about three inches thick. Areas so treated have fairly complete and lasting protection from muskrats. The barrier also protects the shoreline against wave erosion and improves the area for swimming.

Miscellaneous pond animals

Frogs or salamanders (newts) or sometimes both are common in many ponds. Strangely, enough, frogs, tadpoles, and salamanders are rarely found in the stomachs of pond trout, bass, or bluegills. These animals are entirely harmless to humans and are a natural and interesting part of any aquatic environment. There is no practical way of eliminating them from the pond that would not also eliminate the fish. Even if total eradication were achieved, the pond would very soon become repopulated. Although frogs and salamanders consume a portion of the pond's plant and animal life that might otherwise become fish food, their effect on management of a pond for fishing is negligible. Furthermore, they serve an important function as food for various predatory birds and reptiles that may visit the pond and which, without this ready source of food, might make more serious inroads on the fish population.

Occasionally water snakes take up residence near a pond, although this is common only in ponds located close to streams. To date there is no evidence that these snakes noticeably affect pond fish populations, although they do eat fish. Water snakes are less docile than some other kinds and may strike if cornered and sufficiently provoked. However, they are nonvenomous.

Snapping turtles occasionally inhabit larger ponds and, in a few instances, have been known to do some damage to fish populations. Snappers can be distinguished from other turtles by the saw-tooth rear edge of the upper shell. Other kinds of turtles are more common in New York ponds and are entirely harmless. Information on pond turtles and their capture is found in *Turtle Trapping,* Fishery Leaflet 190, available from the United States Fish and Wildlife Service, Washington, D.C. 20240.

Various wild birds occasionally visit farm ponds. As far as is known, most of them do not seriously affect the fish population, with the exception of the great blue heron and kingfisher. There have been occasional instances of ponds well removed from roads or buildings where herons or kingfishers have killed considerable numbers of fish and inflicted wounds on many of the remainder. However, it is virtually impossible for these birds to eliminate a fish pond population unless the pond is extremely small and shallow. Herons and many other migratory birds are protected under federal law. Requests for information or assistance on protecting a pond from these birds should be directed to the regional game manager for your county (see page 20 for addresses).

By far the most damaging bird predator noted in New York ponds has been the domestic Muscovy duck. In farm ponds where Muscovies have been present, trout survival over a five-month summer period has frequently been as low as 10 percent. If it is necessary to give these ducks access to a fish pond, they should be fenced and wing-clipped so that their activities are confined to a very small fraction of the total pond area.

Moles are occasional farm pond pests. Their tunnelling activities may destroy patches of the sod cover on pond banks, with consequent erosion. Mole control by trapping and information on the habits of moles are presented in Cornell Cooperative Extension Information Bulletin 176, *Control of Wildlife Damage in Homes and Gardens*. Moles also can be successfully killed with poisoned bait.

Commercial fish ponds

Sometimes individuals become interested in the possibility of operating a fish pond for financial profit.[5] At present there is little information available from such ventures in New York State. However, certain general considerations and precautions can be mentioned.

For any kind of commercial operation, owners should obtain as much detailed information as possible about the actual profits they can expect. For this, they would need accurate information on the existing or potential mar-

[5]A useful reference on this general topic is *Fish Culture as a Livelihood,* Fishery Leaflet 97, available from the United States Fish and Wildlife Service, Washington D. C. 20240. For further information on fish raising, consult *Culture and Diseases of Game Fishes,* by H. S. Davis, Univ. of California Press, Berkeley, Calif.

ket for their product. Using the average figures on growth, survival, and prices of fish given in this bulletin, owners can estimate the expected cost and yield. They should try to determine as accurately as possible the profit they might realize, taking all of the above factors into consideration, balanced against the cost of the pond and its maintenance. For production on a commercial scale, higher stocking rates than those given here can be employed if supplemental feeding is done or if the fish are cropped heavily and fairly continuously.

For a variety of reasons, New York fish ponds, as defined in this bulletin, are not well adapted to raising and harvesting fish for sale to restaurants, hotels, and the like. Anyone contemplating such a venture should first obtain information from the State Department of Environmental Conservation on legal requirements for this sort of commercial operation.

If fish ponds can be successfully managed for profit, it appears most likely that this management will be in the form of offering fishing for a set fee or for a certain price per fish caught or perhaps a combination of the two. Operation of a fish pond for this purpose (referred to in the Fish and Wildlife Law, Section 11-1913 as a "fishing preserve") requires an annual license from the Department of Environmental Conservation ($25.00 fee), and no fish from federal or state hatcheries can be used in such a venture. There are a number of detailed regulations concerning operation of fishing preserves, particularly with regard to fishing, transporting fish caught, and maintenance and submission of records and reports by the operator. A pond owner considering embarking on a fee-fishing venture should become thoroughly acquainted with Section 11-1913 of the Fish and Wildlife Law.

Addresses of Regional Offices of the New York State Department of Environmental Conservation

Region 1—Stony Brook
Building 40, SUNY

Stony Brook, NY 11794
(516) 751-7900

Region 2—New York City
2 World Trade Center
61st floor
New York, NY 10047
(212) 488-2755

Region 3—New Paltz
21 South Putt Corners Rd.
New Paltz, NY 12561
(914) 255-5453

Millbrook Suboffice
Route 44
Millbrook, NY 12545
(914) 677-8268

Region 4—Schenectady
2176 Guilderland Ave.
Schenectady, NY 12306
(518) 382-0680

Stamford Suboffice
Route 10
Stamford, NY 12167
(607) 652-7364

Region 5—Ray Brook
Route 86
Ray Brook, NY 12977
(518) 891-1370

Warrensburg Suboffice
Hudson St., Box 220
Warrensburg, NY 12885
(518) 623-3671

Region 6—Watertown
State Office Building
317 Washington Street
Watertown, NY 13601
(315) 782-0100

Utica Suboffice
State Office Building
Utica, NY 13501
(315)793-2554

Region 7—Syracuse
7481 Henry Clay Blvd.
Liverpool, NY 13088
(315) 428-4497

Cortland Suboffice
P.O. Box 1169
Fisher Avenue
Cortland, NY 13045
(607) 753-3095

Region 8—Avon
6274 E. Avon-Lima Rd.
Avon, NY 14414
(716) 226-2466

Region 9—Buffalo
600 Delaware Avenue
Buffalo, NY 12402
(716) 847-4565

Olean Suboffice
128 South Street
Olean, NY 14760
(716) 372-0645
(716) 372-8678

FISH CONTAMINANTS

WHAT IS A CONTAMINANT?

The general definition of a contaminant is "any material that makes a substance impure or unclean." For our use, more restricted definition is needed. We will refer to contaminant as *any substance present in fish flesh that decreases public use or viability of the species.* Thus, both chemicals that taint flesh flavor and substances potentially harmful to humans are fish contaminants, as are substances that threaten the survival and reproduction of fish themselves.

Both naturally occurring and manmade materials can be contaminants. For example, mercury is a contaminant when it approaches or exceeds the accepted permissible level of 0.5 part per million in fish flesh since it may exceed currently accepted levels for "safe" food, regardless if the source is natural weathering or industrial pollution. Any substance present in fish that is not a "normal" constituent of the flesh is "contaminating" the flesh to a degree. Currently acceptable health standards for a substance provide a reference point for determining degree of contamination.

HISTORICAL PERSPECTIVE

Fish contaminant problems have typically evolved in three phases. First is a *discovery phase* during which the presence of a particular contaminant is identified. Next comes an *evaluation period* during which health and resource management agencies assess the contaminant's risks to human health. Often, the data available in this phase is severely limited. In the final stage of *refinement*, the data base is expanded and evaluation phase actions are substantiated, removed, or modified as necessary to provide the public with the fullest possible safe use of their resource.

For example, mercury was recently identified in the flesh of some New York fish. Preliminary findings indicated that most freshwater species potentially could have unacceptable levels of mercury. Data gathered allowed the New York Departments of Health, Agriculture and Markets, and Environmental Conservation to issue a joint advisory which specified that most freshwater fish caught in New York could be eaten (only once per week). Further restrictions were placed on certain fish from certain waters and for consumption by pregnant women.

Both PCBs and Mirex went through similar phases of initial discovery, alarm, and subsequent data expansion, followed by some liberalization of health advisories.

A primary effect of the discovery and evaluation phases of contaminant information is the development of information crises. Because basic information is not available, full explanations are often not given to fish consumers who are asked (or told) not to eat certain fish species. Agencies frequently are reluctant to release data that is in developmental stages. Too often, the result is an incredulous sport-fishing public.

Assuming that contaminant problems are likely to occur on a somewhat continuing basis, informational crises and "scares" might be avoided if the public were provided with a continuous flow of objective information as situations develop. One purpose of this source is to assist in providing a base for that information.

IMPACTS OF CONTAMINANTS

Health Impacts

The obvious concern about consuming contaminants is whether they might have some influence on human health.

Toxic effects of subtle pollutants are very difficult to assess in humans. Health effects produced by all but severe cases of exposure are likely to be long-term and possibly indistinguishable from effects produced by other causes. Laboratory testing of animals often is the sole basis of evaluation.

In addition, certain substances are transferred to offspring during gestation, and others affect reproduction itself, effects that further complicate assessment of contaminant problems.

The methodologies for assessing human health risks of toxic substances are far from routine. Thus, the basic question of health impacts of contaminants is the most difficult to answer.

Social and Economic Impacts

Any health advisories established for consumption of freshwater fish will likely produce social and economic impacts. The financial value of commercial and sport fisheries are documented and can be threatened directly if key species are involved. In addition, there may be less obvious social costs in the form of restricted recreational opportunity and freedom of choice in selecting foods.

Social and economic costs should be incorporated when contaminant problems are evaluated, but they are extremely difficult to assess. Balancing social and health considerations is a most formidable task of the regulatory agencies involved.

TOXIC SUBSTANCES POLLUTION

Sources and Characteristics of Contaminants

The United States Environmental Protection Agency has estimated that up to 1,000 new chemicals enter commerce each year in the United States. Hundreds of thousands of chemicals are already in use with little or no toxicological testing conducted before most entered commerce, sometimes many years ago.

Obviously, not all those chemicals currently in use have the characteristics of problem fish contaminants—toxicity to animal life, long retention in waters or animal flesh, and widespread use or direct routes to aquatic environments.

Discovery of Toxic Substances in the Environment

Many currently unrecognized fish contaminants are likely to be "discovered" as our analytical and toxicological techniques are refined. Lake Ontario's contaminant problems are an excellent example of this phenomenon.

Lake Ontario fish were analyzed recently to detect DDT accumulations. It was then discovered that early DDT analyses were blocking out the presence of a second group of contaminants, PCBs. At a later date, it was discovered that standard PCB analyses were masking the presence of a third contaminant, Mirex.

Toxic Substances Control Act

Passage of the Toxic Substances Control Act helped pollution control agencies anticipate toxic substances problems "before the pipe" by requiring prior screening of new substances before they went into use. In addition, several states (including New York) initiated aggressive programs on their own to assess current use of toxic substances.

The Toxic Substances Control Act helped assure that we do not use toxic materials without toxicological screening by currently accepted techniques. However, it will be a long time before our knowledge of chemicals in prior use and aquatic ecosystems allows us to predict contaminant problems with reasonable accuracy.

IMPLICATIONS

Fishery Management Alternatives

Clearly, fish contaminant problems will continue to be a burden on resource managers and users for some time. It will be necessary to assume new emphases in sport-fishing management until contaminant problems are corrected or until medical research provides clarification of contaminant health risks.

Instead of striving for maximum harvest or opportunity to harvest fish from a given water, we should emphasize maximum "safe" use of the resource. To do so, we might have to stress species less subject to accumulation of contaminants, close certain fisheries for highly contaminated species, limit or stop fishing in certain waters, regulate size of catch based on contaminant content, and allow only trophy fishing for highly contaminated fish of a given species.

Extent of the Problem

Many questions about fish contaminants remain unanswered. It seems likely that additional waters and fish species will become involved as we expand our knowledge and refine our study techniques.

Toxic substances in freshwater fish flesh have transformed from single discovery or crisis problems to long-term, complex dilemmas of water resources management. The status of single, current contaminant situations is only one phase of a complex question. Rather, the central issue becomes another question, How do we interpret presently known contamination, anticipate future discoveries, and yet allow fullest safe use of our aquatic resources?

SOURCES OF FISH CONTAMINANTS

TYPES OF CONTAMINANTS

Pollutants can be classified on the basis of their effects on living organisms. Pollutants can act as direct poisons, produce chronic (long-term) effects, accumulate in animal tissues and produce potentially subtle physiological changes, change animal behavior, or cause habitat damage. A given substance can produce a variety of effects when it occurs at different strengths, in alternative forms, or in different environments.

Most fish contaminants are accumulants, materials that build up as residues in fish flesh. Organic chemicals (particularly those containing chlorine and other halogens), heavy metals (such as mercury, lead, etc.), and radionuclides (e.g., strontium-90) are common accumulants.

Chlorine-containing organic chemicals (organochlorines) include such substances as the pesticides DDT, Dieldrin, and Mirex as well as the group of compounds known as PCBs (polychlorinated biphenyls). Organochlorines are generally stable and therefore can build up in the environment. Many organochlorines are toxic to fish at relatively low levels and can accumulate n the tissues of fish and other animals.

Many other (nonchlorinated) organic chemicals also have the potential for producing fish-contaminant problems.

Heavy metals also can accumulate in the tissues of aquatic animals. The toxicity of heavy metals to fish is highly variable depending on the chemical form of the metal, presence of other chemicals, water hardness, and other water-quality factors. There are both natural and human-induced sources of heavy metals in our waters. Metallurgy, medicine, gasoline additives, and pesticides all have been important uses for heavy metals.

There are both natural and man-produced radionuclides as well. Humans release radionuclides in many ways including detonation of nuclear weapons, improper disposal of nuclear wastes, and through certain medical and biological research. The toxicity of low levels of radionuclides is not well understood. Human-produced radionuclides have been identified in fish flesh and could be a significant problem.

HOW FISH CONTAMINANTS ENTER WATERS

Until recently, we thought that direct discharge or spillage of toxic substances into water could account for most fish contaminant problems. However, air pollution and other sources are major contributors also.

For example, PCB contamination of fish in the Great Lakes originally was attributed to direct water-pollution sources. Now we feel atmospheric pollution is a very significant source of PCBs in the Great Lakes.

Detecting sources of contaminants is much more difficult than simply "searching for the pipes." Sources of contaminants are varied and include obvious spills, leachate from improperly constructed landfills, natural weathering of contaminant-containing soils or bedrock, improper incineration of chemicals, surface runoff, and others.

The primary sources of a given contaminant problem depend on the properties of the contaminant, its uses, and the watershed involved. There is no single explanation for all contaminant problems in one body of water, nor for the same contaminant problems in different bodies of water.

ACCUMULATION OF CONTAMINANT RESIDUES

In many cases, contaminants are present in waters or underwater soils at very low levels (often well below levels required to produce toxic effects in animals). Unfortunately, aquatic animals can have much higher levels of contaminants than are found in water because of a process called bioaccumulation or biological magnification.

Fish and other aquatic organisms can take in contaminants directly from the water in which they live. For example, fish can accumulate PCBs across their gill tissues and skin even though PCBs are virtually insoluble in water and present only in minute quantities. Tiny aquatic plants and animals also take in contaminants directly from the water or from water sediments.

Problem contaminants do not break down easily and are retained in living tissue. Each fish retains (and therefore accumulates) a portion of the contaminants it takes in directly from the water. Some contaminants are soluble in fats and are stored in fatty tissues. Others are dispersed throughout the flesh. In addition, contaminants contained in the fish's food are often retained after entering the body.

Plankton can extract a contaminant directly from the water, and alewives or other plankton-eating fish can retain contaminants from the large volume of plankton they consume. For example, Lake Ontario alewives can have PCBs in their flesh at concentrations more than 500,000 times higher than in the Lake's water. Larger fish then eat the alewives, and so on. Through this process, top-of-the-line predators such as salmon and trout can ingest and accumulate contaminants at much higher levels than those found in surrounding waters.

The basic reason for concern over fish contaminants is that humans also tend to accumulate toxic substances. The accumulated contaminants in a fish can be passed on to the person who consumes it – raising the possibility of human health problems.

INTERACTION OF CONTAMINANTS

Knowledge of the health effects of individual contaminants is limited. Analysis of fish contaminant problems is further confounded when more than one toxic substance appears in the same body of water.

In some cases, two substances can work together to increase toxicity problems. For example, either of the heavy metals, copper and zinc, is more toxic to fish when the other is present than when one acts alone. Also, there are some indications that Mirex may suppress the elimination of PCBs from laboratory animal tissues. In other cases, contaminants can tend to cancel out each other's effects.

The entire spectrum of contaminants present in fish flesh should be considered in terms of possible interactions when health rulings are being considered.

CORRECTIVE MEASURES

The obvious first step in correcting an existing contaminant problem is identifying sources. In some cases this may be possible simply by checking existing industrial discharge permits. Things are not that simple in most cases.

Often, ambitious programs of water and sediment analysis are required to track sources of contamination. Even this may be fruitless if air pollution or other nonconcentrated sources are involved. Refinements in the discharge permit process will assist in identifying point sources (such as a single polluting plant), but will not remove the difficulties in identifying diffuse sources (such as air pollution).

4/17

Once sources are identified, the primary corrective agent may well be nature itself. Even persistent toxic substances such as DDT often become unavailable for biological accumulation with time. Some substances are actually destroyed by microbial action, whereas others may accumulate in deep waters where they become overlain with sediments, effectively sealing them from the waters above.

The effectiveness and rapidity with which nature cleanses itself of contaminants are directly dependent on the properties of the substance, the amounts involved, and the characteristics of the body of water involved. In some cases, we can assist nature in the cleansing process. For example, dredging of contaminated sediments has been suggested as one possibility for correcting PCB pollution problems. Such options are generally limited and very expensive.

The emphasis in avoiding contaminant problems needs to be on prevention rather than correction. In many cases the best corrective option is waiting.

—

ANSWER SHEET

EST NO. ______________ PART ______ TITLE OF POSITION ______________________________
(AS GIVEN IN EXAMINATION ANNOUNCEMENT - INCLUDE OPTION, IF ANY)

LACE OF EXAMINATION ______________________________ ______________ DATE __________
(CITY OR TOWN) (STATE)

RATING

USE THE SPECIAL PENCIL. MAKE GLOSSY BLACK MARKS.

1 A B C D E	26 A B C D E	51 A B C D E	76 A B C D E	101 A B C D E
2 A B C D E	27 A B C D E	52 A B C D E	77 A B C D E	102 A B C D E
3 A B C D E	28 A B C D E	53 A B C D E	78 A B C D E	103 A B C D E
4 A B C D E	29 A B C D E	54 A B C D E	79 A B C D E	104 A B C D E
5 A B C D E	30 A B C D E	55 A B C D E	80 A B C D E	105 A B C D E
6 A B C D E	31 A B C D E	56 A B C D E	81 A B C D E	106 A B C D E
7 A B C D E	32 A B C D E	57 A B C D E	82 A B C D E	107 A B C D E
8 A B C D E	33 A B C D E	58 A B C D E	83 A B C D E	108 A B C D E
9 A B C D E	34 A B C D E	59 A B C D E	84 A B C D E	109 A B C D E
10 A B C D E	35 A B C D E	60 A B C D E	85 A B C D E	110 A B C D E

Make only ONE mark for each answer. Additional and stray marks may be counted as mistakes. In making corrections, erase errors COMPLETELY.

11 A B C D E	36 A B C D E	61 A B C D E	86 A B C D E	111 A B C D E
12 A B C D E	37 A B C D E	62 A B C D E	87 A B C D E	112 A B C D E
13 A B C D E	38 A B C D E	63 A B C D E	88 A B C D E	113 A B C D E
14 A B C D E	39 A B C D E	64 A B C D E	89 A B C D E	114 A B C D E
15 A B C D E	40 A B C D E	65 A B C D E	90 A B C D E	115 A B C D E
16 A B C D E	41 A B C D E	66 A B C D E	91 A B C D E	116 A B C D E
17 A B C D E	42 A B C D E	67 A B C D E	92 A B C D E	117 A B C D E
18 A B C D E	43 A B C D E	68 A B C D E	93 A B C D E	118 A B C D E
19 A B C D E	44 A B C D E	69 A B C D E	94 A B C D E	119 A B C D E
20 A B C D E	45 A B C D E	70 A B C D E	95 A B C D E	120 A B C D E
21 A B C D E	46 A B C D E	71 A B C D E	96 A B C D E	121 A B C D E
22 A B C D E	47 A B C D E	72 A B C D E	97 A B C D E	122 A B C D E
23 A B C D E	48 A B C D E	73 A B C D E	98 A B C D E	123 A B C D E
24 A B C D E	49 A B C D E	74 A B C D E	99 A B C D E	124 A B C D E
25 A B C D E	50 A B C D E	75 A B C D E	100 A B C D E	125 A B C D E

ANSWER SHEET

TEST NO. ______________ PART ______ TITLE OF POSITION ______________________________
(AS GIVEN IN EXAMINATION ANNOUNCEMENT - INCLUDE OPTION, IF ANY)

PLACE OF EXAMINATION ______________________________ ______________ DATE ______________
(CITY OR TOWN) (STATE)

RATING

USE THE SPECIAL PENCIL. MAKE GLOSSY BLACK MARKS.

	A B C D E		A B C D E		A B C D E		A B C D E		A B C D E
1	:: :: :: :: ::	26	:: :: :: :: ::	51	:: :: :: :: ::	76	:: :: :: :: ::	101	:: :: :: :: ::
2	:: :: :: :: ::	27	:: :: :: :: ::	52	:: :: :: :: ::	77	:: :: :: :: ::	102	:: :: :: :: ::
3	:: :: :: :: ::	28	:: :: :: :: ::	53	:: :: :: :: ::	78	:: :: :: :: ::	103	:: :: :: :: ::
4	:: :: :: :: ::	29	:: :: :: :: ::	54	:: :: :: :: ::	79	:: :: :: :: ::	104	:: :: :: :: ::
5	:: :: :: :: ::	30	:: :: :: :: ::	55	:: :: :: :: ::	80	:: :: :: :: ::	105	:: :: :: :: ::
6	:: :: :: :: ::	31	:: :: :: :: ::	56	:: :: :: :: ::	81	:: :: :: :: ::	106	:: :: :: :: ::
7	:: :: :: :: ::	32	:: :: :: :: ::	57	:: :: :: :: ::	82	:: :: :: :: ::	107	:: :: :: :: ::
8	:: :: :: :: ::	33	:: :: :: :: ::	58	:: :: :: :: ::	83	:: :: :: :: ::	108	:: :: :: :: ::
9	:: :: :: :: ::	34	:: :: :: :: ::	59	:: :: :: :: ::	84	:: :: :: :: ::	109	:: :: :: :: ::
10	:: :: :: :: ::	35	:: :: :: :: ::	60	:: :: :: :: ::	85	:: :: :: :: ::	110	:: :: :: :: ::

Make only ONE mark for each answer. Additional and stray marks may be counted as mistakes. In making corrections, erase errors COMPLETELY.

	A B C D E		A B C D E		A B C D E		A B C D E		A B C D E
11	:: :: :: :: ::	36	:: :: :: :: ::	61	:: :: :: :: ::	86	:: :: :: :: ::	111	:: :: :: :: ::
12	:: :: :: :: ::	37	:: :: :: :: ::	62	:: :: :: :: ::	87	:: :: :: :: ::	112	:: :: :: :: ::
13	:: :: :: :: ::	38	:: :: :: :: ::	63	:: :: :: :: ::	88	:: :: :: :: ::	113	:: :: :: :: ::
14	:: :: :: :: ::	39	:: :: :: :: ::	64	:: :: :: :: ::	89	:: :: :: :: ::	114	:: :: :: :: ::
15	:: :: :: :: ::	40	:: :: :: :: ::	65	:: :: :: :: ::	90	:: :: :: :: ::	115	:: :: :: :: ::
16	:: :: :: :: ::	41	:: :: :: :: ::	66	:: :: :: :: ::	91	:: :: :: :: ::	116	:: :: :: :: ::
17	:: :: :: :: ::	42	:: :: :: :: ::	67	:: :: :: :: ::	92	:: :: :: :: ::	117	:: :: :: :: ::
18	:: :: :: :: ::	43	:: :: :: :: ::	68	:: :: :: :: ::	93	:: :: :: :: ::	118	:: :: :: :: ::
19	:: :: :: :: ::	44	:: :: :: :: ::	69	:: :: :: :: ::	94	:: :: :: :: ::	119	:: :: :: :: ::
20	:: :: :: :: ::	45	:: :: :: :: ::	70	:: :: :: :: ::	95	:: :: :: :: ::	120	:: :: :: :: ::
21	:: :: :: :: ::	46	:: :: :: :: ::	71	:: :: :: :: ::	96	:: :: :: :: ::	121	:: :: :: :: ::
22	:: :: :: :: ::	47	:: :: :: :: ::	72	:: :: :: :: ::	97	:: :: :: :: ::	122	:: :: :: :: ::
23	:: :: :: :: ::	48	:: :: :: :: ::	73	:: :: :: :: ::	98	:: :: :: :: ::	123	:: :: :: :: ::
24	:: :: :: :: ::	49	:: :: :: :: ::	74	:: :: :: :: ::	99	:: :: :: :: ::	124	:: :: :: :: ::
25	:: :: :: :: ::	50	:: :: :: :: ::	75	:: :: :: :: ::	100	:: :: :: :: ::	125	:: :: :: :: ::